Quest for Democracy

Since the uprisings of 2010 and 2011, it has often been assumed that the politics of the Arab-speaking world is dominated, and will continue to be dominated, by orthodox Islamic thought and authoritarian politics. Challenging these assumptions, Line Khatib explores the current liberal movement in the region, examining its activists and intellectuals, their work, and the strengths and weaknesses of the movement as a whole. By investigating the underground and overlooked actors and activists of liberal activism, Khatib problematizes the ways in which Arab liberalism has been dismissed as an insignificant sociopolitical force, or a mere reaction to Western formulations of liberal politics. Instead, she demonstrates how Arab liberalism is a homegrown phenomenon that has continued to influence the politics of the region since the nineteenth century. Shedding new light on an understudied movement, Khatib provokes a re-evaluation of the existing literature and offers new ways of conceptualizing the future of liberalism and democracy in the modern Arab world.

Line Khatib is a fellow at the Center for Syrian Studies, the University of St Andrews. She was previously Associate Professor of Political Science at the American University of Sharjah. Her research and teaching interests lie within the fields of comparative politics, religion and politics, democratic transitions, and authoritarianism and liberalization in the Arab World. She is the author of *Islamic Revivalism in Syria: The Rise and Fall of Ba'thist Secularism* (2012) and has published book chapters and articles in *Syria Studies*, the *British Journal of Middle Eastern Studies*, and the *Middle East Journal*.

D1556301

Quest for Democracy

Liberalism in the Modern Arab World

Line Khatib

University of St Andrews

CAMBRIDGE
UNIVERSITY PRESS

CAMBRIDGE
UNIVERSITY PRESS

University Printing House, Cambridge CB2 8BS, United Kingdom

One Liberty Plaza, 20th Floor, New York, NY 10006, USA

477 Williamstown Road, Port Melbourne, VIC 3207, Australia

314–321, 3rd Floor, Plot 3, Splendor Forum, Jasola District Centre,
New Delhi – 110025, India

103 Penang Road, #05–06/07, Visioncrest Commercial, Singapore 238467

Cambridge University Press is part of the University of Cambridge.

It furthers the University's mission by disseminating knowledge in the pursuit of
education, learning, and research at the highest international levels of excellence.

www.cambridge.org
Information on this title: www.cambridge.org/9781108482813
DOI: 10.1017/9781108591331

First published 2023

A catalogue record for this publication is available from the British Library.

Library of Congress Cataloging-in-Publication Data
Names: Khatib, Line, author.
Title: Quest for democracy : liberalism in the modern Arab world / Line Khatib.
Description: Cambridge, United Kingdom ; New York, NY :
Cambridge University Press, 2023. | Includes bibliographical references and index.
Identifiers: LCCN 2022025080 | ISBN 9781108482813 (hardback) |
ISBN 9781108591331 (ebook)
Subjects: LCSH: Liberalism – Arab countries. | Arab countries – Politics and
government. | BISAC: POLITICAL SCIENCE / World / General
Classification: LCC JC574.2.A6 K53 2023 |
DDC 320.510917/4927–dc23/eng/20220724
LC record available at https://lccn.loc.gov/2022025080

ISBN 978-1-108-48281-3 Hardback
ISBN 978-1-108-71097-8 Paperback

To Adam and Leo, and all those who make the world a better place

Contents

Acknowledgments

So many people were willing to share their knowledge and experience for this book, including activists, writers, academics, doctors and law-yers, teachers and students, friends, and friends of friends. They did so without any hesitation, in a manner so characteristic of their kindness but also bravery, sometimes without even any knowledge of me and my work. Most of them now live in exile and are no longer allowed to go back home. A few activists I talked to have since passed away and I am particularly indebted to them for their generosity, which will never be forgotten. This book is the result of my getting to know their dreams, their values, and their determination, but also their profound sense of sadness, of their time in prison that was accompanied by torture for some, and their feelings of helplessness. I thank them for being so open and honest about their ideas, their hopes, and their activism.

I would also like to thank the people at Cambridge University Press, Maria Marsh who took on the project, and Atifa Jiwa, Rachel Imrie, Emily Sharp, Laheba Alam, Amala Gobiraman from Lumina Datamat-ics, and many others who helped me to finalize the book. A research grant from LSE to replace an LSE Middle East Centre Arab University Collaborative Grant that was denied to me for political reasons at the time also allowed me to do extensive research from 2016 to 2018, and for that grant, I am especially grateful.

I thank my wonderful friend Robert Stewart for taking the time, as always, to read and comment on the entirety of the book. His patience, and overall support are incredibly helpful and appreciated. My student Maryam Mushtaq has done a lot of the initial research for this book and I thank her for her excellent work and her uplifting dedication.

I could never have written anything without my mom, especially because being a mom myself of two very young children has made aca-demic work extra challenging. Her dedication and love were a crucial support for the research and writing, as was the example of her feminism in action and resolve that I finish the work I start. My husband has also made sure I can work by taking on too many responsibilities himself, in addition to taking care of the baby every second he could, and so allowing me to sit in my office and just write for hours at a time. It takes many people for a mother to write a book! Lastly, I thank my dad, whose formidable knowledge and passion and his own intellectualism and activism set me on an academic path. Without my family and their support, none of this would be possible.

Introduction

Since the onset and subsequent faltering of the so-called Arab Spring, a key question has re-emerged to occupy the writings of many political scientists in particular and social scientists more generally: will the Arab region remain in the throes of authoritarianism and of conservative and radical "Islamic" thought? To answer this question, many have asserted the continued relevance of the authoritarian resilience paradigm in which defensive autocratic rulers remain powerful and proactive societies remain weak. Indeed, in the wake of the Arab Spring, the apparent immutability of some of the political structures as well as assumptions and mindsets both held and propagated by autocrats as well as by conservative and religious actors in the region have disillusioned many. The vexing relationship between "Islam," the region's citizens, and liberalism has been emphasized on multiple occasions, and the rise of Islamic State (IS) and other Islamist radicals has further confirmed for many that citizens of the Arabic-speaking Middle East are almost "doomed" in that they seem to be intellectually, socially, and politically trapped within an autocratic status quo. Further, many analysts have wondered if liberal freedoms and liberalism(s) in general are even widely desired in the Arab region, given that elections in Egypt, Tunisia, and Libya gave power to the illiberal political Islamists. A few studies have dismissed the entire question of liberalization and democratization because of its teleological bias. Other studies have wondered why authoritarian regimes allow for any kind of liberal opposition, thus dismissing the agency of activists in its entirety with political contestation within authoritarian settings being qualified as self-interested, complicit in some ways, and not truly "anti-system," in other words, not liberal democratic. In more conceptually inclusive studies, Arab citizens are described as seeking "democratic change," "societal change," "liberties," "secularism," "order," "rule of law," "reforms," and even "secularism" and "progress"; but they are still rarely portrayed as complex enough to seek "liberal democratic" outcomes, in other words to be pursuing freedoms and political liberties methodically the way other nations were/are able to.

The colonial divide and some of its major assumptions about Arab "backwardness" and predilection for authoritarianism as well as having a "different" and monolithic culture are still present some 80 years later in the majority of studies on the region.[1] The result is an assumption, an assertion, and a conviction that true liberals are a few Westernized intellectuals who are caught up in the tradition of the "other," or simply absent from the scene. Indeed, the entry "liberal" and "liberalism" is absent from most dictionaries on the region. This selective historical reading is in itself based on an inability or unwillingness to perceive the original work of the region's activists and intellectuals, which may be distinct from the work of other liberals worldwide, as fitting within the analytic category of liberalism. Yet these activists and intellectuals are advancing liberal ideas and pursuing liberal outcomes, and the region's relationship with liberalism is considerably more nuanced, complex, and indeed richer, than suggested, as will be shown throughout this work.

Thus, the main goal in this book is to explore and demonstrate the existence and the complexities of an under-studied movement, and in so doing to problematize the dismissal and the lack of works on Arab liberals, and the conventional reading of authoritarianism and contentious politics in the region including giving consideration to the implications for the praxis of liberalism in the region given its invisibility. The aim of

---

[1] Many articles, books, and comments emerged in the aftermath of 2011 announcing the intellectual and moral failure of the self-proclaimed liberals in the region; *Arabs and the Contradictions of Liberalism* is an example. One writer contends, "At its noblest, the Arab Spring was propelled by a Trillingian version of liberalism. Most of its young protagonists, who risked death to defy some of the world's cruelest regimes, did not appreciate liberalism as a complex, philosophical commitment to popular dignity and individual rights. Yet, intuitively, they aspired to something better than the suffocating repression and corruption that had surrounded them since birth under the rule of entrenched dictators. If beneath the rage on the streets the Arab Spring contained a liberal kernel, it was very much a liberalism of sentiments." Sohrab Ahmari, "The Failure of Arab Liberals," *Commentary* (May 1, 2012), www.commentarymagazine .com/articles/the-failure-of-arab-liberals/ Another observer writes, "Four years after Arab Spring protests spread across the Middle East and Northern Africa, the hopes of those initial demonstrators seem more distant than ever. It's no secret that, with the exception of Tunisia, there is little democracy to show for the millions of people who protested and the hundreds of thousands who have died across the region since 2011. In Syria, no fewer than 200,000 people have been killed and another 10 million have left their homes ... The Egyptian economy is in ruins; Yemen is overrun by militants; Libya has become a permanent battlefield; and Bahrain is mired in low-level unrest ... Unlike their rivals, no liberal spokesperson or umbrella group has emerged to carry their principles into politics. Left on the sidelines, those ideals have languished ... liberals and progressives were easily outplayed." Elizabeth Dickinson, "What Happened to Arab Liberalism? Four Years after the Arab Spring, Activists Are Trying to Revive an Enfeebled Movement," *Politico Magazine*, December 17, 2014, www.politico.com/magazine/story/2014/12/arab-spring-anniversary-113637

the book is not, however, to portray the region's current liberal phenomenon as being more significant[2] or more powerful than it actually is or to make it more palpable to liberal and illiberal sensibilities in the West, but to help understand the scale and importance of liberal ideas and praxis, their strengths and weaknesses, and to inform an assessment of the extent to which these ideas and praxis or activism have traction and relevance in society.

To do so, this book rereads historical, intellectual, and political trends, as well as intellectual, political, and civic activism, a rereading that indeed reveals that both autocracy and liberalism are rooted in and have shaped concomitantly social and political developments in the region, even though they have embodied different communities and occupied different – and at times parallel – sociopolitical and cultural spaces. This rereading also reveals a liberalism that is rooted in the region's political history and exposes an original, organic, dynamic and adaptable, enduring, important, and yet contentious relevant movement that is hidden in plain sight.

What has made the movement even more difficult to detect and study is that it has emerged and re-emerged and re-invented itself many times, in response to the region's sociopolitical predicaments such as Western colonialism and the rise of authoritarianism in the 1950s. One conclusion is asserted throughout: the region's relationship with liberalism and liberal and democratic ideas is in fact considerably more complex, local, and indeed richer, than most studies suggest.[3]

A key contention being made in the book is that without examining Arab liberalism and Arab liberals thoroughly, one cannot possibly produce a complete map of the intellectual, cultural, social, and political landscape of the Middle East, nor for that matter understand its current state of affairs or foresee its possible future paths. More importantly, the contemporary movement is particularly important to look at because, as the book argues, it is reflective of and responsible for a number of political and intellectual changes and dynamics at the core of the region, including the authoritarian regimes' liberalization attempts (no matter how cosmetic they are), and the revolutionary events of and since 2011 and 2012.

---

[2] There is plenty of theoretical literature on formal and informal political opposition and participation within authoritarian settings.

[3] For instance, in *Liberalism without Democracy: Nationhood and Citizenship in Egypt, 1922–1936* (Durham and London: Duke University Press, 2006), Abdelslam Maghraoui argues that Egyptian liberals went to great lengths to dismiss Egypt's culture and heritage in order to link Egypt to the West, hence liberalism's failure in the region. As we will see throughout this book, I disagree with this reading of Egyptian liberalism and argue that Arab liberals' intellectual and political history is multivocal, inspired by its local contexts, predicaments, and circumstances, and offers homegrown solutions.

Backdrop of the Project

This is not an easy project to undertake. After all, the Arabic-speaking region appears quite settled in its autocratic status quo, and conservatism seems to be the region's dominant if not sole vibrant intellectual tradition and driving force. At the same time, the classical liberal tradition that had emerged in the nineteenth and early twentieth centuries seems to have effectively suffered a loss of ideological inspiration and vitality as well as political direction. Indeed, the classical liberals' "colonized," "Westernized," "paternalistic," "elitist," and "statist" vision of the future of the Arab world is accused of paving the way for the rhetoric and practice of the pan-Arab populists and authoritarian leftists, which became dominant in the 1950s and 1960s.[4] The argument goes that the populist rhetoric was driven by a sense that the liberals were unable to safeguard independence from the Western powers, and to address issues of economic exploitation and more general economic weakness/inequalities, class conflict, urban exodus, and population growth at home. The reformulation of priorities and attempts to address obstacles to independence led to the rise of illiberal ideas and reactionary actors, and to the sidelining of the proponents of classical liberalism. More importantly, the reformulation of priorities devalued liberal notions of parliamentarianism and constitutionalism and citizens' freedoms rooted in a notion of tolerance and accepting of the "other," and helped to give rise to the authoritarian order and monist systems that the region still grapples with today.

The events of the 1960s, including the breakup of the United Arab Republic between Syria and Egypt in 1961 and the 1967 Arab defeat by Israel, complicated the situation by emboldening the conservatives, namely Islamists who located the solution to the region's many persistent problems in conservative and orthodox Islam rather than in liberalism (including liberal Islam) and leftist ideologies.[5] At the social level, money arriving from an emergent conservative and powerful Gulf region helped to ensure that liberal viewpoints were de-emphasized, because affluence (read: social success) had a conservative, traditional, insular, and reactionary face.

This environment of authoritarian rule, ideological purists including conservative Islamists, rentier states, and petro-dollars suffocated liberal intellectuals and ideas and blunted their impact. The result was that liberals were effectively forced to hide in plain sight, harassed, silenced,

---

[4] See Maghraoui, *Liberalism without Democracy*.
[5] The 1979 Islamic Revolution in Iran reinforced and accelerated these trends.

and eliminated by their states, and attacked from both sides by their conservative and leftist counterparts, who accused liberals of perpetuating imperialist Western ideals and who claimed – and indeed still claim – that they alone speak in the name of the Arab peoples.[6]

With the Arab Spring of 2010–2012, the region initially witnessed what appears today to be a curious phenomenon: the re-emergence of liberal ideas and of liberals as a force on the political scene, to challenge the region's established autocrats and their apologists. But this was short-lived, as the collapse of dictators quickly led to the rise of the Islamists, who demonstrated more stamina, experience, and strategic and organizational skills. And in Syria, Egypt, and the Gulf region, the dictators never relinquished power and used all the forms of structural violence at their disposal to halt the liberal-led uprisings.

Indeed, of the many Arab countries where protests and uprisings have taken place, only Tunisia has seemed able to overcome hurdles toward a genuine liberal democracy most notably visible in the peaceful transfer of power from an Islamist-led coalition to a more liberal coalition and the adoption of a new constitution in January 2014. In Egypt, the army ousted the elected president Muhammad Mursi on July 3, 2013, and the presidential elections that followed in June 2014 brought to power the head of the army, Abdelfattah al-Sisi, which quickly resulted in a return to authoritarian governance. And the Bahraini uprising was shot down before it even started with the help of the Saudi army. Meanwhile, the peaceful uprisings in Syria, Libya, and Yemen have turned into civil wars and regional conflicts that at the time of writing have yet to be settled. The Syrian civil war has attracted armed fundamentalist groups from Iraq, Lebanon, and Turkey. And the conflict has triggered foreign military interventions by illiberal powers such as Russia, Iran, and Turkey. In Yemen, the civil war that erupted in early 2015 has seen Saudi and Emirati military interventions; and Libya continues to struggle with widespread instability and violence, and has yet to make a successful transition toward united and stable governance.

The recapturing of the State by autocrats, on the one hand, and the rise of the Islamists at the expense of the liberals, on the other hand, are no surprise given their historical, fiscal, and organizational dominance in the past 60 years or so. Yet the brief but powerful emergence of the liberal intelligentsia and of liberal ideas and assertions reveal a different

---

[6] One conservative group from Saudi Arabia has taken on the posting of the names and pictures of Arab liberals and to regularly updating the list, named *Qa'imat al-'Ar* (the list of shame), so that the public is aware of the "destructive" and "evil" individuals working against them and their States from within the region.

dimension to Arab society and political life and so provide insight into a parallel reality and movement bubbling along beneath the surface. And while the conservatives and the autocrats quickly took over the popular uprisings, liberal notions, ideas and actors enjoyed immense popularity and displayed vitality, courage, and defiance in that moment before their forced eclipse. The question thus emerges: where did these ideas and people come from, and where are they now?

It is indeed in this context of instability and regional conflagration and the resurgence of a movement of emboldened and yet still repressed activists and thinkers that it becomes even more important to better understand the intellectual and political trajectory of liberalism in the region, and liberals' sociopolitical action, groups and projects, through a study like that undertaken in this book. The examination reveals narratives and a level of sustained activism and conceptualizations that sometimes transcend simplistic registers of nationalism, Islam, and liberalism. As will become clear, the liberals whose texts and activism are examined perceive these registers to be connected and intertwined rather than mutually exclusive. What emerges then is the authenticity and distinctiveness of liberalism as an ideology and as a philosophy in the region.

As such, Arab liberals' discourses converge around a core set of principles that embody the key features of classical and modern liberalism including progress and the inevitability of change, rationalism, constitutionalism, individualism, freedom, equality before the law, democratic rule, secularism, social justice, and the confrontation of puritanical and radical thought[7], and yet do so in a manner informed by the particularities of the region including its heritage and the political oppression that is endemic to the region. This awareness of the complexity of their environment as well as the limited space in which they can assert their ideas compels them to resort to transformative methods and tactics over time, in an attempt not just to survive their illiberal context and secure relative gains[8], but also to continue propagating liberal principles.

Liberalism Defined

Arab liberalism is not a monolithic phenomenon; it is dynamic, multivocal, and complex. One may even speak of a number of liberalisms embodying theoretical tensions, notably over the appropriate role of the

---

[7] More on the key features of political liberalism hereinafter.

[8] In much of the literature on contentious politics, the opposition is portrayed as weak and co-opted, mostly hoping to "secure relative gains" within a context that is dominated by the authoritarian regime.

State and individual versus collective rights and responsibilities. Indeed, even Western liberalism has largely united in its ties Millian utilitarianism, Hegelian idealism, and Rawlsian welfarism, as well as social liberalism and market liberalism.[9] It is a philosophy and an ideology that mixes left-leaning and right-wing values and that is thus dynamic and heterogeneous, with many elements that are rooted in the particular experience, time, and context from which it emerged. The same is true of liberalism in the Arab world, that is, the movement also reflects a multiplicity of traditions, discourses, and homegrown concepts.[10] Comparing both Western and Arab movements here is not meant to assert the default or normative status of Western liberalisms in relation to other movements, but to assert that the dynamic and adaptable configurations of the movement do not dismiss it from the liberal analytic category. Thus, some Arab liberals draw on the strong tradition of social and political justice within Islam and other spiritual traditions to articulate a liberal point of view, such as Abdel-Rahman Kawakibi, Ali Abd al-Raziq, and Jawdat Said[11]; this is what I call Endogenous Liberalism, so-called because of its clear local roots.[12] Others draw on leftist, secular, and humanistic norms of justice such as the signatories of the Damascus Declaration in Syria and the Tomorrow the Revolution Party (Ghad al-Thawra) in Egypt, which I call Intricate Liberalism due to its more universal focus. Thus, some challenge *istibdad* (tyranny) and undue power through reformulation and reinterpretation of religious history and established traditions and political customs; others do so by challenging authoritarian and monist structures and dissecting the monolithic elements within that claim to be "natural," "religious," "nationalistic," and "sacred." Finally, many oscillate between and draw on both endogenous and intricate liberalism in order to advance liberal conceptual imaginations and configurations.

---

[9] See Edmund Fawcett, *Liberalism: The Life of an Idea*, 2nd ed. (Princeton and Oxford: Princeton University Press, 2018).

[10] For a discussion of works that have addressed the multiplicity of the liberal intellectual phenomenon in the Middle East region, see Wael Abu-'Uksa, *Freedom in the Arab World: Concepts and Ideologies in Arabic Thought in the Nineteenth Century* (Cambridge, UK: Cambridge University Press, 2016), pp. 8–12.

[11] For instance, Shaykh Abd al-Rahman al-Kawakibi wrote that the correct Islam promotes a political order that defies *istibdad* (despotism) and that promotes freedoms.

[12] Some may argue that Islamic thinkers should not be included within a book on contemporary liberalism as they do not fit within the liberal analytic category. I choose to include them because their thought is advancing the key concepts and principles of classical and modern Liberalism. To ignore their work then is to ignore an important contribution to the liberal culture emerging in the region. As examples of liberal religious leaders, one might think of Jawdat Said, a Syrian pacifist and humanist shaykh, as well as Muhammad Shahrur and Muhammad Habash, both prominent Islamic scholars.

self-declared "liberals" are not examined. For instance, Al Arabiya news channel is branded a liberal channel, and the Egyptian leader Anwar Sadat identified himself as a liberal reformer – but the definition of liberalism provided earlier clearly excludes such channels and individuals from the liberal category. More specifically, Al Arabiya does not fit within the liberal category since even though it has provided a platform for foreign and domestic liberal democrats to express their views, and despite espousing some aspects of the liberal ideology, it also acts as a mouthpiece for the Saudi autocrats and thus falls short of the "comprehensive test" (see above). Further, a number of Egyptian activists who had challenged the dictatorship of Hosni Mubarak in the name of liberalism and who then endorsed the leadership of Abdel Fattah al-Sisi to bring to an end the democratically elected Islamist government of Mohammed Mursi are not considered liberal because of their latter endorsement. Thus, the definition of liberalism in this book deliberately excludes entities, outlets, and individuals who claim to be liberal – usually because they espouse one or a few of the liberal principles – and yet fall short on the comprehensive set of core principles.[20]

Political Liberalism, Classical Liberalism, Modern Liberalism, and Neoliberalism

In this book, the term "political liberalism" evokes both classical liberalism (the era that spans from the nineteenth to the middle of the twentieth century in the region) and modern liberalism (from the 1960s to the present) in their focus on the political sphere to achieve a liberal political order. Both classical liberalism and modern liberalism are mainly concerned with political issues of individualism, equality, and liberty. As we will see later on in this introductory chapter (see Map of work) and

---

[20] It would be problematic, analytically speaking, if anyone claiming to be liberal for political reasons such as Saudi King Muhammad Bin Salman is then considered liberal in the book since doing so would have the effect of treating liberalism as a shapeless and incoherent system of thought. More specifically, there are two problems that arise if I am to rely on self-claimed adherence to liberalism as a way to study the movement: first, many political parties and leaders want to be considered liberal for political reasons – mainly because they want to distance themselves from the autocratic reality in the region – even though they are in fact only paying lip service to liberalism while actively suppressing freedoms associated with it. Second, considering only self-proclaimed liberals would exclude many of the leftists and reformist Islamists who define themselves as Islamist and yet whom I still categorize as liberals due to their commitment to liberal values such as freedom of speech and assembly, and their focus on social justice and pluralism. And so, it is of utmost importance that the category is defined in such a way as to allow for both openness and coherence, and to account for the particular context of the Middle East.

then within the body of the book, classical liberals adopted an elitist, "top down," state-centric approach that focused on the institution of the State, and did not consider the public masses to be central to the struggle for representative government and the rule of law. Modern liberals, however, have advanced a less elitist outlook in which the focus turned to the rights of citizens and human rights more generally, as well as integration of and reliance on the public masses in their struggle for reforms and democratic rule. For instance, we will see how modern liberalism becomes associated with social liberalism (different from socialism as social liberals do not place society before the individual).

A challenge encountered while conducting research for this book was the conflation in Arabic and non-Arabic sources of political liberalism and neoliberalism.[21] Many commentators posit that the two are the same. But in this book, it is important to distinguish between liberalism and neoliberalism. For instance, while classical liberalism's embrace of free markets and neoliberalism's laissez-faire approach intersect in certain ways, classical liberalism's economic stance stemmed from its initial distrust of power and a pursuit of as much liberty as possible. Neoliberalism's laissez-faire approach, however, flows from the idea that self-regulating markets deliver general prosperity and thus are overall better for societies. Indeed, neoliberalism is primarily an economic ideology that prioritizes the expansion of market forces as a tool for creating material wealth. It is also a modern phenomenon that tends to be endorsed by socially conservative political parties (most famously, Margaret Thatcher's Conservatives in the United Kingdom, and Ronald Reagan's Republicans in the United States) and autocratic leaders (such as Anwar Sadat of Egypt) who aim to marry traditional and hierarchical political and social views with free trade.[22] Thus one might argue that neoliberalism and liberalism are in contradiction with one another when it comes to their priorities: most liberals have asserted that it is essential to create an environment that promotes social justice, individual liberties, and constitutional democracy even if this means some regulation of market forces (welfare capitalism), while neoliberals' priority is the imposition of free markets regardless of the social inequality this strategy might end up creating in the short run.[23] In other words, political liberalism is driven

---

[21] See for instance Burhan Ghaliyoun, "rad ʻala al-liberalyin al-ʻarab," *Voltairenet* (July 5, 2005), www.voltairenet.org/article90638.html

[22] Hence for instance the adoption by Egypt's National Democratic Party of neoliberal policies.

[23] For instance, conservatives and neo-conservatives in North America tend to advocate and propagate neoliberal policies. Anwar al-Sadat of Egypt would be considered a neoliberal, not a political liberal.

by a concern with social justice that the neoliberals deem a byproduct of economic policies. For neoliberals, the market remains always a superior force to government.[24] It is due to these significant differences that I do not look at neoliberals as part of the current politically liberal tradition in the region. The overall focus of this book is thus on political liberalism throughout.[25]

Why Is This Study Important?

There are a variety of reasons why a study examining Arab liberalism is important. First of all, because it is important to study what *is* there (liberal democrats, for instance), instead of only what is missing (democracy)[26], and in so doing to shine light on actors and work that are all too often ignored and greatly understudied. This is because, as was stated earlier, liberals are often hidden in plain sight within Arab societies, silenced by their authoritarian states and conservative counterparts and labeled unfit for the liberal analytical category or dismissed as irrelevant by those studying Middle Eastern societies. For instance, there is no entry on liberalism in the *Encyclopedia of the Modern Islamic World*, nor in the *Encyclopedia of Islam*.[27] Yet as the book will demonstrate, this lacuna ignores the very real activities of Arab liberals and the durability of the liberal movement of which they are a part.[28] It also ignores recent changes in the liberals' methods and level of engagement, which has seen them become very vocal critics of the ways things are interpreted and done in the region from a cultural, social, and political perspective. And significantly, despite the fact that their so-called "eclectic" discourse is being articulated within an extremely hostile environment where it faces considerable political and social obstacles, there is significant conceptual

---

[24] For an excellent summary of neoliberalism, see Andrew Heywood, *Political Ideologies: An Introduction*, 5th ed. (New York: Palgrave Macmillan, 2012), pp. 49–50 and 87–91.

[25] Although outside of the scope of this book, certainly more studies on neoliberalism in the Arabic-speaking world are necessary in order to fully understand political developments in the region.

[26] See Eva Bellin, "The Robustness of Authoritarianism in the Middle East: Exceptionalism in Comparative Perspective" *Comparative Politics* 36, 2 (2004), pp. 139–57.

[27] See Christoph Schumann, "The 'failure' of radical nationalism and the 'silence' of liberal thought in the Arab World," in Schumann (ed.), *Nationalism and Liberal Thought in the Arab East: Ideology and Practice* (New York and London: Routledge, 2010), p. 188.

[28] As Hatina explains, "Indeed, liberal thinking showed historical resilience, remaining a constant part of Arab discourse without the need to reinvent itself or start from scratch." Hatina, "Arab Liberal Thought in Historical Perspective," p. 26.

and institutional groundwork that is being laid by these actors that could, in turn, have larger impacts, particularly on the region's middle class who tend to support the movement. Indeed, while the extent of this impact is contingent on the extent to which it can be propagated, given existing limits on freedom of action, the extent to which the public internalizes the message, and the contextual factors that affect its ultimate roll-out, the Arab Spring movement has clearly shown that it captured the hearts and minds of many people and particularly youth, and thus that it will be difficult to reverse.

Additionally, such a study is important because these liberals' methods and democratic positions are the result of indigenous factors and local developments. As such, they are distinct from those of Western liberals – if not, moreover, undermined by Western liberal leaders' actions and neocolonialist assumptions about the region at times – and thus deserve to be studied as separate phenomena so as to ensure that they are properly understood. Importantly, unlike some earlier liberals in the region, these liberals are engaging in processes of self-criticism and self-appraisal that are not captive of their encounters with the West and that do not need to declare a culturally authentic uniqueness in comparison with the colonizer. As a result, these writers and activists are expanding debates about liberalism beyond a dialogue with and reaction to the Western experience and its conceptualizations of liberalism.

Finally, this examination is important because it adds nuance to some of the most prominent academic literature on the Arab Middle East, which has tended, despite being aware of and even claiming to work against neo-orientalist assumptions and tendencies, to somehow assert and reproduce etic positions that insinuate ontological and epistemological distinctions between the democratic West and the autocratic Arab/Muslim Middle East, and more recently – and one may say more wittingly – between contentious politics under authoritarianism and under democracy; this has the effect of entirely ignoring the agency and principled commitment of activists and leaders. The rise of the populist conservative right in Europe and the United States may in time demonstrate the complexity and resemblance of the assumed self to the Other, but for now, scholars still tend to study the Middle East in terms of its difference relative to some ideal that is explicitly or implicitly Western, and its inability to move beyond a certain point of reference other than by regressing.

A Focus on Egypt and Syria

The following chapters focus on the liberal tradition and movement in two states in the Middle East: Egypt and Syria. The use of a focused case study approach makes it possible to capture the granular detail of the movement within these two countries over the period from the mid-1850s to around 2018, detail that a high-level overview of more countries would miss. Furthermore, Egypt and Syria are particularly instructive for understanding the liberal movement because they are countries with considerable stature and intellectual influence in the region, and that thus are indicative of trends within the larger movement in the region. Egypt and Syria also share many similarities, including of a liberal movement occurring within a larger European postcolonial, authoritarian context with a majority Muslim population though also with an important number of other religious groups and a significant secular population. And yet they are also very different: Egypt is a country that has been seen to be more or less liberalizing and democratizing for a long time, while Syria is considered to be fully autocratic, with very little hope for liberalizing democratic change. As will emerge in the book, these similarities and differences make it possible to more fully explore the various dimensions that are central to liberalism in the region.

Literature Review

Studies on liberalization and contentious politics in the Middle East region have looked at the interplays of culture, political economy, and democratization and have for decades portrayed the region as stuck in a difficult process of cosmetic political liberalization without democratization and as an exceptional region that exhibits many elements that halt practices of social and political justice and contribute to locking the region within a sociopolitical stasis defined by authoritarianism and strong men. In some accounts, reminiscent of Ernest Renan's depiction from the nineteenth century of the illiberal Orient, societies are portrayed as naturally predisposed toward a culture of tribalism and orthodoxy that reinforces illiberal, irrational, and authoritarian trends (Abu Rabi', 2003; Lewis, 2002; Ajami, 1981; Kedourie, 1994; and Laroui, 1976). In other accounts that are less culturally inclined, societies are portrayed as diverse and even active (for instance Bellin 2012; Cavatorta and Aarts, 2012; Rutherford, 2008; Anderson 2006; Brumberg, 2002a, b; Eickelman and Piscatori, 1996; Brynen, Korany and Noble, 1996 to cite a few), but still illiberal and condemned to struggle within the jaws of authoritarian rule and under the influence of conservative Islam due to the resources available to their leaders, their rentier economies, and their nation-building projects and paths

(Heydemann, 2014; Bellin, 2012, 2004; Hinnebusch, 2012, 2000; Guazzone and Pioppo, 2009; Schlumberger, 2007; Anderson, 2006; Brumberg, 2002). Significantly, political outcomes are emphasized in these examinations, and less attention is paid to the ideas and work of the liberal movement itself.

Studies that have focused specifically on the vibrancy or lack thereof of civil societies and their emancipatory role have examined the activism of groups who either challenge (Kubba, 2000), adapt to, or reinforce state and societal trends within the current structures of power and oppression (Albrecht 2013; Cavatorta and Aarts, 2012; Gengler et al., 2011; Wiktorowicz, 2000; Jamal, 2007; Lynch, 2006). Within this approach to questions of liberalism in the region, some analysts perceive the presence of civil society as necessary to pave the way for liberalization, while others question the "normativity that is implicit in the use and application of the term" (Cavatorta, 2011, p. 2). According to the latter accounts, dynamics and events within the region's states should be examined beyond the teleological "transitology" paradigms whereby States are seen as moving toward a liberal democratic order, and the desirability of the liberal democratic end result or democracy promotion, in general, and civil society should be defined more neutrally as an analytic category (Carothers, 2002; Brumberg, 2002; Berman, 2003; Cavatorta, 2011). An ensuing conclusion is that associational life is generated by the context in which it exists and can thus produce a different type of civil society, one that is distinct from that which has flourished in the West, and that is illiberal and undemocratic even though effective in many other ways (Cavatorta and Durac, 2011; Lust-Okar, 2005; Jamal, 2007; Zubaida, 2001; Wiktorowicz, 2000). In these accounts, radical Islamists and other illiberal forces are part of the region's civil society. Indeed, in-depth studies of different countries have shown that Islamists are the region's most powerful civil society actors who, unlike their secular and liberal counterparts, have developed effective outreach methods allowing them to play a significant role within politics following the Arab Spring. In such an environment, the liberals have lost both ideologically and concretely, and their work is often only parenthetically mentioned. Even when liberals and secularists are mentioned, overall analyses contend that the nature of the state in the Arab Middle East has stifled the liberals' ability to effect any significant change and has weakened these groups via restrictive rules and a "divide and rule" strategy that is an intrinsic part of the authoritarian order (Albrecht 2013; Lust-Okar 2005). During the Arab Spring, a few observers and analysts backtracked in the sense that they agreed that the liberal middle class was entirely missed in their analysis, but this backtracking soon came to an end with the rise of the Islamists to power in Egypt, Tunisia, and Syria (see for example: Dickinson, 2014; Bitar, 2014; Ahmari, 2012, to name but a few).

The literature on democracy and liberalism in the Middle East and North Africa also includes writers who have looked at the intellectual history of the region. For example, Hourani (1962), Ajami (1981), Schumann (2010), and Hanssen and Weiss (2016) trace the roots of Arab nationalism, Islamic reformism, and Islamic radicalism by examining the "thought" and the main thinkers of the region through the twentieth century. These authors assert that liberals had put more emphasis on national independence than on civil liberties and social justice. Abdelslam Maghraoui (2006) accuses Egyptian liberals of trying to attach Egypt to Europe and of devaluating local culture and social practices, which according to him, explains their failure to make any significant changes to society and politics. Michaelle Browers argues that although there is opening up to liberal ideas in Egypt and Yemen, this does not translate into rearticulation of values and changes in practice (Browers, 2009).

Others have looked more specifically at how religion and the Islamic tradition in particular have stifled liberal projects. They distinguish between conservative Islam, liberal Islam, and progressive Islam. In so doing, they attempt to answer questions related to pluralism, social justice, and human rights in the region via insights into the Islamic creed, and how it has been interpreted in order to facilitate or block social and political change and liberalism more generally. Authors such as Leonard Binder (1988) and Gudrun Krämer (1996) make it clear that conservative Islam is the most vibrant actor in the region and that consensus and conservative interpretations of the Quran and of Hadiths are the most prevalent trends. Emmanuel Sivan and Bassam Tibi furthermore assert that the alternative of liberal Islam has failed to galvanize the masses and that the real struggle in the region is between Islamic radicalism and the autocratic state (Tibi, 1997; Sivan, 1997 and 2003).

Other authors including Safi, Sachedina, Kamrava, and Ali focus on issues of social justice within the Islamic faith. They argue that Islamic humanism engages with Islamic thought and practices in order to "speak truth to power" (Sachedina, 2001; Kamrava, 2011; Ali, 2006; Safi, 2014: 487). But these authors assert that most of what they perceive as "progressive," "reformist," and "liberal Islam" is developing in the United States and Canada rather than in the Middle East. Khaled Abou El Fadl writes, "the contemporary Islamic world has been intellectually impoverished, and so there have been far too few influential philosophical or critical intellectual movements emerging from the Muslim World in the modern age."[29] In these works, Islamist ideology is over-emphasized, and the region's liberals are either treated as non-existent or are given very little attention.

Thus the marginalization of liberals is not only carried out by regimes and in the media, but within academic scholarship as well. Some claim that this is the reality on the ground, after all, some 45% of the region's population supports the conservative Islamist project.[30] But there are other groups and other projects: over 250 atheist groups exist in the Middle East,[31] and over 80% of the region's people say they support liberal democratic rule.[32] That this liberal democratic component should not be ignored in examinations of the region's sociopolitical dynamics and actors is of course a central contention driving this book.

A few recent works by Schumann (2008), Gershoni and Jankowski (2010), as well as Hatina and Schumann (2015) and Abu-ʿUksa (2016) give consideration to this liberal democratic component. Abu-ʿUksa's work shed significant light on the political semantics of the word freedom and in doing so demonstrates the rich and changing intellectual history of liberalism in the region. Although these four books seem entirely different in scope and content, they are united in their rereading of historical, intellectual, and political trends, and they demonstrate that contemporary liberal thought in the region is more vibrant, layered, original, and involved than is assumed – even though different from its Western counterpart. They look at various facets of liberalism in order to capture liberal actors, moments, spaces meanings, and outcomes. In so doing, they depict liberalism as the common thread between a variety of wide-ranging and diffuse worldviews, although Hatina (2011 and 2015),

---

[29] Khaled Abou El Fadl, "The Ugly Modern and the Modern Ugly: Reclaiming the Beautiful in Islam," in Omid Safi (ed.), *Progressive Muslims: On Justice, Gender and Pluralism* (Oxford: Oneworld, 2003), p. 37.

[30] Based on numbers compiled in the 2000s for Algeria, Yemen, Morocco, Tunisia, Iraq, Lebanon, Kuwait, Palestinian Authority, Bahrain, Turkey, and Egypt (year of poll varies for each state). Numbers available in: Robert Lee and Lihi Ben Shitrit, "Religion, Society, and Politics in the Middle East," in Ellen Lust (ed.), *The Middle East*, 13th ed. (Los Angeles, London, Singapore, Washington, DC: Sage, 2014), p. 240.

[31] Ahmed Benchemsi, "Invisible Atheists: The Spread of Disbelief in the Arab World," *New Republic*, April 24, 2015, https://newrepublic.com/article/121559/rise-arab-atheists.

[32] See Mark Tessler and Amaney Jamal, *Arab Barometer Project*, 2010, www.arabbarometer.org; and the Arab Opinion Index 2019–20 made available by the Arab Center for Research and Policy Studies (ACRPS), available at www.dohainstitute.org/en/Lists/ACRPS-PDFDocumentLibrary/Arab-Opinion-/index-2019-2020-Inbreef-English-Version.pdf; see also Mohamad al-Masri, "Populisme et opinion publique: une lecture du barometer de l'opinion arabe 2019–2020," Presentation at the Arab Center for Research and Policy Studies' Annual Colloquium (January 29, 2021).

Abu-'Uksa, and Gershoni and Jankowski (2010) are more careful than Schumann to avoid treating liberalism as a loose analytic category that is too ambiguous or all-encompassing. Hatina's multipronged approach maintains the integrity of the liberal category without rendering it so rigid as to dismiss the nuances and dynamism within liberal thought in the Middle East.

Other works such as Elizabeth Thompson's *How the West Stole Democracy from the Arabs* (2020) and Elizabeth S. Kassab's *Contemporary Arab Thought* (2010) present nuanced, complex pictures and discuss different aspects of the liberal movement and thought in the region. Like Gershoni and Jankowski, Thompson's work covers the early period, 1918–1922 to be precise, and makes a revolutionary argument that liberal democratic ideas were flourishing but aborted in Syria because of the French colonialists. Meanwhile, Kassab's rich work on contemporary Arab thought covers a few of those intellectuals that are considered liberal in this book. Both works, Thompson's and Kassab's, contribute enormously to our understanding of liberal democratic actors and thought within the region.

This present book builds upon the work of Hatina, Schumann, Abu-'Uksa, Thompson, Gershoni and Jankowski, as well as of Kassab in an attempt to broaden the scope of the study of liberalism and its significance, and to nuance some of the conclusions by placing them within the broader literature and the body of theory it asserts. In so doing, this contribution neither aims to erase nor to belittle the distance between the liberals and their societies and regimes, but to help delineate the productive and promising space that these often-astute writers and thinkers and committed activists are able to create. In this narrative, the gaps and tensions between the liberals and large parts of their societies are not overstated, and doom-laden scenarios not inevitable.

Finally, it is important to reiterate that the purpose of the book is to shed light on liberalism in the region, including the liberal episodes and actors. In so doing, the book might be accused of disregarding the rest of the picture; yet this is purposely done, for the simple reason that the rest of the puzzle is well examined elsewhere and does not need reiteration here. This said, the narrative does also somewhat engage with illiberal actors and activities, if only to appropriately contextualize its exposition of liberal dynamics and developments.

Methodology

In order to address the topics covered by the book, I adopt a multi-methods approach incorporating both qualitative and quantitative data. The qualitative data includes open-ended interviews and conversations with individuals who consider themselves to be "liberal activists," "liberal intellectuals," and "liberal students." Interviewees were identified purposively, based on their (potential) knowledge related to the book's areas of focus, with snowballing somewhat used to identify further interviewees from existing interviewees.

These conversations were undertaken between 2010 and 2020, and included individuals who resided in the Gulf region, mainly the United Arab Emirates, as well as others who were there in transit. Other conversations were conducted in Jordan, Egypt, France, and the United Kingdom, as well as via Skype and Messenger with key actors (journalists, civil society activists, intellectuals, and academics) who identify as liberals. One of the central aims in the interviews was to understand liberal activism and whether and how liberal observers anticipate regional changes at the political and social levels.

The quantitative data looked at and drawn upon for this study includes surveys related to political and social attitudes in the region, many of which are cross-national and available on arabbarometer.com, on the Arab Reform Initiative, as well as the Arab Opinion Index launched by the Arab Center for Research and Policy Studies (ACRPS) and presented at the Centre Arabe de Recherches et d'Etudes Politiques de Paris (CAREP).

In addition to the interviews and survey data, the book draws upon content analysis of primary documentary sources available in Arabic that outline the ideas and commentaries of liberal actors in the region. This has included content analysis of recorded speeches, TV and radio interviews, pamphlets, online conversations available to the public, Facebook and other social media posts, and political programs and promises, which I gathered remotely in order to understand the current liberal landscape and to ascertain its vibrancy within the region.[33]

My research also relied on a large variety of secondary materials in Arabic, English, and French, including print and online media, memoirs, as well as historical and analytical works. Secondary sources examined also focused upon the topic of liberalism and conservatism in the Arab region. The aim in considering these works is to assess the variances and shifts within liberal activism and work at a local, national, and regional level and more broadly to fully understand the liberal landscape and analysis of it, including understanding the recent intensification of liberal activism and some palpable changes in society and in social relations.

---

[33] Please note that the videos and social media links and posts referenced in the text were live at the time of writing.

Map of the Work

The book assesses the liberal movement's struggles, focus and values, its strengths and weaknesses as well as its transformation by looking at the activism, written work, commentaries, art, and forms of reasoning and approach of liberal politicians, intellectuals and civil society activists. The book thus alternates between providing a historical and political narrative about the region's liberal legacy and practice as a movement in motion, and describing the work and thought of the liberals that formed this movement, going from the nineteenth century until the present. Each chapter thus combines a political history account and a look at some of the thinkers and activists that shape the movement.

The first chapter offers historical context and an overview of the intellectual and political history of Classical Liberalism during the nineteenth century and early twentieth century in the region. It serves as an introduction for those who are not aware of the earlier liberal tradition and the liberal political elite of the time. The focus of the chapter is unique in that it looks at how classical liberals approached questions of despotism, civil freedoms, rights and democracy, and on how they have conceived of political change and state building. These questions have been ignored within most of the academic literature, which has tended to focus on these intellectuals and politicians' pan-Arabist and nationalist agendas instead of on their liberal and democratic outlooks. Overall, the chapter provides an essential historical and analytical background about the region's earliest liberal intellectual and political history and episodes; it shows that liberal concepts were not "foreign concepts" imposed suddenly on an unsuspecting public. The chapter intends to inform the rest of the study and set the boundaries of the movement.

Chapter 2 focuses on the period from the 1960s to the 1990s. The chapter shows how liberalism continued its path in the midst of authoritarianism, and how liberal activisms, although entangled in the authoritarian political structure, helped to modify the political configurations of authoritarianism and bring changes to the region's political culture. Thus the chapter argues that, despite their seeming absence and silence, the liberals were still active on the ground. The chapter shows that the triumph of the new illiberal forces meant that liberals had to change and adapt, working differently and cautiously. They began to turn away from their focus on the institutions of the State and change from above, and realized that they needed to direct their attention to mobilizing reform through liberal non-governmental institutions, through social activism, and a focus on cultural transformation, if they were to exist at all. In other words, with the recognition that the liberal ethos in Arab political and intellectual culture had eroded, it became important to enact change, not from above as had the classical liberals done, but from below by enhancing the awareness and power of the citizen. This necessitated a move away from the elitist paternalism of the previous generations. The liberals also reconnected with their leftist national progressive counterparts. In fact, in both Egypt and Syria, the possible coalition between liberals, conservatives, and leftists would turn out to be too threatening for the authoritarian regimes. The chapter concludes that dismissal of the region's liberal intellectual and activist work throughout the 1970s, 1980s and 1990s by much of the Arabic, English and French speaking academy distracts us from the significance of this period in laying the foundations for a more liberal political culture, and from the liberals' immense contribution to the events of the Arab Spring in 2011 and 2012.

Chapter 3 then discusses the phase spanning from the 2000s until the start of the Arab Spring in 2011–2012, including the renewal and revitalization in the 2000s. It pays particular attention to how activists and communities have come together in pursuit of shared liberal notions and goals, and how they have impacted political conduct and affairs. Critique continued to be inward-looking and led to renewed ideas in books, art, the printed press, on the internet, and on Satellite television about what a nation, a community and a *muwaten* [citizen] are or should be.[34] Intellectuals and activists began to move beyond dogmatic and rigid interpretations in their attempts to reappropriate, make sense of, and reclaim liberal values. Activists and thinkers created illegal public forums to galvanize the public masses as they took to the streets, and engaged in debates about separation of powers, pluralism, and individuality, stressing issues of civil rights and political freedoms and individuals' right to self-rule. Even leftist thinkers who lost faith in the contentions of the radical era turned to a "liberal-ish" agenda that emphasized liberal rights and freedoms and criticized state monopolies over power and the economy.

Chapter 4 looks at the restitution of liberalism as a potential model for political change during the Arab Spring and then its inability to take power. The chapter refutes the narrative that the Arab Spring was the result of a leaderless movement of an alienated youth and loose associations of activists who lacked an ideological drive and who were merely driven by their profound malaise. The chapter argues that this overall analysis ignores years of liberal and pro-democracy activism against the

[34] Roel Meijer, "Liberalism in the Middle East and the Issue of Citizenship Rights," in Meir Hatina and Christoph Schumann (eds.), *Arab Liberal Thought After 1967: Old Dilemmas, New Perceptions* (New York: Palgrave Macmillan, 2015), p. 71.

extant patterns and nature of domination and authority in the region, and the fact that protestors rallied behind a set of ideas that were consistently and categorically different from the ones rallied behind in the 1950s and 1960s.[35] What is missed in most studies is the deep and consistent transformation and reformulation of the object of discontent; in other words, the protestors' demands no longer reflected the post-colonial discourse and its emphasis on questions of economic egalitarianism, public ownership, rapid industrialization, class conflict and the economically marginalized, and imperialism, even though all of these questions remain concerns of the majority. Millions confronted their States despite the threat of the regimes' violent security apparatuses, and in so doing they disseminated the liberals' ideas and activism, and showed that liberalism is alive, vibrant, and hiding in plain sight within youths groups, NGOs, television shows, theatre, art, schools and universities, political forums and online discussions, and literature.

The last chapter of the book recapitulates the general themes and advances a number of concluding remarks.

The four core chapters of the book juxtapose the different time periods, answering the questions of who are the protagonists of Arab liberalism and what are some of their sociopolitical initiatives and approaches? They also help shed light on the social, ideational, and structural reasons behind the liberals' defeat at the hands of illiberal forces and their renewal attempts, paying particular attention to how liberalism has impacted the nature of both state and society and political life more generally. In so doing, the four chapters pay particular attention to the work of individual liberals and groups as well as some of their narratives and initiatives.[36] This examination provides insight into how liberal were/are advancing their objectives and changing the nature of State-society relations in the region, and how the authoritarian settings in which they found themselves altered their tactics and practice.

The range of activists, scholars, intellectuals, groups, and initiatives examined in the book is far from exhaustive since it leaves out many other relevant Arabic-speaking liberals from Egypt and Syria and from around the region. Indeed, the intent of the book is not to be a comprehensive intellectual and political history of all liberals and liberal initiatives and groups in the region, but to provide a consistent narrative that allows a better examination of some of the liberal trends and activists

---

[35] Meijer, "Liberalism in the Middle East and the Issue of Citizenship Rights," p. 66.

[36] Narratives are especially important for providing insight into how these actors organize, interpret events, and attempt to advance their objectives (Patterson and Monroe, 1998).

and their transformation over time. Finally, some may argue that Islamic thinkers should not be included within a book on liberalism as they do not fit within the liberal analytic category. I choose to include them because their thought is advancing the key concepts and principles of modern liberalism. To ignore their work then is to ignore an important contribution to the overall liberal narrative in the region.

Thus the choice of people focused upon makes it possible to depict the diversity of liberal scholars' opinions and the transformations of the liberal movement over time. These people were also focused upon because they lived most of their lives in the region, they write mostly in Arabic and are thus able to reach a broader Arabic-speaking audience while tending to be relatively ignored by non-Arabic speaking scholars and analysts, and they express their ideas through writing and scholarly articles and have also been quite active and vocal in promoting their ideas on Arab TV channels and programs. Their appearances have pitted them directly against the region's established conservatives, have attracted quite a bit of attention, and have placed them under attack (and sometimes physical threat) from illiberal forces and particularly from the regime and from regime loyalists.

1   Nineteenth to Mid-Twentieth Century
Paternalistic Liberalism and Planting the Seeds of Democracy

Freedom is the ultimate virtue of humankind: Democracy is the only political system of modern man and modern society
Abbas Mahmud al-Aqqad[1]

Liberalism is the product of a yearning to be free, free from tyranny and from forces that are perceived to be uncompromising and unjust.[2] Defined this way, it would be impossible to talk about liberalism as only a modern movement whether in the Arab World or elsewhere. Indeed, liberalism, if understood as using our rational faculty to end political injustice and expand freedom of thought and expression, is as old as humanity. If, however, the focus is on norms of achieving peace, and of institutionalizing equality, individual freedom, constitutional democracy, and rule of law, then liberalism should be viewed as a nineteenth- and twentieth-century movement (*haraka*). It is this modern understanding and political movement within the context of the Arabic-speaking world that this book discusses, with a particular focus on Egypt and Syria, a region in which liberalism dates back more than two centuries and is the result of a yearning to be free from foreign occupation and a rejection of political and religious absolutism.

But in contradiction with what is often assumed, Arab liberalism is not just an imported intellectual system of thought. Modern Arab liberalism emerged, and has been appropriated, then recreated, modified, merged, contextualized, and regenerated to fit and serve the context in which it operated.[3] In other words, like other ideologies that saw the light in the region, such as nationalism and communism, liberalism is both the

---

[1] Israel Gershoni, "Liberal Democratic Legacies in Modern Egypt: The Role of the Intellectuals, 1900–1950," *IAS* (2012).

[2] Edmund Fawcett, *Liberalism: The Life of an Idea*, 2nd ed. (Princeton and Oxford: Princeton University Press, 2018), p. 201.

[3] See Wael Abu-'Uksa, *Freedom in the Arab World: Concepts and Ideologies in Arabic Thought in the Nineteenth Century* (Cambridge, UK: Cambridge University Press, 2016).

product of intellectual and political exchange and continuity between the different civilizations and of an organically conceived desire for sociopolitical emancipation and for political justice.[4]

To show this endogenous nature, the following sections of this chapter provide a historical and political narrative about the region's liberal legacy. They present a discussion of classical liberalism and its beginnings as an intellectual and political movement in the Arabic-speaking world in the nineteenth and early twentieth centuries, and they show how intellectuals and political actors deliberated liberal – not Western – solutions to perceived problems. Although this information is general and familiar to some readers, this chapter is important because it is focused on the liberal moments: on how the classical liberals approached questions of despotism, civil freedoms, rights, and democracy; and on how they have conceived and designed political change – questions that have been ignored within most of the academic literature, which has tended to focus on setbacks and on the intellectuals and politicians' pan-Arabist and nationalist agendas instead. We will see, for instance, that Arab liberalism was developing a democratic theory of governance, even if paternalistic and elitist in its methods, and that liberal concepts were not "foreign concepts" that the intellectuals wished to impose promptly on an unsuspecting public. We will also see how the nineteenth to the early twentieth centuries is not only a period of self-definition, and thus struggle, but also of grand achievements and of control of the State by liberal actors. While this was a passing phase in the sense that it failed to institutionalize liberal democratic institutions, it nonetheless set the boundaries of the movement and tells us about today's democratic liberalism and its aspirations.

Overall then, the narrative emphasizes the liberals' ideas of reform and liberalism's success stories – as opposed to their failures, which are well documented elsewhere – as well as the centrality of the issues of despotism, freedom, and political representation in their thinking and political activity, in an attempt to showcase the movement's endogenous nature

---

[4] Meijer makes the point that no ideology exists in pure form in the Middle East. It is important to note here that European liberalisms are also the product of other intellectual traditions and works before those of the Renaissance, and some liberal ideas can be traced back to Greek and Alexandrian scholarly traditions, and to Islamic philosophy. For example, in the tenth century, al-Farabi spoke of the "rational faculty" (*quwwa 'aqliyya*) of humans through which we are able to find happiness in the arenas of individual action and social interaction. The overall point then is that there is far less of a rupture in intellectual activity than is assumed, with intellectual traditions often proving to be (more or less) inter-civilizational.

and specific characteristics. This chapter also sheds more light on the reasons for the ultimate failure to establish the liberal political framework that was aimed at. In so doing, the chapter does not aim to dispel the grand narrative advanced by scholars of the classical period in their focus on elites and their central role in the advancement of nationalist and pan-Arabist ideas in the region – indeed, we will see how different groups and parties have constructed liberalism based on their own interests and needs.[5] It does, however, aim to emphasize the politically liberal element within the nationalists' accounts, as well as drawing attention to the role of the colonizers in sabotaging the liberal project in the region and specifically in Syria and Egypt, the two states that are the primary focus of the historical and political analysis.

It is difficult to definitively establish when liberal concepts really started in the Arabic-speaking region. Most accounts, however, place them in the early nineteenth century, a time of both political and social challenges and transformations in the region, which saw the rise of a vibrant intellectual and political elite that was inspired by hopes of independence from the Ottomans as well as by the Europeans' industrial and scientific achievements. That elite pursued and encouraged the production of new knowledge, especially through the channels of education as well as through books and newspapers, facilitated by "benevolent autocrats" such as the ambitious viceroy of Egypt, Muhammad 'Ali (1769–1849), his son, Ibrahim Pasha (1789–1848), as well as other khedives such as Isma'il Pasha. As stated above, this elitist start produced a movement that was paternalistic and focused on the institution of the State, but that was also focused on individual and collective freedom and that was egalitarian and even democratic in its outlooks.

Nineteenth to Early Twentieth Century: The Era of Muhammad Ali and of the Liberal Intellectual

Although one could make a case that ideas to reform and modernize[6] based upon liberal ideas preceded the time of Muhammad Ali, most accounts on Arab liberalism date its emergence back to 'Ali's attempts to

---

[5] See Philip S. Khoury, *Syria and the French Mandate: The Politics of Arab Nationalism, 1920–1945* (Princeton: Princeton University Press, 1987).

[6] An attempt to establish new ways of doing things, thinking, and organizing society. For more on modernization and modernism, see Hisham Sharabi, *Arab Intellectuals and the West: The Formative Years 1875–1914* (Baltimore, MD: John Hopkins University Press, 1970); and John F. Wilson, "Modernity and Religion: A Problem of Perspective," in William Nicholls (ed.), *Modernity and Religion* (Waterloo, ON: Wilfrid Laurier University Press, 1987).

secure his own rule by modernizing Egypt and gaining its independence from the Ottoman Empire.[7] Muhammad Ali had risen to power in Egypt in 1805 following the departure of the French – and interestingly for this work, his rise was the outcome of an assertion of the popular will. Ali was chosen by Egyptians who felt he better represented their aspirations – as Chalcraft puts it, "commoners (al-'amma), neither controlled or entirely led by the ulema … assembled and demanded to depose the Ottoman-appointed Pasha and appoint the Albanian military man Mehmet Ali in his stead."[8] Ali had promised to serve the people and to respect their will.[9]

He was indeed a modernizer. His policies and decrees built new forms of political community from above based on a centralized system of governance, professional bureaucracy, a state of citizenship, and a representative council. His State streamlined and monopolized the economy and established a military-based manufacturing sector and an industrial base for Egypt. Tax collection was reorganized in a more egalitarian manner without distinction between Muslims and Christians.[10] The State also modernized the infrastructure (communications, utilities, education, agriculture, and transport) and established new types of political institutions including creating a Consultation Council in 1829 consisting of 156 members, 99 of them dignitaries that were elected directly by the people. The State also established new schools that inaugurated public education in Arabic and universities that specialized in a variety of emerging fields including government administration, engineering, law, and medicine.[11] Hospitals were also established, as was a medical school for women in 1832. In 1866, the Advisory Council of Representatives was created under Khedive Isma'il, who had pursued his grandfather's reforms.[12] The Advisory Council marked a commitment to liberal politics as it established a full-fledged election system and would soon become a place of debate and political opposition.[13]

---

[7] See Khaled Fahmy, *All the Pasha's Men: Mehmet Ali, His Army and the Making of Modern Egypt* (Cairo: American University in Cairo Press, 2002).

[8] John Chalcraft, *Popular Politics in the Making of the Modern Middle East* (New York: Cambridge University Press, 2016), pp. 83–84.

[9] The Tanzimat period under the Ottomans (1839–1876) would make similar promises reflecting the attitudes and expectations of the time.

[10] Karim Atassi, *Syria, the Strength of an Idea: The Constitutional Architectures of Its Political regimes* (translated from French by Christopher Sutcliffe) (Cambridge: Cambridge University Press, 2018), p. 15.

[11] Albert Hourani, *Arabic Thought in the Liberal Age: 1798–1939* (Cambridge: Cambridge University Press, 1983), pp. 51–54.

[12] Although also leading to British occupation of Egypt in 1882. See The Editors, "Isma'il Pasha: Ottoman Viceroy of Egypt," in *Encyclopedia Britannica* (February 26, 2021), www.britannica.com/biography/Ismail-Pasha.

[13] Editors, "Isma'il Pasha."

These measures and institutions, while meant to strengthen the position of the ruler vis-à-vis his subjects and the Ottomans, encouraged the creation of a dynamic society[14] and promoted a true *nahda*[15] (renaissance) by virtue of advancing intellectualism, science, and social change, including by sending promising male students to study in Europe and learn foreign languages, measures that in turn facilitated the translation of a formidable number of European works into Arabic. At the same time, the collapse of traditional institutions such as the urban guilds, coupled with the inability of the old knowledge networks to manage the changing needs of society, accelerated the process of producing and integrating new ideas.[16] All this rendered Islamic society better equipped for the demands of the modern world, and just as importantly, more open to liberal ideas as well as more egalitarian in its outlooks.

The ensuing political and intellectual transformations were impacting the entire region. Revolts and uprisings took place in attempts to resist new repressive Ottoman economic and political measures.[17] New liberalizing ideas about representative government, the rule of law, and justice translated into promises of self-rule and political representation by emerging leaders, and the creation of new forms of political community. Even the Turkish Ottomans became fully aware that reforms in the function of government were necessary and promised liberalizing changes: Ottoman subjects were to be transformed into equal citizens, modern laws were promised, and associational life was on the rise, as well as the need for representative parliaments. These ideas would lead to the creation of a burgeoning civil society, voluntary associations, and parliamentary life as early as the 1820s; and as stated above, it led to Egypt, in particular, pioneering its own representative parliament, the Consultative Deputies Assembly, in 1866.[18] Elections for parliament would constantly refer to the wishes, hopes, and interests of the people.[19]

Promises of the projected ideals of egalitarianism, civic respect, autonomy, and political decentralization facilitated the occupation of Syria by the forces of Muhammad Ali's son, Ibrahim Pasha, in October 1831. The idea that different regions can engage in self-rule and have control

---

[14] Hourani, *Arabic Thought in the Liberal Age*, pp. 52–53.

[15] The *nahda* was a political and sociocultural response to Ottoman political centralization and repression and Western interventionism and colonization.

[16] Abu-'Uksa, *Freedom in the Arab World*, pp. 83–84.

[17] Chalcraft, *Popular Politics*, pp. 67–69.

[18] Bahgat Korany, "Restricted Democratization from Above: Egypt," in Bahgat Korany, Rex Brynen, and Paul Noble (eds.), *Political Liberalization and Democratization in the Arab World: Comparative Perspectives* (vol. 2) (Boulder CO: Lynne Rienner, 1998), p. 40.

[19] Chalcraft, *Popular Politics*, p. 120.

over their own political projects turned Ibrahim Pasha into a liberator from repressive Ottoman rule, and a much needed modernizer.[20] And he did deliver on some of his promises to Syrians. Under him, the Syrian province with Damascus as its capital stretched from the Taurus Mountains in the north to Sinai in the south, and from the Mediterranean in the west to the Euphrates in the east. It thus asserted a Syrian identity that transcended communal differences; and for the first time in centuries, power was shifting hands from the Turks to the locals, whether Syrian or Egyptian, who began to redefine their identities and political projects outside of the Ottoman ones.[21]

New avenues of political and economic participation were established, opening up the flow of communication, ideas, and trade between and within Syria and Egypt, and between the two nations and Europe. Egalitarian and democratic ideals were spreading and meant that representatives of the people gathered in councils in which minorities were treated equally and sat alongside Muslims. Syria witnessed the opening of public schools for boys and girls, and thousands of students were now able to attend institutions of higher learning in Damascus, Aleppo, and Antioch. Commitment to the ideal of civic respect[22] was asserted through the imposition of equal rights and duties and the regularization of tax collection. Syria was witnessing its first modernization and industrial development in hundreds of years.[23] Newspapers and periodicals would soon emerge, such as *Hadiqat al-Akhbar* of Khalil al-Khuri (1836–1907), *Nafir Suriya*, and *al-Jinan* of Butrus al-Bustani (1819–1883). These publications shunned intercommunal violence, engaged with issues of governance, and called for unity, equality, tolerance, citizens' rights including "the basic right for freedom," and secularism.[24]

Yet the unitary and liberalizing experience within and between Egypt and Syria would ultimately fail in Syria, due to coinciding European and Ottoman interests, foreign intervention and, importantly for this work, Ibrahim Pasha's betrayal of his liberalizing promises.[25] The Syrian and

---

[20] Although Ibrahim Pasha betrayed his promises and his military regime was dismantled soon after in 1841. See Chalcraft, *Popular Politics*, p. 69; and Ussama Makdisi, *The Culture of Sectarianism: Community, History, and Violence in Nineteenth Century Ottoman Lebanon* (Berkeley: University of California Press, 2000).

[21] Hourani, *Arabic Thought in the Liberal Age*, pp. 56–61; Atassi, *Syria*, p. 15; Fruma Zachs, *The Making of a Syrian Identity: Intellectuals and Merchants in Nineteenth Century Beirut* (Leiden and Boston: Brill, 2005), pp. 86–88.

[22] Meaning that the State is legally committed to respecting the wishes and projects of its constituency.

[23] Atassi, *Syria*, pp. 15–18.

[24] Zachs, *The Making of a Syrian Identity*, pp. 89–90.

[25] Muhammad Ali had to evacuate Syria in December 1940.

Lebanese leaders would in fact cite tyrannical authority, oppression, and the recovery of their freedom to explain their revolt. "By a paradox," writes Hourani, "it was the modern nature of Muhammad Ali's government which in the end aroused Syrian opposition, and the new sense of religious equality ..."[26] which the Ottomans were now promising for all within the Empire. Nonetheless, the experience would still facilitate fundamental changes to the structure of the political system. And the mid-nineteenth century would witness the rise of political participation and of a new class of Arab (and Ottoman) intellectuals and statesmen who worked to superimpose liberal values – such as representative government, self-rule, political justice, basic citizenship rights, civic tolerance, and respect of others in general – on the multiplicity of other identities that governed the lives of the Arabic-speaking peoples of the region.

One of those first intellectuals was Rifa'a al-Tahtawi (1801–1873), who was sent by Muhammad Ali on an educational mission to Paris in 1826. Tahtawi would go on to become one of the first pioneers of the renaissance and progressive thinkers of the modern era. In his efforts to learn about the West, Tahtawi had to rethink the relations between the self and the new knowledge and relations of power that were presented to him in France. As part of this process, he praised the French for their use of reason to produce new ideas and knowledge, and for being free from the shackles of orthodoxy and tradition.[27] Two liberal elements that he noted in 1826 were first, that the French king did not hold absolute power and that he was accountable to his people through representative bodies that created the laws, which he praised, and second, that Islamic principles are not incompatible with European modernity. In the preface of his meticulous translation of the French Constitution, Tahtawi writes: "We should like to include this book – even though most of what is in it cannot be found in the Book of Almighty God, nor in the *sunna* of the Prophet ... – so that you may see how their [the French's] intellect has decided that justice (*'adl*) and equity (*insaf*) are the causes for the civilization of kingdoms ..."[28] Tahtawi believed that principles of good governance, justice, freedom (*hurriyya*), and reason could be found within Islamic principles and could thus be adopted and applied. Kassab notes that although the equivalencies he established were conceptually and epistemologically questionable, "he must have considered change

---

[26] Hourani, *Arabic Thought in the Liberal Age*, p. 60.
[27] Hourani, *A History of the Arab Peoples*, pp. 304–305.
[28] Cited in Elizabeth Suzanne Kassab, *Contemporary Arab Thought: Cultural Critique in Comparative Perspective* (New York: Columbia University Press, 2010), pp. 23–24.

and improvement to be possibilities within reach."[29] Indeed, Tahtawi's observations presented France as a civilized equal, not a threatening and superior force. In his description of the Greek revolt against the Ottoman sultan, he used the word *hurriyya* to explain the reason for the revolution "emphasizing the conceptual association between freedom, revolution, and sovereignty, in contrast with absolutism."[30] Tahtawi's focus on the importance of political representation and social justice would become recurring themes within the *nahda* literature and mood, as well as principles expected to be incorporated within the emerging political constructs.

In Syria, the concept of freedom was also becoming more prominent and increasingly comprehensive, emphasizing the rule of law, popular sovereignty, and political freedoms, and articulating the individual's relation to society, religious institutions, and State.[31] Physician and thinker Francis Marrash (1837–1874) published his *Ghabat al-Haqq* (the *Forest of Justice*, 1866) in which he presented his ideas about how to achieve the Kingdom of Liberty – as opposed to the Kingdom of Slavery. That same year, a certain Muhammad Rashid Pasha was warmly welcomed in Syria as Governor General by both the elite and the rest of the people "who believed that such a 'liberal man' could contribute to the Vilayet of Syria and that 'now Syria stood to win a better future.'"[32]

In the 1850s and 1860s and following Muhammad Ali's death, a split could be identified among the intellectuals about how to conceptualize and organize politics and society broadly speaking. This split was between those who supported liberal reforms and those who worried about maintenance of the moral order they cherished. The latter group feared the loss of morality and solidarity if new generations were no longer grounded in the traditional knowledge of their ancestors.[33] For those who advocated reform, however, both institutional and cultural, change was not as foreign or alienating as some made it sound. Among these reformers, two distinct trends emerged: the secularists who endorsed revolutionizing the sociopolitical system in the region, and the Islamic and Christian modernists who believed that religion could – and should – still remain a legitimate basis of modern life if it was re-interpreted according to modern human reason instead of relying on old teachings and applications. Both the secularist and the faith-based trends were undoubtedly

[29] Kassab, *Contemporary Arab Thought*, p. 25.
[30] Abu-'Uksa, *Freedom in the Arab World*, p. 109.
[31] Ibid, p. 102 and pp. 116–117.
[32] Cited in Zachs, *The Making of a Syrian Identity*, p. 106.
[33] Hourani, *A History of the Arab Peoples*, p. 307.

liberal. They asserted ideas about the need to use reason and science in order to create a new sociopolitical order, to ensure freedom of the press and of speech, to protect the individual against the repressive State and tyranny, and to create a modern citizen with inalienable rights and civic liberties, as well as a representative State. And all this was part of an attempt to catch up with and to achieve the technological progress and economic and scientific development that Europe was seeing, but also to ensure political justice and religious tolerance were served. Both trends agreed that one main reason for the region's stagnation was political and religious despotism (*istibdad*), so much so that the two movements initially overlapped and cooperated in order to achieve change.[34]

While hundreds of works and newspapers could be looked at, two works by two prominent thinkers, Abd al-Rahman al-Kawakibi (1855–1902, Syrian) and 'Ali Abd al-Raziq (1888–1966, Egyptian), are particularly useful for highlighting the era's liberal direction. They focus on questions of governance in Islam and discuss the concept of despotism and the people's inalienable rights to create their own laws. In their studies, both thinkers challenge the traditionalist absolutist links between the political and religious domains. They argue that Muslims need to revise the assumed relationship between political and religious authority according to modern necessities, and by relying on their rational capacities and renewed understandings of the sacred texts instead of relying on traditionalist interpretations.[35]

Abd al-Rahman al-Kawakibi's liberal contribution to the Arab region is still felt today even though he is a little-known pioneer of the classical liberal age and the *nahda*.[36] He came from a well-educated and prominent family from the northern Syrian city of Aleppo, and was a thinker, a philosopher, and a daring journalist. He occupied a number of high government positions in Aleppo before turning to private practice and political activism in 1888. In his practice, he paid special attention to the

---

[34] For more on their overlap and cooperation, see Elizabeth F. Thompson, *How the West Stole Democracy from the Arabs: The Syrian Arab Congress of 1920 and the Destruction of Its Historic Liberal-Islamic Alliance* (New York: Atlantic Monthly Press, 2020).

[35] Hicham El Haddaji, "The Congruent Critique of Despotism in Abd Al-Rahman Al-Kawakibi and Shaykh Ali Abdel-Raziq," *AlMuntaqa*, Vol. 1, No. 3 (2018), pp. 92–103, www.jstor.org/stable/10.31430/almuntaqa.1.3.0092. Accessed August 5, 2020.

[36] Kawakibi's work was generally dismissed by Western academics for a number of reasons, amongst them a focus on Egyptian reformists and those who produced their works in Egypt, as well as claims that his work is influenced by Western Enlightenment thinkers. But as Weismann so eloquently puts it, "The claim about his lack of originality ultimately derives from the Orientalist inclination to see all innovative ideas as coming from the modern West." See Itzchak Weismann, *Abd al-Rahman al-Kawakibi: Islamic Reform and Arab Nationalism* (London: Oneworld, 2015), pp. 4 and 102.

needs of the poor and assisted them "in their dealings with the government and in forwarding petitions against corrupt provincial officials to Istanbul ... an activity that gained him the sobriquet 'father of the weak' (*abu al-du'afa*)."[37]

When discussed in Western academia, Kawakibi is presented mostly as an Arab nationalist and an Islamic reformer, but his political vision and his work on autocratic governance and democratic rule are equally impressive. He wrote his book *Taba'i' al-istibdad wa masari' al-isti'bad* (1902) [*The Characteristics of Despotism and the Destructions of Enslavement*][38] about what he perceived as the main problem facing the region and its people,[39] and he influenced entire generations of Syrian and Arab thinkers and reformers in the process. The book is a liberal manifesto par excellence; it advances a forceful condemnation of Ottoman autocracy and repression, and offers a scientific enquiry into and denunciation of despotism (*istibdad*) in general. Weismann explains,

For Kawakibi, tyranny is the antithesis of politics. If politics is the prudent conduct of public affairs, tyranny is their capricious conduct. By his definition, tyranny ... may apply to religious leaders, family heads, and guild masters, but it is especially used in the case of governments, the most powerful factor in rendering human beings the most miserable creatures on earth![40]

Indeed, Kawakibi considered tyranny an affliction, he explains, it "is unaccountable, unlimited, arbitrary, self-serving and exclusive rule."[41] Already in the preface of his work he asserts that the origin of backwardness in the region is "political despotism" and its cure is "constitutional democracy."[42]

Political and social backwardness, "the malady" as he puts it, are the product of despotism, which fosters slavery [*isti'bad*], and ignorance. Al-Kawakibi explains the intimate relationship between the triad: despotism prevents knowledge and promotes ignorance – especially ignorance of the social sciences and philosophy, which teach people their rights and that freedom is essential in life.[43] Ignorance in turn cements slavery and destroys the social body in its entirety.[44] Despotism is thus the source of

---

[37] Weismann, *Abd al-Rahman al-Kawakibi*, p. 51.
[38] The book has no English official translation yet.
[39] The book and other texts by Kawakibi were translated into French in 2016 by Hala Kodmani (Abd al-Rahman al-Kawakibi, *Du despotism et autres textes*, Arles: Actes Sud) with a postscript by Kawakibi's grandson, Salam Kawakibi.
[40] Weismann, *Abd al-Rahman al-Kawakibi*, p. 104.
[41] Kassab, *Contemporary Arab Thought*, p. 37.
[42] Abd al-Rahman Al-Kawakibi, *Taba'i' al-Istibdad wa-Masari' al-Isti'bad* [*The Nature of Despotism*], with introduction by Majdi Said (Cairo, Egypt: Dar al-Kitab al-Masri, 2011), p. 3.
[43] Al-Kawakibi, *Taba'i' al-Istibdad*, p. 51.
[44] Ibid, pp. 43–45.

all depravity: "it corrupts the mind, religion, education, science, and morals. It is the source of injustice, humiliation, ignorance, poverty, unemployment, and ruin."[45] Crime, he asserts, diminishes because it becomes hidden rather than prevented as the tyrannical State creates lesser despots (clergymen, ignorant fathers, and stupid husbands), and removes man's natural drive to improve, "turning the march of progress into decline, and growth into annihilation."[46] For Kawakibi, human progress is necessary and natural if allowed, and without it, humans would only face annihilation. He explains, "The people are put to death with their own hands as a result of the fear that ignorance fosters. When ignorance is expelled and reason flourishes, fear disappears" and thus free life can begin [author's translation][47] This is only possible, explains Kawakibi, if the people's opinion, individuality, and freedom, are respected.[48] He writes that the remedy begins with the establishment of a "democratic" government[49]; the people's will and democratic rule being the only legitimate basis for governance.[50]

Kawakibi then bridges liberal and Islamic ideals. In so doing, he draws on the strong tradition of social and political justice within Islam, claiming that *istibdad* is not Islamic and that the un-Islamic authoritarianism and the resultant imbalance of power relations that emerged between the people and the State was one main reason for the collapse of many regimes and empires, and will necessarily lead to the collapse of the Ottoman Empire.

And so *istibdad* can only lead to doom and demise but then it is *not* inevitable. Humans can create better political and social orders in which they can thrive and live harmoniously together. In his justificatory narrative, Kawakibi proclaims that Islam is committed to science, and morality, and renewal and change, and that it advances principles of conciliation, social justice, rule of law, and liberty, asserting that the truest form of Islamic governance is indeed constitutional governance. As such, religion can be the cornerstone of sociopolitical reforms. In so arguing, Kawakibi made a clear case for an Islamic liberal republic, making the case for what I call an "endogenous liberalism." This endogeneity does not mean for Kawakibi that the appropriation of enlightened ideas from the West is to be shunned. Quite the opposite, since there is no clash between liberalism and Islam; the region can learn from these

---

[45] Kassab, *Contemporary Arab Thought*, p. 38.
[46] Wesmann, *Abd al-Rahman al-Kawakibi*, p. 114.
[47] Al-Kawakibi, *Taba'i' al-Istibdad*, p. 46.
[48] Ibid, pp. 16–17.
[49] Ibid, p. 34.
[50] Ibid, p. 16.

ideas without necessarily adopting a hedonistic and overly materialistic culture.[51]

Kawakibi's critical stance and promotion of democratic and egalitarian ideals would not go unnoticed by the Ottoman rulers. His work was censored and the many newspapers he founded were closed because his ideas directly challenged the despotism of the Ottoman regime – at the time led by Sultan 'Abd al-Hamid II (1876–1909), whose governance was characterized by his contemporary intellectuals as engaging in absolutism in the name of pan-Islamism – and more importantly for this book, because his ideas had traction among Syrian and Arab thinkers and reformers. Kawakibi's activism and intellectual defiance led to him being arrested twice and then accused of high treason and of plotting to kill the governor of Aleppo. While he was acquitted, like other contemporary thinkers, he was forced into exile in Egypt in 1889. There he frequented the circle of Muhammad Abduh and other Egypt-based Syrian reformers such as Rashid Rida.[52] He died a few years later at the age of 48, allegedly poisoned on the orders of 'Abd al-Hamid in Cairo.

Kawakibi has influenced many in the region, including Arab nationalists and Islamic modernists, and certainly more recently the group of Arab and Muslim liberals who have recognized Kawakibi in their conferences and writings as a liberal pioneer, a champion of human rights, and an original thinker with concrete propositions for democratic change.

Ali Abd al-Raziq agreed with al-Kawakibi's endorsement of constitutional democracy, and his work was equally liberal and influential. Raziq was an Egyptian philosopher and religious scholar from al-Azhar university who took the reformist Islamic scholar Muhammad Abduh's[53]

---

[51] Weismann, *Abd al-Rahman al-Kawakibi*, p. 103.

[52] Ibid, p. 4.

[53] Muhammad Abdu (1849–1905), Grand Mufti of Egypt (1899) [*Mufti al-diyar al-masriyya*], an Islamic scholar of traditional education, who was one of those concerned with liberalizing society and revising religious practice and interpretation, writes about his mission, "to liberate thought from the shackles of imitation ... to return, in the acquisition of religious knowledge, to its first sources, and to weight them in the scale of human reason, which God has created ... so that God's wisdom may be fulfilled and the order of the human world preserved; and to prove that, seen in this light, religions must be accounted a friend to science, pushing [humans] to investigate the secrets of existence, summoning [them] to respect established truths and to depend on them in [their] moral life and conduct." (Quoted in Hourani, *A History of the Arab Peoples*, pp. 307–308). Muhammad Abduh's writings advocated distinguishing between the fixed and the changing within Islam: the fixed are related to belief in God, in revelation and in moral responsibility, while the changing are the laws and traditions of Islam. These are contextual and thus constantly changing according to human reason, whose challenge is to accommodate change while remaining loyal to the fixed principles of Islam (Hourani, *A History of the Arab Peoples*, p. 308).

analysis a few steps further and initiated an intellectual revolution in the process. Raziq came from a prominent and well-educated family. He had become a judge in 1915 in Cairo, and so his assertions were particularly impactful. Indeed, he was expelled from his position as judge and as a scholar of al-Azhar by the Higher Council of Ulama at the request of Egypt's King Fuad, following the controversy, political debate, instability and resignation of liberal ministers, and the governing coalition that followed the publication of his book in 1925.[54]

Al-Raziq studied the relationship between Islam and politics, and the claim by religious traditionalists and some modernists that the political office of the Caliphate – which has historically been a repressive office – is a religious requirement under Islamic Law. In his book, *al-islam wa usul al-hukum* (1925) [Islam and the Foundations of Governance], Abd al-Raziq questions if there is an Islamic system of governance that is sanctioned by the foundational texts, namely the Quran and the collection of hadiths. He cites these foundational texts and traditional scripture in arguing that political rule is not part of the prophetic mission of Muhammad, which belongs to the spiritual realm.[55] Al-Raziq explains that Islam is a religious and spiritual message, not a political one, and that the prophet Muhammad is a religious and a spiritual messenger, not a political ruler or "king" [*malek*].[56] He also notes that there is no hadith or Quranic verse that mentions the concept of *khilafa* (Caliphate) in the political sense or that requires unification between the temporal and the spiritual worlds, and thus politics and Islam.[57] He further notes that there is no consensus between the religious scholars on the legitimacy of any of the Caliphs that followed the first three caliphs. This leads him to refute the inseparability of Islam and politics declared by Islamic jurists, and to refute the assertion that Islam is both *din* and *dawla* (religion and state). He deduces that there is no religiously required order to political affairs in Islam, that Muslims are "free" to devise their own systems of rule based on "social and political sciences" as well as the most advanced insights flowing from human reasoning and experience of governance.[58]

[54] Mahmud al-Wardani, "Al-Islam wa usul al-hukum li al-shaykh Ali Abd al-Raziq: al-kitab allazi wallada alaf al-kutub," *Al-Khaleej newspaper* (UAE), File 32, No. 7534 (January 4, 2000), pp. 8–12.

[55] Andrew McDonald, "Ali Abd al-Raziq: A profile," *Jadaliyya* (September 4, 2018), www.jadaliyya.com/Details/37930

[56] Ali Abd al-Raziq, *Al-Islam was usul al-hukum: bahth fi al-khilafa wa al-hukuma fi al-Islam* [Islam and the Foundations of Governance: A Study of the Caliphate and Government in Islam], with commentary by Mamduh Haqi (Beirut, Lebanon: Dar Maktabat al-Hayat, n.d.), pp. 143–153.

[57] Al-Raziq, *Al-Islam wa usul al-hukum*, p. 42.

[58] Ibid, p. 201.

In so doing, Raziq challenges institutionalized religion and promotes a very modern and liberal idea: that people are entitled to create their own systems of governance and to modernize their political system in liberal and secular ways, and that they are free to choose their own leaders and to express their ideas freely. In so doing, Raziq also challenged orthodox and monolithic interpretations of religion, and advocated for the primacy of human reason.[59] Indeed, by proclaiming the Islamic Caliphate a human innovation (*ijtihad*), not only is he able to interpret Islamic sources in ways that contradict many claims and assumptions within the Islamic tradition about the body politic in Islam and thus to challenge the imposed monolithic interpretation, but also to declare the Caliphate to be a corrupt system, established by means of violence and the sword, a "*jinaya*" [crime], and a source of *istibdad* [despotism] for Muslims:[60] "[t]hat is the crime of the kings and their despotism against Muslims, they steered them away from the right way [*al-huda*] and blinded them to the paths of truth [*wujuh al-haq*] ..." [author's translation].[61] He concludes that God could not have wished the fate and well-being of the Muslims to be dependent or under the mercy of one ruler.[62]

In his work, Raziq reasserted many of the arguments of his liberal predecessors such as Kawakibi about *istibdad* and democracy, and yet also started a religious and a political revolution about what would soon be dubbed "Islamic secularism." His assertions are not only theoretical, since al-Raziq was writing as a jurist against the backdrop of the ambition of Egypt's King Fuad to become the region's new Caliph, with British blessing. Al-Raziq's book was a clear challenge to the British attempts to reinstate the Caliphate. He accused Caliphs of acquiring rule illegitimately by silencing intellectual enquiry and the will of their people.

Al-Raziq's work set off significant political debate in 1925. After all, he had referenced traditional scholarship, and the writings of historically reputable Muslim scholars and jurists to support claims against a political institution that had come to be considered an intrinsic part of the Islamic religion.[63] Many newspapers (such as the Liberal

---

[59] Ibid. For more on al-Raziq, see Jamal Barut. *Harakat al-Tanwir al-'Arabiyya fi al-Qarn al-Tasi' 'Ashar: Halaqat Halab Dirasa wa-Mukhtarat* [*The Arab Enlightenment Movement in the Nineteenth Century: A Study and Extracts from the Aleppo Circle*], (Damascus, Syria: the Syrian Ministry of Culture Publications, 1994); Al-Raziq, see Souad T. Ali. *A religion, not a state: Ali Abd al-Raziq's Islamic justification of political secularism* (Utah: University of Utah Press, 2009).

[60] Al-Raziq, *Al-Islam wa usul al-hukum*, pp. 74–75.

[61] Ibid, p. 200.

[62] Ibid, p. 86.

[63] For more on this, see Souad T. Ali. *A Religion, Not a State: Ali Abd al-Raziq's Islamic Justification of Political Secularism* (Utah: University of Utah Press, 2009).

Constitutional Party newspaper al-Siyasa) and thinkers (including Muhammad Husayn Haikal) came to al-Raziq's rescue and accused the committee of 'ulama chosen to adjudicate the case against him of restricting freedom of opinion and speech, and of contradicting the Constitution.

Politically speaking, despite the fact that the 1919 revolution is accused of achieving only a few of its goals, a democratic transition was asserting itself as will be discussed hereinafter, and King Fuad was increasingly ceding power to the Egyptian Parliament and government (an issue which will be explored in more detail later in this chapter). And this context made Raziq's case particularly important. Indeed, both Kawakibi and Raziq had contributed to this democratic transition and emphasized a very liberal idea, the essential nature of freedom and democracy, as well as the need to use human reason rather than religious customs to challenge orthodoxy and to shape change in the organization of society and politics.

Other authoritative thinkers such as Butrus al-Bustani (1819–1883), Rashid al-Dahdah (1813–1889), Hind Nawfal (1860–1920), Qasem Amin (1865–1908), Farah Antun (1874–1922), Nazik al-Abid (1887–1959), and Mary Ajami (1888–1965) advocated for political justice and representative government, freedom of thought and the press, for advances in gender equality, and the need to base political practice on scientific studies rather than established religious precepts and orthodoxy.[64] They all agreed with Kawakibi that despotism corrupts the mind and destroys virtue and morality.[65] And they all viewed change away from despotism and sociopolitical oppression as necessary for society's success. Some adopted a more secular outlook than others, and a few were entirely inspired by the European liberal experiment.

Among the latter was Taha Hussein (1889–1973) who picked up where some of his predecessors left off. Hussein was considered the "Doyen of Arab Culture" and is one of the most authoritative and prominent proponents of liberal democracy of his day. He published *The Future of Culture in Egypt* in 1938, in which he argued that democracy is not a foreign concept but one that has its roots in Greek, Roman, and Mediterranean civilizations, of which Egypt is a part. He contended that democracy was sovereignty of the people for the people and that it is preferable to any other system of rule such as monarchy and communism. He also held that citizens possess inalienable natural rights to freedom and to

---

[64] For more on Bustani and Dahdah, see Abu-'Uksa, *Freedom in the Arab World*, pp. 175–181.

[65] Kassab, *Contemporary Arab Thought*, p. 33.

self-rule.[66] Then Hussein asserted that science and democratic rule, as conceived in Europe, are essential to adopt if Egypt is to overcome its failures and become a modern independent nation. Hussein was a prolific author, translator, linguist, modernist, and editor. He became professor of Ancient History at Cairo University in 1919, and was an active reformist and advocate of free schooling for everyone throughout his career. He was later able to implement his ideas as Minister of Education from 1950 to 1952.[67] Further, in his earlier, controversial book analyzing pre-Islamic poetry (fi al-shi'r al-jahili, 1926), he had argued that Arabic poetry was falsified after the establishment of Islam in order to lend outside support to Koranic stories, thus suggesting albeit indirectly that the Quran was written by people, and that it should not be read as an objective source of history. Hussein is thus less interested in redefining an Islamic relation to governance than were Kawakibi and Raziq. His vision of change is entirely secular, which he argues Egyptian culture supports. In so doing, he advances a more intricate liberalism rooted in secular rationality to argue against heritage and customary views and to emphasize human experience and history over divine claims and authority.[68]

His writings angered some of the traditionalists at al-Azhar university, and led to him losing his job at Cairo University in 1931 even though the public prosecutor at the time reflected the prevailing liberal culture of the time in stating that Taha Hussein's opinions were those of a researcher and an academic, and should thus not be censored. Indeed, Hussein went on to establish the University of Alexandria in 1942, and was appointed Minister of Education in 1950. That he was able to continue working shows the continued presence and influence of liberals and of liberal thinking in the early twentieth century.

Tahtawi, Kawakibi, Raziq, and Hussein were authoritative intellectuals and their work and experiences are representative of the many others with whom they together initiated the liberal political debate about the intertwined topics of the rule of the people, secularism, free thought, political justice, public education, and pluralism in the Arabic-speaking region. Their thought would help challenge orthodoxy and monolithism, and would galvanize civil society and fuel the liberal political movements

---

[66] Gershoni, "Liberal Democratic Legacies."
[67] Kassab, Contemporary Arab Thought, p. 42.
[68] Ahmed Abdel Meguid and Daanisch Faruqi, "The Truncated Debate: Egyptian liberals, Islamists, and Ideological Statism," in Dalia F. Fahmy and Daanish Faruqi, eds., Egypt and the Contradictions of Liberalism: Illiberal Intelligentsia and the Future of Egyptian Democracy (London: Oneworld Publications, 2017), pp. 256–257.

for independence and sociopolitical emancipation that emerged in the early to mid-twentieth century in the entire region.

Early to Mid-Twentieth Century: Liberal Politics in Egypt and Syria

Ideas about reform materialized in the late nineteenth and early twentieth centuries within a nationalistic and paternalistic type of liberal politics and within a context of fading empires, systems and orders, of European colonizers, and of the rise of the nation-state and the working middle class.

Democratic transitions had started in both Egypt and Syria, this happened despite the monarchical rule and British occupation in Egypt and the unwillingness of the Ottomans followed by the French to allow for liberal democratic governance in Syria.[69] And so in addition to the intellectual liberal movement and its appeal to principles and ideas of popular consultation, a parallel political movement was taking shape that had as its main goal liberation from the occupier (whether through institutional autonomy or complete withdrawal of foreign forces), parliamentary rule and overall political emancipation. Political leaders and elites agreed with intellectuals and thinkers such as Kawakibi, Raziq, and Hussein that one of the main reasons for society's ills and backwardness was the lack of representation and access to the institutions of the State, which were dominated by Turkish, French, and English colonists. Egyptians and Syrians – as well as others in the region – rose up to demand their right to self-rule, rationalizing that dignity and justice would then naturally follow.[70]

And yet in general, the early liberals perceived liberal change as a movement from above rather than from below, focusing on the need for political autonomy and reasoning that only once the political framework and laws had been completely transformed in a liberal democratic direction could there be a transformation of the socioeconomic situation within the region. This was a moment of opening and decolonization,

---

[69] For more on the French's work against the institutionalization of democracy in Syria, see Thompson, *How the West Stole Democracy from the Arabs*.

[70] See the Tunisian Constitution of 1860 for example, which was the first written constitution in the region separating executive, legislative, and judiciary powers and limiting the powers of the Bey. For more on Egypt's liberal era in the nineteenth and early twentieth centuries in general, see Afaf Lutfi al-Sayyid Marsot, *Egypt's Liberal Experiment: 1922–1936* (Berkeley: University of California Press, 1977); Israel Gershoni and James Jankowski, *Egypt, Islam, and the Arabs: The Search for Egyptian Nationhood, 1900–1930* (London: Oxford University Press, 1986); Nathan J. Brown, *The Rule of Law in the Arab World: Courts in Egypt and the Gulf* (Cambridge University Press, 1997).

and so for many liberals, most of whom came from the traditional oligarchic elite, the State was an instrument and an ally rather than a foe.

Egypt: A Focus on the State and the Rise of Liberal Institutions

In Egypt, the need for representative government and a constitution in which rights would be secured and equality safeguarded was invoked as early as the 1860s. Senior politicians, namely provincial notables and merchants, allied themselves with Egyptian intellectuals such as Muhammad Abduh, the press, and army officers in order to demand representative government and to oppose Turco-Circassian privilege, European influence, and the authority of the khedive over them.[71] For instance, a Chamber of Deputies (*majlis shura al-nuwab*) was established in 1866 under Khedive Ismail, the ruler of Egypt after Muhammad Ali, and very quickly gave rise to hopes amid its attempts at meaningful representation. One of the leading figures in the Chamber, a merchant from Cairo, said in 1879,

We the delegates and representatives of the Egyptian people, the defenders of its rights, and the promoters of its welfare ... [thank the *khedive* for the convocation of the *majlis* which] ... represents the basis for civilization and order ... [and] the necessary means for the achievement of freedom (which is the source of progress and advance), and the true driving force for the development of legal equality, which in its turn brings about the essence of justice and the spirit of equity.[72]

The *majlis* hoped to achieve its goals of limiting the powers of the Khedive, of political reforms and the establishment of a constitutional monarchy through the institutions of the State. The first political party, the National Party, was established in 1879 and promised political freedoms, social justice, and the rule of law.[73] Yet the British invasion would put a halt to these ambitions. British rule, especially under consul-general Evelyn Baring (1883–1907), was exploitative, tyrannical, and undermined Egypt's sociopolitical and educational development.[74] Like the Ottoman rulers before them, the British perceived Egyptians as illiterate *fellahin* (peasants) incapable of rational thought.[75] This did not stop the liberal

---

[71] The French invasion of Tunisia in 1881 added to the Egyptians' fears.

[72] Quoted in Chalcraft, *Popular Politics*, p. 161 from Alexander Schölch, *Egypt for the Egyptians! The Socio-Political Crisis in Egypt 1878–1882* (London: Ithaca Press, 1981), p. 80.

[73] Abdelslam M. Maghraoui, *Liberalism without Democracy: Nationhood and Citizenship in Egypt, 1922–1936* (Durham: Duke University Press, 2006), p. 127.

[74] The Dufferin Report created a puppet parliament and asserted British control. The Egyptian army was disbanded.

[75] See Edward W. Said, *Orientalism* (New York: Vintage Books), pp. 38–41.

intelligentsia and a variety of institutions from fanning ideas about rationalism, representative government, natural rights and inalienable freedoms, self-determination, and the need to reconfigure the State. Among those was Abbas Hilmi II, a new khedive who rose to power in 1892 and who advocated for independence from the British. The College of Law, established around the same time (in 1886), and a French School of Law that was founded in 1890 were also advocating for liberal ideals.[76] And so while Baring was actively restricting access to primary and secondary education,[77] lawyers and judges were still studying the ideals of the liberal discourse and political thought – in both its European and Arabic versions – and became passionate proponents of liberal reform.[78] Thus the most prominent advocates of liberalism at the turn of the twentieth century in Egypt would turn out to be lawyers and judges such as Sa'ad Zaghlul (1859–1927), Qasim Amin (1863–1908), Ahmad Lutfi al-Sayyid (1872–1963), Mustafa Kamil (1874–1908), Mustafa al-Nahhas (1879–1965), and Huda al-Sha'rawi (1879–1947).[79] Other proponents of liberalism were journalists and literary figures such as Nabawiya Musa (1886–1951), Muhammad Husayn Haykal (1888–1956), Abbas Mahmud al-Aqqad (1889–1964), and Tawfiq al-Hakim (1898–1987).

To the liberals, constitutionalism, patriotism, political justice, and progress were not mere ideals; they served to unite Egyptians of different socioeconomic classes together and form the basis of a powerful movement against the British occupier and against autocratic rule. And while censorship and harassment struck at the liberal nationalists, the protests and support of the workers and the peasants throughout Egypt against the British in the early 1900s emboldened them further.

The liberals would go on to form an Egyptian delegation (al-Wafd) that was meant to head to Versailles for the Paris Peace Conference of 1919 in order to negotiate the end of the British Protectorate and Egyptian independence. The Wafd was led by a charismatic lawyer, Sa'ad Zaghlul, who toured the country with other Wafdists such as Mustafa al-Nahhas in order to mobilize Egyptians and garner support for the country's independence.[80] In so doing, the Wafd had staged a peaceful

---

[76] Farhat J. Ziadeh, *Lawyers, the Rule of Law, and Liberalism in Modern Egypt*, (Stanford: Hoover Institution, 1968), p. 150; Bruce K. Rutherford, *Egypt after Mubarak: Liberalism, Islam, and Democracy in the Arab World* (Princeton and Oxford: Princeton University Press, 2008), p. 37.

[77] For more on Baren's role in restricting education in Egypt, see Leila Ahmed, *Women and Gender in Islam* (New Haven: Yale University Press, 1992), pp. 137–153.

[78] Rutherford, *Egypt after Mubarak*, pp. 37–38.

[79] Ibid, p. 38.

[80] Chalcraft, *Popular Politics*, pp. 206–207.

revolution against the British occupation, peaceful because the movement was massively popular and thus garnered widespread support in uniting together under one umbrella a broad national coalition of political and social groups such as the law school students and the railway workers, all of whom demanded Egypt's independence, liberty, and the establishment of a democratic State.[81]

The British responded to the unrest with violence against the protestors, and the arrest and deportation of Zaghloul and other members of the coalition. But the arrests not only failed to calm the unrest, they would ignite a nation-wide insurrection. Law students and lawyers as well as other civilians (ulema', high status women, school teachers, tramway workers, electric company workers, customs employees and government employees) took to the streets *en masse* in support of the Wafd, initiating what would become known as the 1919 Revolution.[82] The Wafd leaders used their homes to organize rallies and meetings and the Wafd was able to distribute money to workers who went on strike in their support. The movement became so massive that it would end British occupation of – although not its presence in – Egypt and would hurl the Wafd party into power in 1920. Soon after, the party would win parliamentary elections (179 out of 211 seats), declare Egypt a modern and independent nation-state (1922), and promulgate a liberal constitution (1923) that called for a two-house Parliament and the immediate establishment of a constitutional monarchy.

The Wafd would go on to become the embodiment of parliamentary democracy in Egypt,[83] with an ideology that was committed to democratic principles of governance. Indeed, article 3 of the party's statute read, "The Wafd draws its power from the will (*raghba*) of the people, expressed directly and through their deputies in elected bodies."[84] With these words, the transition to democracy was effectively initiated. The new constitution was indubitably liberal. It guaranteed freedom of expression and assembly and the equality of all before the law regardless of race, language and religion. An Egyptian Parliament with legislative

---

[81] Abdel-Fattah Mady, "Student Political Activism in Democratizing Egypt," in Dalia F. Fahmy and Daanish Faruqi, eds., *Egypt and the Contradictions of Liberalism: Illiberal Intelligentsia and the Future of Egyptian Democracy* (London: Oneworld Publications, 2017), p. 203.

[82] Joel Beinin and Zachary Lockman, *Workers on the Nile: Nationalism, Communism, Islam and the Egyptian Working Class* (Princeton, NJ: Princeton University Press, 1998), pp. 93–99; Beth Baron, *Egypt as a Woman: Nationalism, Gender, and Politics* (Berkeley: University of California Press, 2007); Chalcraft, *Popular Politics*, pp. 207–208.

[83] Korany, "Restricted Democratization," p. 40.

[84] Quoted in Maghraoui, *Liberalism without Democracy*, p. 127.

power alongside the King was established, and it included a Senate as well as a chamber of deputies. The structure and political formula were meant to restrict the power of the King, broaden the powers of Parliament, increase the proportion of the people who could vote in order to move toward universal suffrage and greater popular sovereignty, and advance citizens' civil rights.[85] The Wafd was aided by the Bar Association and the Liberal Constitutionalist Party,[86] who played an important role in drafting the 1923 Constitution and in curbing the powers of the King and of British officials.[87]

But these radically democratic moves made the 1923 constitution too liberal to tolerate within the context of imperial and monarchical rule. Powerful opponents including the King and the British abolished it in 1930, reinstating the King's original powers. The liberals fought back, and an uprising that united students, teachers, journalists, trade syndicates, and judges, as well as all main national political parties restored the 1923 constitution in December 1935.[88] In the May 1936 elections, and despite the powerful opposition of the British, the Wafd won 89% of the votes and 157 seats in Parliament.[89] The liberals were back in power.[90]

Although conflicts between the liberals and those who supported King Fuad continued to stall the democratic process, liberalism's vibrancy was felt in Egypt throughout the 1920s, 1930s, and 1940s and animated its schools, coffee and tea houses, and social clubs, as well as the pages

---

[85] R. A. Hinnebusch, "The Reemergence of the Wafd Party: Glimpses of the Liberal Opposition in Egypt," *International Journal of Middle East Studies*, 16 (1984), pp. 99–100; Hourani, *Arabic Thought in the Liberal Age*, pp. 175–177; Rutherford, *Egypt after Mubarak*, p. 39.

[86] The Liberal Constitutionalist Party (*Hizb al-ahrar al-dasturiyun*) was another liberal institution founded in April 1922 by Zaghlul's rival within the Wafd party, Adli Yakan, and other nationalists also mainly from the Wafd Party such as Muhammad Mahmoud, Muhammad Husayn Haykal, and Ahmad Maher. The Party's main purpose was initially to provide a liberal alternative to the Wafd, although one that is more willing to work with the Monarchy. Its official organ was a newspaper, *al-Siyasa* (The Politics) in which the members asserted their belief that a civilized nation like Egypt would flourish with constitutional governance and individual freedoms.

[87] See Maghraoui, *Liberalism without Democracy*, p. 128.

[88] Mady, "Student Political Activism in Democratizing Egypt," p. 204.

[89] For more on the Wafd, see James P. Jankowski, "The Egyptian Blue Shirts and the Egyptian Wafd, 1935–1938," Middle Eastern Studies, Vol. 6, No. 1 (January 1970), pp. 77–95; Marius Deeb, "Labour and Politics in Egypt, 1919–1939," *International Journal of Middle East Studies*, Vol. 10, No. 2 (May 1979), pp. 187–203; Donald M. Reid, "The National Bar Association and Egyptian Politics, 1912–1954," *The International Journal of African Historical Studies*, Vol. 7, No. 4 (1974), pp. 608–646.

[90] Rutherford, *Egypt after Mubarak*, p. 42. See also Ziadeh, *Lawyers, the Rule of Law, and Liberalism in Modern Egypt*.

of prominent political journals such as *al-Risala* (1933–1958), *al-Hilal* (1892-), *al-Ahram* (1875-), and *Ruz al-Yusuf* (1925-), and the writing of some of the most widely read and esteemed thinkers in the Arab World, such as Taha Hussein, Ahmad Amin (1878–1954), Muhammad Zaki Abd al-Qadir (1906–1982), and Abbas Mahmud al-Aqqad (1889–1964).[91]

Aqqad was a member of the Wafd Party and one of the most active representatives of the liberal movement in Egypt from the 1920s to the 1940s. He had written hundreds of articles and books in which he expressed and developed his liberal democratic views and dissected absolutist ideologies and systems of rule.[92] In his book, *Hitler fi al-Mizan* (Hitler in the Balance), published in 1940 at the height of Hitler's political and military success, Aqqad writes that Hitler's racist and dictatorial project is not only dangerous for freedom and democracy but for enlightened culture in general.[93] Gershoni explains Aqqad's viewpoints, "In Aqqad's view, the merits of a liberal democracy were rooted in: individual freedoms and civil liberties, constitutionalism, a parliamentary and multiparty system, the separation of powers, equality for all citizens, cultural pluralism, and the unquestionable legitimacy of political opposition."[94]

Some of the liberals' ideas caused them to be accused by their rivals of elitism, paternalism, and of internalizing the outlook of the colonizers. But a closer look at discourse and events shows that even the early phase of liberalism in Egypt included thinkers who criticized the paternalistic elements within the liberal movement and additionally that they were hardly mere privileged emulators of Westerners.[95] Indeed, many Egyptian liberal intellectuals advanced homegrown and intricate conceptualizations of liberalism, as shown earlier. They were also critical of their

---

[91] See previous section for more on these thinkers' thought.

[92] See for instance his book *Al-Hukum al-Mutlaq fi al-Qarn al-'Ishreen* [Absolutist Governance in the 20th Century] published in 1929.

[93] Gershoni, "Liberal Democratic Legacies."

[94] Ibid.

[95] For instance in *Liberalism without Democracy*, Maghraoui argues that Egypt's reformers embraced the language of liberalism as their own, they adopted social prejudices built into the language of European liberalism to the extent that they alienated the people of Egypt who considered Arabic and Islamic cultures (and subcultures) part of their cultural and historical heritage. Thus, Maghraoui argues that efforts to achieve liberalization failed within the realm of culture, rather than politics.

See also the chapter on "Egypt's secularized intelligentsia and the guardians of truth" by Khaled Abou El Fadl, in Dalia F. Fahmy and Daanish Faruqi, eds., *Egypt and the Contradictions of Liberalism: Illiberal Intelligentsia and the Future of Egyptian Democracy* (London: Oneworld Publications, 2017), pp. 235–252.

Western counterparts and of Western imperialism more generally. For instance, many liberals asserted that liberal democratic powers "were far from blameless in international affairs; first among their flaws was their imperialism."[96] Indeed, the Egyptian liberal intelligentsia successfully led the fight against European totalitarianism and radicalism in Egypt and the Arabic-speaking world, even when liberal European leaders were contemplating a compromise with fascist forces.[97] One prominent journalist addressed Arabic-speaking readers and reminded them of why Hitler's project is to be rejected: "... if you treasure individual liberties and believe in the value of freedom – freedom of thought in literature, ethics, philosophy, and religion – then there is no doubt that you will hate the regime which supports economic efficiency over freedom, or in other words sacrifices the latter for the sake of realizing the former."[98] His statement also reveals a belief that Egyptians and Arabs cherish their individual freedoms. Furthermore, as discussed earlier, a number of thinkers such as Muhammad Husayn Haykal incorporated religious history and precepts in advancing their liberal viewpoints, thus reasserting a liberal trend that is different from the ones advanced in the West at the time.

But while Egyptian Liberals differed on tactics – meaning for instance whether religion should inspire liberal change or not or whether they should use diplomacy over confrontation with the British and the King – they agreed on and were committed to liberal constitutionalism and pluralism, to the rule of law, and to individual freedoms and freedom of speech and opinion. The result was that Egypt's political environment was effectively transforming into a liberal one that allowed for open intellectual debate, for individual freedoms, free press, and the organization of free and fair elections. And from 1922 to 1952, parliamentarianism served as a framework within which liberals impacted social and political life.[99] Gershoni concludes, "The [liberal] system ... dismantled the autocracy of the khedival rule, eroded the authoritarian political culture of the late Egyptian-Ottoman oligarchy, and weakened British colonial rule. It encouraged ethnic pluralism and religious tolerance, reduced the presence of the police and army, and cultivated rich cultural activity with minimal state intervention."[100]

---

[96] See the remarkable work of Israel Gershoni and James Jankowski, *Confronting Fascism in Egypt: Dictatorship versus Democracy in the 1930s* (Stanford: Stanford University Press, 2010), p. 85.

[97] See Israel Gershoni, "Egyptian Liberalism in an Age of 'Crisis of Orientation': al-Risala's Reaction to Fascism and Nazism, 1933–39," *International Journal of Middle East Studies*, Vol. 31, No. 4 (1999), pp. 551–576; Gershoni and Jankowski, *Confronting Fascism in Egypt.*

[98] Quoted in Gershoni and Jankowski, *Confronting Fascism in Egypt*, p. 128.

[99] Gershoni, "Liberal Democratic Legacies."

[100] Ibid.

But the liberals would fail to manage issues of class and economic hardship that accompanied the exponential population growth and the rural exodus witnessed in the 1930s and 1940s. They would also fail to offer meaningful socioeconomic reforms at the domestic level, causing dismay and disbelief, and leading a few prominent Wafdists to leave the Party.[101] The youth would also feel betrayed by the liberals' inability to secure full independence from the British and to effectively challenge the autocratic tendencies of the King, who continued to sabotage the liberals' efforts to create a viable democratic State.[102] The result is that liberal constitutionalism became less attractive, replaced by issues of alienation, poverty, and unemployment, leading to the rising tide of radical nationalism of Young Egypt, of right-wing pan-Islamism, and the populism of the leftist parties.

The rise of Gamal (Jamal) Abdul Nasser to power in 1952 would effectively put an end to the power and political principles of the liberals. Nasser's rise would also effectively end the independence of the Bar Association, and the other liberal institutions and parties in Egypt. Some liberals, still hopeful, turned to Nasser, rationalizing that an enlightened temporary dictator could create the needed liberal order that they had not been able to create yet.[103] Indeed, one thing remained true for the liberals until the rise of Nasser and the realization that his rule was anything but temporary is their belief that a liberal order could be started through the state.

Syria: A Liberal Beginning

In Syria, like in Egypt, the need for representative government and a constitution in which rights would be secured and equality safeguarded was invoked as early as the 1860s, and in 1867, a *Majlis 'Umumi* (General Council) was established which was to convene every year in Beirut and to submit its resolutions to the Vali, Rashid Pasha at the time, who would then inform the government in Istanbul of his final decisions. The departure of Rashid Pasha in 1871 and the rise of Ottoman Sultan Abdul Hamid II marked a turning point in Syria, and the political environment

---

[101] Ahmed Abdalla, *The Student Movement and National Politics in Egypt 1923–1973* (Cairo and New York: The American University of Cairo Press, 2008), p. 12.

[102] Abdalla, *The Student Movement*, p. 14.

[103] One of those liberals is Ihsan Abd al-Quddus, the then-editor of the prominent magazine *Ruz-al-Yusuf*. See Meguid and Faruqi, "The Truncated Debate: Egyptian Liberals, Islamists, and Ideological Statism," p. 263; Joel Gordon, *Nasser's Blessed Movement: Egypt's Free Officers and the July Revolution* (New York: Oxford University Press, 1992), p. 33.

soon deteriorated. This led to a movement of politicians, notables, and merchants allying themselves with Syrian intellectuals in an attempt to oppose Turkish and European authority over them, with the movement reaching its zenith in the early twentieth century.

The history of early to mid-twentieth century Syria is often focused on struggle: the end of Ottoman rule, the nationalist pan-Arab and the class-based movements, and negotiations with the French colonizer in an attempt to build a new independent state. And yet while it was a time of struggle, it was also a time of creative expression, renewal, and hope for the newly created nation of Syrians, a time in which ideas about respecting individual rights, honoring ideological pluralism, and sanctioning freedom of thought and expression were flourishing and seen as achievable goals.

Several factors had combined in the twentieth century to create a fairly unified elite that would end up dominating Syrian politics with little challenge from rival forces until the mid-twentieth century.[104] It is during the time of the collapse of the Ottoman Empire that this elite would cohesively assert itself, and would quite easily manage to secure its position and influence during the reign of King Faysal (1918–1920), to subsequently play the role of mediators between the people and the French during the process of decolonization, and finally to act as leaders of newly independent Syria beginning in 1946. This elite, which included intellectuals, businessmen, and politicians, mobilized under the banner of liberalism, patriotism, and Arab nationalism, effectively uniting the highly diverse constituencies of Greater Syria (the Levant).[105]

This commitment to a nationalist tinged liberalism was clear from the outset. On October 3, 1918, the forces of the Arab revolt that were fighting for independence from the Ottomans entered Damascus and terminated Ottoman sovereignty with the help of the Syrian notables. Those notables then welcomed the Arab forces leader, Amir Faisal, son of the Grand Sharif of Mecca, and immediately began their state-building project. That project, known as the Arab Kingdom, was based on principles

---

[104] Philip S. Khoury, "Syrian Political Culture: A Historical Perspective," in Richard T. Antoun and Donald Quataert (eds.), *Syria: Society, Culture, and Polity* (New York: State University of New York Press, 1991), p. 16. For more on the era of the Syrian notables, see C. Ernest Dawn, *From Ottomanism to Arabism: Essays on the Origins of Arab Nationalism* (Urbana: University of Illinois Press, 1973); Philip S. Khoury, *Urban Notables and Arab Nationalism: The Politics of Damascus, 1860–1920* (Cambridge University Press, 1983).

[105] At the time, the terms "Arab" and "Syrian" were used interchangeably. Both qualifications denoted the people of Greater Syria, namely current day Palestine/Israel, Lebanon, Syria, and Jordan.

of representation and constitutionalism, on a separation of powers, and on the establishment of democratic institutions such as the Syrian General Congress.

Khoury explains that the choice of creating a liberal environment stemmed from the notables' desire to maintain their lifestyles, but also their privileges and particular interests as a group. A liberal environment allowed them to battle and settle their sociopolitical and economic disputes in a "genteel" fashion: "Apart from the aim of independence, nationalism incorporated the liberal bourgeois language of constitutionalism, parliamentary forms, and personal freedoms ... parliament was an ideal, genteel place in which factions could play out their struggles and ambitions."[106]

Perhaps another reason for their adoption of a liberal framework is their own education and personal convictions – we have seen how Kawakibi and other prominent thinkers considered despotism to be at the root of all injustice, and saw political participation as indispensable for progress. A liberal environment was in line then with their aspiration to implement the representative political system and citizens' rights that they had hoped for under Ibrahim Pasha and then during the Tanzimat period under the Ottomans (1839–1876), while also echoing their judgment that only a representative and pluralist system of governance would bring about political justice and unite the heterogeneous constituencies of Greater Syria. The result was that liberal ideas and principles prevailed within the different public discourses. Kawakibi was indeed among hundreds of Arab, Egyptian, and Syrian/Lebanese thinkers, such as Rashid Rida (1865–1935), Khalil al-Khuri, Butrus al-Bustani and his son Salim al-Bustani, Francis Marrash, Hind Nawfal (1860–1922), Nazik al-abid (1887–1959), Mary Ajami (1888–1965), and to an extent Shibli Shumayyil (1850–1917), who advocated for the end of despotism and who held that freedom, education, and political participation and justice were the basis for civilizational growth and prosperity.[107] These pioneers founded literary periodicals and political newspapers such as al-Jinan (1860) and Al-Arus (1910), and established a vibrant Arab press[108] in which they expressed and disseminated their ideas throughout the region.[109]

---

[106] Khoury, "Syrian Political Culture," p. 23.
[107] Kassab, *Contemporary Arab Thought*, p. 32.
[108] Often in Cairo, where they had more freedom of expression. For instance, all of the prominent periodicals and newspapers such as *al-Jinan*, *al-Ahram*, and *al-Hilal* were founded by Syrio-Lebanese intellectuals, in Cairo.
[109] These thinkers then relocated to Cairo when Ottoman censorship increased in Greater Syria at the end of the century. Kassab, *Contemporary Arab Thought*, p. 32.

This intellectual liberalism was paralleled at the political level, and the first official session of an independent Syrian General Congress was held on June 3, 1919. Liberalism and egalitarianism defined the overall atmosphere, and Christians and Muslims as well as Jews were represented in the newly created government.[110] Shaykh Rashid Rida, the president of the Syrian General Congress in 1920, writes, "Freedom in all its aspects ruled – including freedom of association, speech, and publishing – which were envied in other parts of Syria and Egypt ... People sensed their own honor and dignity."[111] Constitutions showcased the liberal ambitions of the era. Indeed, the Constitution drafted in 1920, which was tailored to serve the needs of the Syrian constituency, was the quintessence of the nascent liberal environment. The Constitutional Committee charged with writing the Constitution settled on a representative monarchical system. Elizabeth Thompson explains that the Committee agreed on, "a civil, parliamentary form of government because it would balance freedom and rule of law. The proposed regime would mobilize public opinion, but also guard against 'exclusionary and religious elements in politics and government'."[112] A bill of rights ensured primary education, equal citizen rights to all those residing in Syria, freedom of speech and opinion, freedom of religion and association, and freedom from torture and unauthorized entry into homes. Article 9 of the Constitution was nothing less than revolutionary in that it stated, "The King is respected, but not responsible."[113]

This liberal democratic project would be halted almost immediately. This is because the 1920 Constitution and the parliamentary elections that were planned for after ratification never materialized due to the French using violence to stop the creation of an independent liberal Syrian state. The French mandate leaders feared a democratic Damascus would inspire other Arabs. Thompson explains, "Dictatorship came on the heels of British and French colonial soldiers ... by means of brute force. The mandatory regimes uprooted the foundations of democracy laid in 1920 and built obstacles to its return ..."[114] It became clear that the French had a different plan for Syria. They had entered Latakia in 1918 and were able to impose a siege and capture the capital Damascus on 25 July 1920. Very shortly afterward, they toppled King Faisal's newly founded government and imposed a direct form of rule over Syria,

[110] Elizabeth F. Thompson, *How the West Stole Democracy from the Arabs: The Syrian Arab Congress of 1920 and the Destruction of Its Historic Liberal-Islamic Alliance* (New York: Atlantic Monthly Press, 2020), pp. 236–237.
[111] Quoted in Thompson, *How the West Stole Democracy*, p. 240.
[112] Thompson, *How the West Stole Democracy*, p. 242.
[113] Ibid, p. 243.
[114] Ibid, p. xvi.

in so doing destroying the newly created democratic Arab Kingdom. The fall of the Arab Kingdom would subsequently be seen by liberals as having planted the seeds of a new illiberal era, and a reminder of Western imperialism and deceit.

The French project had no major collaborator in Syria, forcing the French to rule by coercion and division. Meanwhile the liberal forces, who would eventually gather under the National Bloc in 1928, continued to seek independence as well as the establishment of a democratic state by garnering the power of an unprecedented coalition that reflected the social, economic, confessional, and regional diversity of Syria.[115] The coalition, spearheaded by the urban intelligentsia along with liberal politicians, would play a major role in the resistance against the French colonizers, and there would be a full-fledged armed confrontation from 1925 to 1927 between the French and the liberal nationalists led by leaders such as Abd al-Rahman Shahbandar, Nasib al-Bakri, Hashim al-Atassi, Saadallah al-Jabri, Jamil Mardam Bey, Shukri al-Quwatli, and Ibrahim Hananu, the founder of the League of National Defense, to name only a few.[116] The Syrian armed resistance was ultimately unsuccessful, but did contribute to the achievement of political concessions from 1927 to 1936 including the securing of indirect rule.

The aim of the political elite at the time under the leadership of the National Bloc was to create the liberal institutions and apparatus needed to ensure sovereignty of Syrians and thus independent rule. And having recognized that war would not lead to the achievement of their aspirations, they treaded defiantly but diplomatically. Their diplomacy would translate into the establishment of a constituent parliament composed of a majority of National Bloc members who were elected in April 1928 and were charged with drafting a constitution. The new constitution they promulgated was democratic, republican, and parliamentary, and it limited the powers of the French in favor of the parliament.[117] This however infuriated the French, who perceived the constitution as a threat and the Syrian leaders as arrogant and insolent. And although Georges Clemenceau had, a few years earlier, considered the Syrian leaders to be fellow liberals,[118] the French authorities now preferred to simply do away with them, resulting in the dismissal of parliament in August 1928 and the

---

[115] Chalcraft, *Popular Politics*, p. 221.

[116] Philip Khoury, *Syria and the French Mandate* (Princeton, NJ: Princeton University Press, 1987), pp. 103–106.

[117] Salma Mardam Bey, *Syria's Quest for Independence 1939–1945*, (Reading, UK: Ithaca Press, 1994), p. 3.

[118] Thompson, *How the West Stole Democracy*, p. 252.

dissolution of the Constitution. It was not until May 14, 1930, that the French submitted the Constitution to the League of Nations, and even then only after extensively revising and redrafting the text, which in turn led to the declaration of the establishment of the Republic of Syria.[119]

The first elections following the creation of the Republic of Syria were held in 1931–1932 under the French revised constitution. The National Bloc had won a minority of seats in the new Chamber of Deputies (16 deputies out of 70) due to extensive manipulation by the French authorities. The Parliament had thus become a French puppet, with National Bloc members in the opposition as a minority.

In 1934, France attempted to impose a treaty of independence on its own terms. It promised gradual independence but kept the Syrian Mountains under French control. The National Bloc spearheaded a fierce opposition to the treaty. They blocked it in parliament, which led to its dissolution and the suspension of the constitution yet again by the French. The National Bloc then called for a national strike in protest. Demonstrations raged at the national level, and the French were forced to back down due to massive popular unrest.

Like their Egyptian counterparts, Syrian liberals still believed that the end of the Mandate could be achieved through communication and negotiations. In 1936, they formed a delegation that went to Paris to negotiate for a new treaty to recognize Syrian independence. The negotiations were a success and the treaty was signed in September of that year. Back in Syria, democratic elections were then held resulting in an overwhelming victory for the National Bloc candidates such as Hashem al-Atasi who was elected president of the Syrian Republic, Fares al-Khouri president of the General Assembly, and Mardam Bey who was asked to form the government.[120] It was a victory for the liberals and for democracy in Syria.

Unfortunately for these liberals, the French parliament would refuse to ratify the treaty in 1939, thus voiding the terms of the treaty and with it the ability of the Syrian government to transition the country toward independence. Jamil Mardam Bey wrote: "le Mandat s'est acharné à éliminer les Syriens du gouvernement de leur pays (the Mandate has tried desperately to eliminate Syrians from the government of their own country [author's translation])."[121] Salma Mardam Bey (the daughter of Jamil Mardam Bey) explains,

---

[119] Atassi, *Syria*, p. 5.
[120] Mardam Bey, *Syria's Quest*, p. 12.
[121] Letter written by Jamil Mardam Bey, available translated in French from Arabic in Salma Mardam Bey, *La Syrie et la France: bilan d'une équivoque (1939–1945)* (Paris: l'Harmattan, 1994), p. 14.

The non-ratification of the Franco-Syrian Treaty by the French parliament was accompanied by yet another disaster, namely the replacement of Comte de Martel by Gabriel Puaux as high commissioner to Syria and Lebanon. Puaux was a member of a political species that one would have imagined to be extinct by the mid-twentieth century. In his memoirs, Deux Années au Levant Puaux wrote of his dream to turn Syria and Lebanon into monarchies: "Why not create in Syria a king? ... A king assuming supreme power 'à l'orientale' will not have to satisfy the demands of demagogues [nationalists] ... But can the French Republic create monarchs?" Indeed he even took steps towards realising his project by contacting Fouad Hamza, a counsellor of King Abdul Aziz: I asked him if his master would consider giving Syria a king in the person of one of his sons.[122]

Despite these challenges, the Syrian liberals still managed to create a republican parliamentarian system, and they continued to settle their differences effectively through open debate and based upon a commitment to individual rights, a free press, and the organization of free and fair elections. But, like their Egyptian counterparts, the Syrian liberals were also faced with the difficult task of leading Syria to total independence and of securing the evacuation of all the occupation forces after the end of World War II. The unwillingness of the French to ratify agreements they had entered into weakened these leaders, who were blamed for the failure to ensure an independent Syria. Also contributing to the generalized instability was that the Syrian political elite and the National Bloc, like their Egyptian counterparts, had not given sufficient attention to the rising issues of poverty, rural exodus, and class-based grievances. The country would as a result witness several coup d'états between 1949 and 1954. The liberals nonetheless stayed committed to their project and continued to target political stability – thus following their return to power in the wake of the first coup d'état against them in 1949, they drafted a new constitution that enhanced limits on the exercise of power by the executive branch so as to ensure parliamentarian inviolability. The 1950 constitution also put agrarian and social issues at the heart of political life in Syria. Yet instability continued to plague the country, and the last liberal assembly was elected democratically in 1961. The result overall was that many became disenchanted with the liberal project and its inability to move the country forward.

In 1962, article 59 of the new promulgated constitution included a provision that granted the president the right to govern by decree, which the 1950 constitution had prohibited. "The coming to power of the Ba'th party turned the page in the history of a liberal, pluralistic, and

[122] Mardam Bey, *Syria's Quest*, p. 15.

parliamentary Syria and ushered in an era of authoritarian, presidential, monolithic regimes of the popular democracy type found in eastern
Europe in Cold War times."[123]

Conclusion

While parliamentary institutions remained weak and were overseen by
hostile colonial powers in both Egypt and Syria, the political environment nonetheless showcased multipartyism and party competition,
periodic elections, democratic norms, popular participation, and free
speech as well as freedom of association at least until the early 1950s in
Egypt and the early 1960s in Syria. Liberal values thus dominated, and
meant that issues and problems were debated and negotiated in parliaments and were reflected and reproduced in constitutions and citizens'
rights as well as the overall civic order. Indeed, liberal values shaped
the emerging public and legal spheres and were in turn shaped by their
interactions. Furthermore, liberalism was not just an imported intellectual and political system of thought, rather it was created, reinvented,
adapted, and reframed in order to fit within the region's specific context
and to address its complex problems. This was done by authors such
as Kawakibi, Raziq, and Haykal with both methodological fluidity and
creativity as well as deep contextual. And so the nineteenth and early
twentieth centuries offered a transparent and hopeful environment, with
many significant sociopolitical transformations that demonstrated an
Arab liberalism that was not simply imported but that had also developed in situ over time, critically engaging with its context and fighting
against the Western powers including sometimes with diplomatic tools,
and advocating for homegrown solutions to local problems.

The liberal democratic legacy of the movement was only weakened
and eventually undone by the strong repression it encountered at the
hands of foreign leaders as well as local leaderships who had an interest
in less liberal projects, and in the 1940s and 1950s, by leftist and conservative groups and parties that saw liberalism as a threat and an extension
of the imperialist Western projects.

The mid-twentieth century would bring about a new set of challenges:
economic and political instability, and with them the birth in the 1950s
and 1960s of authoritarian leaderships that advanced illiberal discourses.
These leaderships were able to quickly amass formidable fiscal and political power, and with the backing of foreign alliances and patrons, to

---

[123] Atassi, *Syria*, p. 6.

repress anyone challenging their authority (see Chapter 2). In Syria and Egypt, these leaderships were the revolutionary populists, the Ba'thists and the Nasserites, who would rise slowly but surely in the immediate post-decolonization era (1950s–1960s). These forces aimed to shape the region in ways that adhered to socialist ideology, but they defined their nationalism through populist rather than liberal concepts, which attracted the emerging middle and working classes that had felt ignored by the liberals.[124]

The rise of the authoritarian left was partly the result of modern realities that the region faced, including the inability of the liberals to secure a dignified independence, but also population growth, a rising poverty gap, rural exodus, and a need to industrialize as quickly as possible, which had meant that the most popular parties were no longer those advancing ideas of democracy, representative government, and civil liberties. Instead, leftist ideologies offering fast, seemingly effective, egalitarian, nationalistic, and totalizing solutions to the poor and middle class were gaining traction. But it is important to emphasize as well that a crucial reason for the ability of authoritarian leftists to gain power was their roots in the officer corps. And then once in power, inspired by Soviet communism and European socialism, they focused on patriotism and unity, power and control of one's destiny as a nation through revolution, a strong ideological political command, and drastic societal change. Thus issues of fiscal health and social mobility took precedence over questions of liberty and citizens' rights. Khoury writes,

The language of nationalism no longer emphasized constitutionalism, parliamentary forms, or personal freedoms, but rather social and economic justice for the masses, neutralism in international politics ... mass education, land reform, social welfare, and rapid industrialization, all of which [was] to be brought about by a strong, dynamic, interventionist state, all for the good of the masses. Government was to be "for the people, but not by the people."[125]

Furthermore, once in power by military coups in both Syria and Egypt, these parties were overtaken by their own radical members, who pushed forward their particular factions as the only patriotic ones

---

[124] For more on the rise of the rural classes, see Hanna Batatu, *The Old Social Classes and the Revolutionary Movements in Iraq* (Princeton: Princeton University press, 1978); Hanna Batatu, "Some Observations on the Social Roots of Syria's Ruling Military Group and the Causes of Its Dominance," *Middle East Journal* 35 (1981), pp. 335–338.

[125] Khoury, "Syrian Political Culture," p. 26.

and thus deserving of legitimate political power.[126] The new leaders also moved to restrict the free press and freedom of speech in the name of unity, nationalism, and the welfare of the masses. In this environment of restricted information, statism, promises of rapid development, and cryptic enemies, the old liberals were vilified and accused of spreading ideas on behalf of the enemies of the Arab nations. They were criticized for failing to maintain the integrity of Greater Syria and to save Palestine, for failing to uphold Arab nationalism, and for fostering diplomatic and economic ties with the imperialist powers of the West.

The fact that the Arab liberals' ideas did not entail servitude or servility to Western powers but rather equality with them would be a forgotten detail. Frustration with Western powers and their history and actions in the region meant that the illiberal message resonated, although not as rapidly and effectively as it is often thought to have done. Indeed Khoury notes, "That elements among the veteran elite managed to retain influence in politics as late as the early 1960s suggests how tenacious and resilient they were in the face of the growing forces of radicalization in the military and in civilian society."[127] Soon enough it became clear that instead of empowering the masses and shedding feudalism, these populist regimes had been hijacked by radicals who were unable to deliver on their promises, and who created corrupt and authoritarian orders throughout the region.

The ability to speak freely contracted quickly throughout Syria and Egypt, though also in Iraq, Tunisia, Algeria, as well as within the newly formed conservative monarchies which, although politically allied to the Western powers, did not allow liberal ideas to spread for fear of losing their own power in the process. By the 1960s, the ideas of the so-called enlightened thinkers of the region were effectively ignored, silenced, removed from schoolbooks, and eclipsed by both self-proclaimed republics and the region's conservative monarchies.

The era of paternalistic liberalism thus came to an end. Yet new liberal voices would soon emerge as a result of the realization that the old liberal democrats had not only failed to achieve change through the institution of the State but had also lost their own privileged position in the process. These new voices began to focus on creating a vibrant civil society that would act as a mediator between the citizen and the state. The focus

---

[126] For instance, the Ba'th party of Syria adhered to a liberal democratic parliamentarian framework before being overtaken by its Marxist-leaning members, who sanctioned the establishment of an authoritarian and personalized regime in 1963.

[127] Khoury, "Syrian Political Culture," p. 27.

was thus slowly shifting away from enacting change from above – which had become effectively impossible anyway – to creating a civil society that would enhance the power of the citizen and curb the powers of the State.[128]

In this new approach and logic, the State is still expected to create an environment that would allow for such a civil society to emerge but the elitist paternalism of the earlier generation was fading.

---

[128] For more on this, see Roel Meijer, *The Quest for Modernity: Secular Liberal and Left Wing Political Thought in Egypt, 1945–1958* (New York and London: Routledge, 2002).

2   1960s to the 1990s

The Loss of the State and the Shift
in Focus and Approach

> Confronting the State in tyrannical countries is like facing a mythical creature, one cannot fathom the amount of harm it can cause nor its shape.
>
> Writer Khairi al-Zahabi[1]

This chapter sheds light on the liberals' public and private work and discourse within the authoritarian and repressive sociopolitical context from the 1960s to the end of the 1990s. It particularly focuses on their "hidden" and not so hidden transcripts,[2] in other words their work beyond their seeming silence and absence, to shed light on their ongoing active engagement despite the contextual conditions forcing them to largely go underground. It argues that while the liberals were eclipsed by the region's authoritarian regimes, by illiberal leftists, and conservatives such as the pan-Islamists, they nonetheless remained vital and continued to have a sociopolitical impact through other means than via direct political engagement.

The rise of regimes that aimed to achieve national independence through a focus on rapid industrialization and authoritarian-nationalist agendas meant that one-party political systems prevailed almost everywhere in the Arab world during the 1960s, with constitutionalism brought to grinding halt. In the newly formed monarchies, such as Saudi Arabia, totalizing authoritarianism became the only option allowed to exist. In Egypt and Syria, populist authoritarian leaders and agendas took over the political apparatus. Overall, the 1960s and 1970s witnessed the conflation of regime and State and thus the impossibility for "true political liberals" (to reuse Ayman Nour's qualification of consistent liberals) to join the State without undermining their own liberalism in the process.[3]

---

[1] Ghassan Nasser, "Khairi al-Zahabi: al-dimucratia wa al-mowatana huma al-bawabaal-wahida li-khalas suriya," *Harmoon Center for Contemporary Studies* (January 28, 2021).

[2] See James C. Scott, *Domination and the Arts of Resistance: Hidden Transcripts* (New Haven and London: Yale University Press, 1990).

[3] Fi al-'umq, "Al-liberaliyun al-arab wa al-dimucratiya," *al-Jazeera* (May 12, 2014), www.youtube.com/watch?v=U_K_w7meM9E

Thus, the 1960s and 1970s became the era in which the liberals had to turn away from their focus on the institutions of the State and change from above, and realized that they needed to direct their attention to mobilizing reform through liberal nongovernmental institutions, through civil society and social activism, and a focus on cultural transformation instead. In other words, with the recognition that the liberal ethos in Arab political and intellectual culture had been eroded – particularly in Egypt and Syria – it became important to enact change from below rather than from above, by enhancing the power of citizens and resisting the authoritarian order in as many ways as possible.[4] This necessitated a move away from the elitist paternalism of the previous generations, as well as working in smaller, scattered, and independent groups in order to avoid the regime's scrutiny.

The liberals also reconnected with their democratic leftist counterparts. And in both Egypt and Syria, the possible coalition between liberals, democratic conservatives (mainly Islamic forces), and leftists would turn out to be too much for the authoritarian regimes to take. This was especially because pro-democracy leftists and Islamists switched to working from within a liberal logic in order to topple the authoritarian regimes, and thus effectively joined the liberal movement.[5] We can thus see the tentative start of an overall shift away from doctrinaire commitments and toward a more critical stance, directed inwards, and in which the focus is on how to establish a system of rule and a society that safeguard plurality and freedoms. More fundamentally, intellectuals began to realize that democracy and citizen freedoms and rights are not mere principles whose merits are to be debated and discussed at a theoretical level, but rather vital requirements for leading a dignified life.[6]

It is important to realize that the onset of the authoritarian era did not erase all the marks of the preceding liberal era. If anything, the liberal era was invoked by many actors in the 1970s and 1980s as a phase that should be returned to, albeit with some improvements. Thus, despite the many twists and turns in liberalism's trajectory in the region, many liberal concepts had been introduced and successfully integrated into constitutions and legal systems. In particular, promises of citizens' rights, of limits on and

---

[4] Lust explains that regimes cannot dictate their opponents' actions but they can create rules and institutions in such a way as to limit their actions and determine who can and cannot exist. See Ellen Lust-Okar, *Structuring Conflict in the Arab World: Incumbents, Opponents, and Institutions* (Cambridge: Cambridge University Press, 2005), p. 35.

[5] Meir Hatina, "Arab Liberal Thought in Historical Perspective," in Meir Hatina and Christoph Schumann (eds.), *Arab Liberal Thought after 1967: Old Dilemmas, New Perceptions* (New York: Palgrave Macmillan, 2015), p. 27.

[6] We will see how important leftists such as Ilyas Murkus and Yasin al-Hafez start integrating liberal elements, such as individual freedom, within their thought.

separation of political powers, and of the need for the creation of multiparty systems permeated political debates and political programs. And so even as emancipation from imperialism and economic malaise took over and the parliamentarian systems were completely manipulated and dismantled, it was done in the name of urgent national needs, resistance to imperialism, and emergency laws. For instance, in the 1962 National Charter, which was the ideological manifesto of his regime, Gamal Abdel Nasser asserted that democracy and free speech were a reaffirmation of the people's sovereignty if properly prepared for. Thus, his objection to the 1922–1952 period was that it "saw [liberal] democracy reduced to the superimposition of a formal constitutional façade to cover up economic exploitation and social subordination."[7] What we can see then is that Nasser – whose regime had established the Egyptian political system of one-party rule – did not deny the merits of "freedom" and "democracy" in the liberal sense of the words. Further, he asserted that civil freedoms are a necessity but noted that they should be linked to economic and social transformations for them to be truly established. Hafez al-Asad, Syria's president from 1970 to 2000, also conceded that pluralism and democracy were desired by many in Syria, but that "the phase through which the country is passing is not suitable for implementing [a fully competitive electoral system] … despite the fact that many in Syria are convinced this is the best method."[8]

One thing is clear, that by the 1960s, most governments in the region had successfully cemented autocratic modes of ruling and ruling coalitions that were especially hostile to political liberals (whether left-wing or right-wing liberals). Political activism was officially constrained in the name of nationalism and unity and state-led development, often echoing classical Marxist and Soviet claims that liberalism does not really liberate society but rather only serves its bourgeois interests, and more fundamentally that liberal democracy is ineffective at best.[9]

---

[7] Korany, "Restricted Democratization," p. 42.

[8] Cited in Raymond A. Hinnebusch, "Calculated Decompression as a Substitute for Democratization: Syria," in B. Korany, R. Brynen and P. Noble (eds.), *Political Liberalization and Democratization in the Arab World*, Vol. 2: Comparative Experiences (Boulder, CO, and London: Lynne Rienner, 1998), p. 224.

[9] For instance the Ba'th party's *Theoretical Foundations*, which was revised in 1963, stated, "… parliamentary government in its liberal bourgeois form could in no way be a means of radical social transformation and was merely a formal façade hiding the influence of feudalism and the upper middle classes … power must be passed from the feudal and bourgeois classes to the working classes. This is why we must go beyond parliamentary government because it is one of the forms of [feudal and bourgeois] class domination over the mass of the people." Translation of the text available in Karim Atassi, *Syria, the Strength of an Idea: The Constitutional Architectures of Its Political Regimes* (Cambridge University Press, 2018), pp. 372–372.

This triumph of the populist leftist and illiberal discourse meant that liberals had to change and adapt, that they had to work differently and cautiously. After all, this new generation of liberals, which included members of the middle and professional classes, women, critical thinkers, and exiles living abroad, was no longer part of the political elite nor espousing the dominant ideology.[10] Their new agenda became inward looking, focused around fighting for human rights, religious moderation, secular laws, and bridging the immense gap between them and the public masses. At the same time, their new positions, focus, and methods meant that particularly since 1967, Arab liberals were seen by some as a "heterogeneous and poorly organized group,"[11] probably because necessity drove them to work in small, scattered, and independent groups, to change course quite often, and to retain a low profile and thus to be at times hidden in plain sight. And yet, as this chapter argues, dismissal of the region's liberal intellectual and activist work throughout the 1970s, 1980s, and 1990s in much of the Arabic-, English-, and French-speaking academy distracts us from the seminality of this period in laying the foundations of a more liberal political culture, and maybe even civic order,[12] and certainly for liberals' immense contribution to the events of the Arab Spring in 2011 and 2012.[13] Indeed, the following sections will show how liberalism re-emerged in the midst of authoritarianism, and how liberal activisms, although entangled in and restrained by the authoritarian structure, nonetheless helped to modify the political configurations of authoritarianism and brought changes to the region's political culture.

---

[10] Emran El-Badawi, "Conflict and Reconciliation: 'Arab liberalism' in Syria and Egypt," in Dalia F. Fahmy and Daanish Faruqi, (eds.), *Egypt and the Contradictions of Liberalism: Illiberal Intelligentsia and the Future of Egyptian Democracy* (London: Oneworld Publications, 2017), p. 292.

[11] Meir Hatina, "Arab Liberal Thought in Historical Perspective," in Hatina and Schumann (eds.), *Arab Liberal Thought after 1967: Old Dilemmas, New Perceptions* (New York: Palgrave Macmillan, 2015) p. 23.

[12] Hatina writes, "Notably, ideological ambiguity and an absence of consistency are also present in Western liberal thought, with its vacillation between individualism and collective purpose, liberty and distributive justice, and free markets and the welfare state, as reflected in John Rawls's theory of justice and its critics. However, Western discourse does not nullify the liberal perception as unworthy of analysis and recognizes this perception as distinct from other ideological streams such as socialism or communitarianism. Why, therefore, should the Arab case be an exception? Although the liberal experience in Arab lands proved to be fragile, beset by retreats and suspensions, it nevertheless endured." Hatina, "Arab Liberal Thought in Historical Perspectives," pp. 25–26.

[13] Indeed, as will be discussed in this and following chapters, the notions that were exclusively liberal slowly came to be adopted by staunch Marxists. Leftists in general realized the need for political liberalization, and some have become liberals.

Egypt: Hope and Repression

In Egypt, the students and workers that had been mobilized within the framework of nationalist liberalism in the 1920s and 1930s were by the 1940s losing their trust in the ability of the Wafd party and the liberals in general to deliver on their promises for sociopolitical reform and independence from the British. The constant British undermining of Egyptian will, their continued military presence, and more broadly the crisis of liberalism in the West during the World War II certainly did not help Egypt's liberals. The Wafd also seemed incapable of managing the newly emerging socioeconomic malaise Egyptians were facing. Liberal nationalism, reformism, and legalistic culture were failing the plebeian masses. New popular mobilizations and alternatives, such as the Muslim Brotherhood, the Socialists, and the Communists, began to emerge, with no one group successfully monopolizing the political field. Thus, the Egyptian State was in crisis throughout the 1940s.[14] Some believed that what was needed was no longer reformism, diplomatic patience, and negotiations, but forceful and direct action through the State.[15]

Direct action would come in the form of a military coup. The army takeover of the Free Officers on July 23, 1952, put an end to the crisis of the weak State but also to Egyptian multipartyism and civil freedoms. The Free Officers promised to restore national independence and to purify the political system. Egypt was turned into a republic. As for the British, Chalcraft explains, "models of imperialism old and new suggested that a military officer was easier to do business with than a democratic politician or a movement with a meaningful social base."[16]

And so the revolution "from above" was successful, prompting no intervention from the British imperial army; but change came with a heavy cost for liberals and more importantly liberal principles of governance. Political activism was almost immediately restricted. Demonstrations and strikes were swiftly quelled, and collective action was crushed. All political parties were banned in 1953 and political participation was suppressed. Youth mobilization was limited to state-controlled organizations such as the Youth Organization and the Youth Vanguard.[17] The unions were absorbed by the State in 1957, and were therefore no longer capable

---

[14] Chalcraft, *Popular Politics*, pp. 296–297.
[15] Ibid, p. 313.
[16] Ibid, p. 318.
[17] Joel Beinin and Zachary Lockman, *Workers on the Nile: Nationalism, Communism, Islam and the Egyptian Working Class* (Princeton, NJ: Princeton University Press, 1998), pp. 421–431; Dina Shehata, "Youth Activism in Egypt," *Arab Reform Initiative* (October 23, 2008), p. 3.

of independent action.[18] The board of the Bar Association was dissolved and replaced by an appointed one. Nasser also decreed that all the board lawyers were now to be recruited from the regime's party, the Arab Socialist Union.[19] The communist parties were dissolved and their leadership joined the regime, and the National Assembly was to be composed of at least 50% workers and peasants.[20] The liberal leaders found themselves subject to harassment, political marginalization, and imprisonment. As Hinnebusch explains, "Party politics was replaced by charismatic leadership, military-bureaucratic rule, and an effort to impose a modernizing revolution from above...[the liberal leaders] were powerless against a regime combining broad support and effective means of coercion...."[21]

It is within this context that Egypt's premier liberal-nationalist independence movement, the Wafd, was put to rest; its leader, Fuad Serag al-Din, was imprisoned in March 1952 for a few months, then again in 1953 before being sentenced to 15 years in prison in 1954, released 2 years later, and again imprisoned in 1961 and in 1965. Muhammad Asfur, a renowned Wafdist and a civil rights lawyer who had declared that "socialism is not a substitute for political freedoms,"[22] was also silenced by the regime.

But not all was lost, or at least this was the feeling at the time. Egyptian liberals continued to advocate for liberalism and to propose solutions through the Bar Association. But they were no longer in control of the very important institution of the State, an institution that was perceived by most movements in the region as the only means for national change and liberation. They thus proceeded with their usual legal methods of educating, writing, critiquing, and negotiating, pushing for constitutional limits on state power, for pluralism and for freedom of speech and of assembly; but this only brought on further restrictions and caused Mustapha ElBaradei, the president of the Bar Association, to be dismissed as president by the Nasser regime in 1966. His dismissal was initially experienced as a major setback, but the Association regained its voice and energy following the 1967 Six-Day War defeat to Israel, calling for the prosecution of those responsible for the debacle. The Association was emboldened following Nasser's March 30, 1968, declaration in which he acknowledged Egypt's predicament. The then-president of the Association, Ahmad Khawaja, wrote an article in the

---

[18] Chalcraft, *Popular Politics*, pp. 322–323.
[19] Rutherford, *Egypt after Mubarak*, p. 42; Ziadeh, *Lawyers, the Rule of Law and Liberalism*, p. 158.
[20] Chalcraft, *Popular Politics*, p. 324.
[21] Raymond A. Hinnebusch, "The Reemergence of the Wafd Party: Glimpses of the Liberal Opposition in Egypt," *International Journal of Middle East Studies*, Vol. 16, Issue 1 (1984), p. 100.
[22] Rutherford, *Egypt after Mubarak*, p. 43.

Association's journal condemning the regime's use of exceptional courts and calling for respect for the rule of law. Other prominent lawyers asserted the right of citizens to have their civil freedoms respected, and demanded immediate liberal reforms.[23] These various measures reflected another shift in the mood, this time in support of liberal democracy. And the shift seemed to gather still more momentum when student protests erupted in February and November 1968, with protesters objecting to the lack of freedom of speech and of the press, and demanding the separation of powers and the right to protest and to freedom of assembly.[24]

The sudden death of Nasser in 1970 seemed to open up new possibilities for the liberal cause. Anwar Sadat rose to power in September 1970 and promised a return to multipartyism and democratic transitions, which was welcomed by the liberals, and more broadly reflected the shift in the popular mood in Egypt since the defeat in the Six-Day War. Sadat went on to invite a number of prominent liberals, such as Ahmad Khawaja, Ibrahim Darwish, and Abd al-Hamid Mitwali, to serve on the committee that drafted the 1971 Constitution.[25] The invited liberal lawyers agreed to serve in order to advance principles of pluralism, personal freedom, human rights, and democratic governance, by integrating them into the new constitution. Meanwhile, the Bar Association brought back the prominent liberal Mustapha ElBaradei as its president, which was seen as a significant victory for liberalism within the country given the reasons for Baradei's dismissal in 1966. The Association quickly established a series of weekly seminars to discuss political affairs and issues of democratization and policy in order to educate the public and to prepare for the return of political rights and multipartyism.[26]

And yet soon enough the regime's party, now called the National Democratic Party (NDP), decreed a series of security laws and regulations to limit freedom of expression as well as freedom of the press. Overall, the NDP's new laws allowed the party to effectively dominate the legislative and executive branches.[27] The liberals within the Bar Association reacted by denouncing these laws and offered pro bono legal representation for anyone charged under them.[28] The Bar Association also worked relentlessly to force the State to respect the independence of the Supreme

---

[23] Ibid.
[24] Ahmed Abdalla, *The Student Movement and National Politics in Egypt 1923–1973* (Cairo: American University of Cairo Press, 2008), pp. 174–176.
[25] Rutherford, *Egypt after Mubarak*, p. 44.
[26] Ibid.
[27] For more on the different measures in place, see Maye Kassem *Egyptian Politics: The Dynamics of Authoritarian Rule* (Boulder, CO: Lynne Rienner, 2004).
[28] Rutherford, *Egypt after Mubarak*, p. 44.

Constitutional Court, which was created in 1979. For two years, the Association lobbied to reverse a draft law that would create a politicized court with close ties to the executive branch and the Ministry of Justice, with the General Assembly of the Bar arguing that such a court would threaten the rule of law and would fail to uphold the Constitution – and the Association was ultimately successful in its bid, thus helping to overcome the regime's desire to control the judiciary. This then was a tangible victory for the liberal camp, a victory that would prove to be important for pro-democracy activists after the Arab Spring.[29] And yet despite this victory, the 1980s would see changes in the membership of the Bar Association that would decrease its power as a force for liberal reform.[30]

Other liberal forces were also attempting to modify the political course under Sadat. In February 1978, a number of elder statesmen came together to revive the Wafd Party – which had been disbanded under Nasser in 1954 – and try to renew it as a political force. Sadat seemed open to the idea, although for illiberal reasons in that he was hoping that a revival of the liberal party would give legitimacy to his rule and would facilitate the imposition of his neoliberal economic plans. But the "New Wafd" would not turn out to be the accommodationist ally Sadat was hoping for, since the Wafdists took advantage of Sadat's partial political liberalization to assemble and organize[31] and they immediately moved to challenge his regime. They demanded

---

[29] Ibid, p. 45.

[30] It is important to note that some analysts consider the Judiciary a liberal force because Egyptian judges continued to defend the Constitution against infringements by the State. For instance, judges curtailed the powers of the state by ruling against the confiscation of private property without adequate compensation under Nasser – citing abuse of power – and voiding security decrees that allowed Sadat to imprison his opponents. Both the Nasser and Sadat governments had argued that their decisions were not subject to "judicial scrutiny" because they were taken to protect the nation and ensure the country's stability. The Supreme Constitutional Court rejected this line of argumentation, asserting that, "the executive authority is not free to decide upon the existence of a state of necessity. Rather, it is subject to the control exercised by the Supreme Constitutional Court, which ascertains the existence of a state of necessity within the limits specified by the Constitution" (see Rutherford, *Egypt after Mubarak*, p. 54). The reasons for not considering the Judiciary as a liberal force in the present work is related to the judges' accommodation of the ideal of a strong state that upholds the morality and traditions of the nation, and because the notion of individual rights is entirely missing in most rulings. And so, for the purposes of this book, although many judges have consistently defended liberal values and although clearly reformist and at times progressive, the judiciary does not pass the liberal comprehensive test outlined in the introductory chapter of this work.

[31] In February 1978, and after months of work by old Wafdist leaders to recruit the number of necessary deputies in parliament, the party received its license. Under the Sadat regime's new parties law, parties were to assemble a minimum of twenty deputies in parliament before the party would be approved, a provision the regime had hoped would prevent the formation of independent parties. One independent, Ahmad Taha, a Marxist, is said to have joined the Wafd to give it the required number of deputies. Hinnebusch, "The Reemergence of the Wafd," p. 104.

a thorough political liberalization, accused the regime of autocratic rule and of lacking legitimacy, and competed with Sadat for the loyalties of Egypt's upper and middle classes. Although their challenge was short-lived since they were repressed a few months later by the regime, Hinnebusch explains, "that short experience permitted a valuable glimpse of Egypt's subterranean liberal opposition, threw light on Egyptian politics under Sadat and allowed another chapter to be added to the odyssey of liberalism in Egypt."[32]

Indeed, the first speech delivered by the Party's old Wafdist leader and former Secretary-General, Fuad Serag ad-Din, to the Lawyers' Syndicate was bold, defiant, and one might even say militant. He gave credit to the Wafd for the British evacuation of Egyptian territory, contrasting it with the Israeli occupation brought on by Nasser's policies. He attacked the 1952 revolution, calling it a mere coup d'état, and contrasting it with the Wafd-led 1919 "popular revolution" (see Chapter 1). He then went on to attack the Sadat regime, claimed that Egypt suffered from a political vacuum and that the existing parties were mere puppets with no real roots, who were making the parliament an obedient body incapable of holding any regime accountable.[33]

Democracy was the Wafd's main demand and most attractive feature in the eyes of those who supported it. As Hinnebusch puts it, "'Democracy' was the overwhelmingly dominant theme stressed by the leaders in their writings and speeches. This was also the main issue on which it attracted its membership; the majority of activists cited as their reason for joining the party either its democratic mission or its status as the genuine representative of the people's will."[34] The Wafdists demanded a representative, liberal political system rooted in the rule of law, an executive accountable to the legislature, a parliamentary system with a leader directly elected by the people following a competitive process, the removal of all restrictions on the formation of political parties, freedom of expression for all citizens, and private ownership as well as no restrictions on the press. Wafdists also demanded the separation of religion from the State, especially the institution of al-Azhar, as well as to modernize Family Law in line with liberal and liberal feminist principles (Family Law at the time relied on conservative Islamic jurisprudence). Economically, the New Wafdists argued that the public sector should be limited to the largest projects, and the private sector should be expanded to include medium and small enterprises.[35]

[32] Hinnebusch, "The Reemergence of the Wafd," p. 99.
[33] Ibid, p. 103.
[34] Ibid, p. 110.
[35] Ibid, pp. 110–111.

In those few months that the New Wafd was allowed to operate, it proved to be quite effective and unexpectedly popular given the socialist regional moment in which it was supposedly operating. And unlike the new political elite of the regime who justified the State's autocratic ways and a limited economic liberalization in which State clients played the most significant role, the leaders of the New Wafd were adamant in their demands for a thorough political liberalization, as well as democratization accompanied by freedom of expression and the press.[36] These ideas gained the Wafd increasing influence within the Bar Association, whose members were emboldened and became openly critical of the regime's policies within Parliament. Wafdists started expressing defiant anti-government opinions during political rallies, "arousing enthusiastic response of the crowds."[37] They also reconnected and began to work closely with their leftist national progressive counterparts. This coalition was, however, seen as becoming too risky by the Sadat regime to its monopoly on power. The regime reacted swiftly. In May 1978, Sadat cracked down on the opposition. New restrictions on political liberties were imposed through a staged referendum. One of the restrictions was to ban "from political activity those who 'corrupted political life before the 1952 revolution,' i.e., Serag ad-Din and several other top Wafd elders."[38] The Wafd was basically ordered to purge its unruly leadership, but instead the party opted to disband. Wafdists also accused the regime of unlawful use of a referendum to violate the spirit of the constitution and impose restrictions on political freedoms and political rights, and deplored the regime's inability to accept democratic opposition.[39] Although the party disbanded, a few Wafdists stayed on as independents; yet the parliamentary elections of 1979 were staged in such a way that all critics of the regime lost their seats, with the ruling NDP winning an overwhelming majority in the 390-seat parliament.[40]

Sadat was determined to and capable of eliminating the liberal political threat, along with the threat posed by other dissenters. He put thousands of activists, students, and thinkers in prison, and used the 1980 so-called Shame Law with its special extra-judicial value

---

[36] Ibid, p. 119.
[37] Ibid, p. 117.
[38] Ibid.
[39] Ibid.
[40] Edward Cody, "Sadat Presses Bill to Punish Dissent," *The Washington Post* (February 21, 1980).

tribunals – which were given sweeping powers – to punish anti-government agitation and violations of Egypt's Islamic tradition, as well as its moral and national values.[41] The Law of Shame stipulated that anyone "who perpetrates what involves the denial of divine laws, or contravenes their rulings, either by inciting children and youth to abandon religious values, or through disloyalty to the nation, shall be subject to punishment according to what is stipulated in article 171 of the penal code...."[42] The Law prompted the liberal activist Mustapha Mare'i, the then head of the Lawyers' Syndicate, to warn that Egypt was returning to the repressive era of Nasser. Other intellectuals protested that the value tribunals and a "socialist public prosecutor" were being given broad and vaguely defined powers.[43] The law targeted pro-democracy actors and in particular the liberals, singling out anyone who had expressed "opposition to, hatred of, or contempt for the state's political, social or economic system, calling for the domination by any one social class over others or for the liquidation of a social class."[44] This formulation of the law clearly targeted most liberal critics of the regime since they were perceived as trying to change the ostensibly socialist sociopolitical and economic system. Sadat also used the law "protecting social peace" to control the opposition and silence thinkers and political opponents.[45] In September 1981, he arrested about 1500 of Egypt's political elite and intelligentsia including liberal figures such as Fouad Serag al-Din, the party's then-chairman, and other founders of the New Wafd.

At Sadat's death in October 1981, his vice president Husni Mubarak took over as Egypt's president, and he immediately declared a state of emergency throughout the country. The onset of emergency laws meant that the government had absolute authority for harassing and detaining critics as it saw fit, this despite the fact that multipartyism was in theory maintained.[46] Indeed, the activation of emergency laws soon led to the many State security apparatuses being tasked with relegating most

---

[41] Ibid.

[42] The law was abolished with the abolition of the Socialist Prosecutor General in the constitutional amendments of 2007. See "Anwar Sadat Issues 'Law of Shame'," translated by Kevin Moore (January 22, 2014), https://edinburgharabicinitiative.wordpress.com/2014/02/09/anwar-sadat-issues-law-of-shame/

[43] Cody, "Sadat Presses Bill."

[44] Ibid.

[45] Korany, "Restricted Democratization," pp. 47–48, 50.

[46] Indeed, the state of emergency would be periodically renewed until the 2011 revolution. Yoram Meital, "The Struggle over Political Order in Egypt: The 2005 Elections," *The Middle East Journal*, Vol. 60, No. 2 (April 2006), p. 259.

citizens and those resisting the authoritarian state to silence.[47] Even in terms of electoral politics, Albrecht writes that when the numbers of tolerated opposition representatives rose remarkably during the 1980s:

from thirty-three in 1979 to sixty-four in 1984 and one hundred members in parliament after the 1987 elections. The most important modifications after the 1987 elections pertained to the change from a party-list system to an individual-candidacy system, which has become the core mechanism of electoral politics ever since and caused the "individualization" of Egyptian politics in general, and of the organizational fragmentation of political parties in particular.[48]

The 1990 parliamentary elections witnessed the starting point of a decade of political de-liberalization, embracing higher degrees of repression toward the entire political opposition.[49]

These measures, which ensured the weakness and "individualization" of the opposition in general, did not mean that the liberal movement and its ideals disappeared; rather, it was transforming, adapting, and reemerging in other ways. Indeed, as liberals realized the political sphere was tightening, they turned their attention to raising awareness about issues of human rights, social justice, and social responsibility. Egyptian activists also connected with their foreign counterparts, and were supported in their work by international declarations such as the Universal Declaration of Human Rights and by international organizations such as the United Nations and the European Union. They created networks of human rights such as the Arab Organization for Human Rights (AOHR) founded in 1983 (the country's oldest independent human rights group), the Arab Women Solidarity Association founded in 1982, the Egyptian Organization for Human Rights (EOHR, established in 1985), the Ibn Khaldun Center for Development Studies (1988), the Cairo Institute

---

[47] Particularly rigid publication and censorship laws bound newspapers and journals published by the opposition parties and NGOs. The internal security forces' harassment and intimidations became extensive and thorough, even on university campuses in which security units were empowered and emboldened. See Meital, "The Struggle over Political Order," p. 259. See also Eberhard Kienle, *The Grand Delusion: Democracy and Economic Reform in Egypt* (London: I.B. Tauris, 2001). The New Wafd attempted a political comeback in 1984 but instead of pushing for democratization and change, it opted to support the status quo and to push for relative gains. In so doing, it legitimized rather than discredited the illiberal dictatorship of Mubarak, and thus lost, for the purpose of this work, its liberal status.

[48] Holger Albrecht, *Raging against the Machine: Political Opposition under Authoritarianism in Egypt* (Syracuse: Syracuse University Press, 2013), p. 136.

[49] Ibid; Jason Brownlee, "The Decline of Pluralism in Mubarak's Egypt," *Journal of Democracy*, Vol. 13, No. 4 (2012), pp. 6–14.

for Human Rights Studies (1993), the Nadeem Center (1993), and the Egyptian Center for Women's Rights (1996), among others.[50]

Their work involved mostly informing the public about their rights and keeping records. They issued press releases about human rights violations and provided support for those who became victims of violations. They raised awareness and informed citizens of their constitutional rights and how to lobby for them. They organized workshops, seminars, conferences, and lectures, and launched campaigns on what human rights are, their covenants, and the many ways Egyptian law was supposed to protect them. They trained lawyers and human rights activists, and they researched cases, and issued reports and pamphlets in order to document violations. Importantly, they took on issues with the institutions of the State such as the Prosecutor General and the Ministry of Interior, and contacted embassies and other international human rights organizations that could provide help or pressure for change. They engaged in fact-finding missions, investigated complaints, visited prisons, and collected testimonies, and they helped victims with representation and free legal counseling. They also filed lawsuits and represented victims – sometimes successfully – in court. And they coordinated with other NGOs and journalists to spread and record information. All this work was a vital part of pushing for greater rule of law and a rights-based culture.

Their determination to continue working and advancing a liberal culture was not easy. They were for the most part operating outside the law, in the sense that they were not legal entities registered as human rights organizations but were rather registered as law firms, medical clinics (such as the Nadeem Center, which is dedicated to combatting violence and torture and rehabilitating victims), and civil companies. What this highlights is that they had to be innovative if they were to continue working under the constant surveillance of a fearful and aggressive State.[51]

Yet despite the surveillance, these organizations were able to raise awareness, educate, and train people in addition to establishing links with other organizations, and providing for much needed legal and financial assistance. Thus, while their work was often under the radar – and maybe at times perceived as beneficial to the regime[52] – they coordinated across national borders and slowly impacted State human rights

---

[50] For more on Egypt's NGOs in general, see Maha Abdelrahman, *Civil Society Exposed: The Politics of NGOs in Egypt* (Cairo: American University of Cairo Press, 2004).

[51] Heba Morayef, "Reexamining Human Rights Change in Egypt," p. 10.

[52] The regime restricts the liberal NGOs work and thus their political impact and outreach while benefitting from portraying itself as allowing dissenting institutions to exist.

practices and youth political culture in Egypt and the region overall.[53] They considered their activities and services to be essential in pushing back against repressive States and the emergency laws that are often utilized by these States.

Their work was also essential in light of the rise in the 1970s and 1980s of Islamist radicalism in Egypt. This emergence of radicals was one of the results of Sadat's policies of endorsement, cooptation, and manipulation of Islamists in an attempt to bolster his image as a pious leader and to weaken his opposition, namely the leftists and the liberals.[54] When Mubarak rose to power in the early 1980s, he attempted to curb the Islamists' activism and militancy, but did so only indirectly because they helped to quell threatening liberal voices as a byproduct of pushing their own agenda. Moreover, their potential threat was used by the Mubarak regime to make the case for ongoing emergency laws and the need to rally behind the State in order to ensure stability and the secular order.[55]

The boogeyman of the Islamist threat was effective in muting most opposition voices, including many self-proclaimed liberals, who truly feared the rising radicalism of some of the Islamist groups and thus sided with the State. Others, including writers, academics, lawyers, journalists, and activists, saw through the threat and reckoned that Islamist radicalism and State authoritarianism were two faces of the same illiberal coin. These activists and intellectuals and the institutions they led continued to negotiate relations of power through their work, activism, and writings – as we will see hereinafter. And in so doing, they were constantly helping to shape the political order and culture in a liberal direction, including working to empower citizens and to restrict any monopoly on power whether by the Islamists or the State.

Indeed, academics and writers such as Farag Fouda (1945–1992) and Nasr Hamid Abu Zayd (1943–2010) became a force to be reckoned with and prominent voices for human rights, "social and political justice," and liberal feminism. Their books and political activism helped advance liberal ideals and pitted them directly against the State and Islamists in

---

[53] Joe Stork, "Three Decades of Human Rights Activism in the Middle East and North Africa: An Ambiguous Balance of Sheet," in Joel Beinin and Frederic Vairel (eds.), *Social Movements, Mobilization, and Contestation in the Middle East and North Africa*, 2nd ed. (Stanford: Stanford University Press, 2013).

[54] Islamist radicals end up assassinating Sadat in 1980.

[55] Abdel-Fattah Mady, "Student political activism in democratizing Egypt," in Dalia F. Fahmy and Daanish Faruqi (eds.), *Egypt and the Contradictions of Liberalism: Illiberal Intelligentsia and the Future of Egyptian Democracy* (London: Oneworld Publications, 2017), pp. 218–219.

the 1970s to the1990s. They were some of the most prominent intellectuals who fought for the de-politicization of religion and the liberalization of the political system and of society in the Arab region. Both religious and political authorities tried to silence them through a number of legal and not so legal methods.

Soon enough these thinkers realized that one way to challenge the authoritarian political culture in Egypt and the region and to disseminate a liberal perspective was by denouncing and dissecting Islamist radicalism which, as stated earlier, was often manipulated and utilized by the State to gain legitimacy and oppress dissenters. In their critique of an orthodox Islamism, these intellectuals also made the case for the virtues of freedom of speech, pluralism and liberal democracy. Their discourse represented a more general liberal trend of challenging culturalist, ahistorical, anti-rational, and patronizing ideas and positions. And unlike their classical counterparts, their strength and popularity lay in their ability to organically challenge the legitimacy of the claims by Islamists and the regime to be the "natural" and authentic representatives of Arab society, often by using their own logic against them.

Farag Fouda was one of the most vocal and famous political activists and writers in the 1980s and early 1990s in Egypt. He was an agricultural economist who dedicated his life to combatting radicalism and oppression. In this latter regard, he was a liberal secularist, a political activist, a human rights activist, and a prolific writer and debater. He helped found the Egyptian Organization for Human Rights and created al-Jam'iya al-Masriya li al-tanweer (The Egyptian Association for Enlightenment), whose main purpose was educating Egyptian citizens about freedom of opinion and expression, as well as citizenship and human rights.

Fouda was perceived as a threat by both the regime and radicals in an environment that cultivated taboos and oppression, because of his audacity and ability to speak clearly, critically, and with humor, and thus to connect with his audience no matter their level of education. He was killed on June 8, 1992, by two members of the Islamist group al-Gamma'a al-Islamiya as he was leaving his office with his son and a friend. On January 6th of that year, he had taken part in a televised debate with conservative Shaykh Muhammad al-Ghazali. The event, entitled al-dawla al-madaniya fi muwagahet al-dawla al-diniya [The civil State in confrontation with the religious State] was attended by more than 30,000 people. It included other liberals and Islamists such as liberal shaykh Muhammad Ahmad Khalafallah, Ma'mun al-Hudaibi, the leader of the Egyptian Muslim Brotherhood at the time, and Muhammad 'Amara from the leftist Tagamu' party. Following the debate, Fouda was accused of being an atheist and a heretic by Al-Azhar Shaykhs, and by the leader of al-Gamaa al-Islamiyya who had stated that "Haza al-rajul, la hal lahu ila al-qatl" [This man, his only solution is death].[56] He was thus assassinated – but his ideas have lived on.

Fouda, like his liberal predecessors who discussed Islam and politics such as Kawakibi and Raziq (see Chapter 1), asserted the importance of separating religion from politics and from lawmaking. He also insisted on the difference between what Muslims do and have done (Islamic history and Islamic civilization) from what the Quran says Muslims ought to do (Islamic creed). In *Al-Haqiqa al-gha'iba* (The Absent Truth, 1986), Fouda tried to answer the following questions: does the Quran promote a specific political State? Do the Quran and the Sunna have a political vision or determine how Muslims are to mandate or remove their political leaders? Is the historical Caliphate system really Islamic? Fouda determined that Islam is a religious creed, not a political project (*din wa laysa dawla*), and that it ought to be free of the burden of the political realm, in which everyone is seeking power.[57] In so doing, Fouda defended the legitimacy of a secular order.

He furthermore refuted certain religious leaders' claims that the application of Islamic law would solve the decadence of Muslim societies. He refuted these leaders' monist views and he invited them and Islamists in general to join in a conversation based on transparency, freedom of expression and thought, and rationality, instead of fear and claims about divine damnation and salvation. Clearly, he said, it is easier to make accusations of apostasy than to rationally discuss the mundane problems Egyptians faced daily such as inflation and poverty.[58] In *al-Haqiqa al-Gha'iba*, Fouda also revisited and laid bare the Islamist past that the radicals claim is ideal (hence the title of the work "The Absent Truth") in an attempt to dismiss their monolithic claims about Truth and the right path. He argued that the Caliphate was marred by *istibdad* (tyranny), injustice, and lack of progress. Here he advances some of his most liberal arguments and in particular his view of the relationship between those in power and the people, arguing that history shows pious and good people have made many mistakes, indeed, even the early Islamic period of the four Rightly Guided Caliphs saw its share of power seeking, civil wars, and violence.[59] Thus, he concluded that good

---

[56] Program Muni'a Min al-Tadawul, "Farag Fouda: Nakun aw la-Nakun," *Al-Ghad TV* (July 29, 2019).

[57] Farag Fouda, *Al-Haqiqa al-Gha'iba*, 3rd ed. (Cairo: Dar al-Fikr, 1988), pp. 11–12.

[58] Elizabeth Suzanne Kassab, *Contemporary Arab Thought: Cultural Critique in Comparative Perspective* (New York: Columbia University Press, 2010), pp. 222–224. Hatina, "Arab Liberal Thought in Historical Perspective," pp. 30–31.

[59] Fouda, *Al-Haqiqa*, pp. 41–72. See also Kharej al-Nas, "Al-Haqiqa al-Gha'iba: al-kitab allazi qatala Faraj Fouda," *Al-Jazeera TV* (September 17, 2017).

governance and justice require more than just pious people being in charge; it requires methods of accountability. He wrote, "Justice is not achieved because the ruler is just, and does not reign because the subjects are good, and it is not the result of Islamic Law, it is established with what we call a system of governance (*nizam hukum*), by that I mean the mechanisms of control (*dawabet*) through which a ruler is held accountable if he commits a wrong, and stops him if he transgresses (tajawaz), and removes him if he overlooks the people's interest..."[60] [author's translation]. Thus only through the implementation of mechanisms that ensure the accountability of those in power to the people they serve can States perfect themselves.

Fouda asserted that he and other liberals will fight for all, including radical Islamists, to have the right to express their views freely as long as political difference is practiced within the framework of democracy and the rule of law, which would ensure they (the liberals and the Islamists) can coexist and work together for the sake of the country.[61] Fouda reasserted this latter idea in his book, *al-Nadhir* (1989), in which he argued that the only solution to radicalism, separatism, and radical infiltration was political inclusion within a democratic State in which everyone could express themselves freely. These prerequisites he calls for, of a democratic State and freedom of expression, could explain why Fouda left the New Wafd when the party's leader decided to cooperate with the Egyptian Muslim Brothers under the Mubarak regime in order to expand the party's reach within parliament.

Fouda's ability to reach the public masses, to simplify matters, to challenge monolithic discourses, and to explain issues and concepts on TV programs, in conferences, and in newspapers with such clarity, audacity, and wit turned him into a serious threat to religious fanaticism, but also certainly to the authoritarian State in light of his tacit critique of repressive authority and his support for civil freedoms.[62] Indeed, his collection of articles "Nakun aw la nakun" (To Be or Not to Be) was condemned by the Islamic Research Foundation of Al-Azhar University[63], but it was also withdrawn from publication and blocked by the State, and Fouda was summoned by the State Security Services for interrogation.[64] While most

---

[60] Fouda, *Al-Haqiqa*, p. 27.

[61] Kassab, *Contemporary Arab Thought*, pp. 222–224. Hatina and Schumann, *Arab Liberal Thought after 1967*, pp. 30–31.

[62] Abd al-Sami' Jamil, "Kuluhum Qatalu Farag Fouda hayan, kuluhum yakhshunahu al'an mayitan," *Daqaeq.net* (May 14, 2020).

[63] TV program Muni'a min al-Tadawel, "Farag Fuda: nakun aw la nakun," *Al-Ghad TV* (July 29, 2019).

[64] Kassab, *Contemporary Arab Thought*, p. 221.

studies of Fouda have focused on his confrontation with the Islamists, they miss his struggle with the State overall, more specifically in its refusal to allow him to create a political party (al-Mustaqbal is the name of his never-legalized party) and thus in restricting his activity and reach. The State thus acted as a behind-the-scenes actor, supervising and banning research, and letting Islamists harass and limit thinkers when deemed useful for ensuring its survival. Notwithstanding these harassments, Fouda's books were best sellers in Egypt and the Arab region, and contributed to the dissemination of secularist and liberal ideas and notions.[65]

Nasr Hamid Abu Zayd also disseminated liberal norms of individual freedom, of freedom of thought and expression, and of rejecting monist systems through his work on political Islamism. He was a professor of Islamic Studies at Cairo University and one of the most renowned Arab thinkers and liberal critics. He challenged political Islam by adopting a literary and hermeneutical approach through which the Quran is analyzed in terms of its textual content and within its historical context. Abu Zayd's criticism was also directed at a number of 'ulama who were supported by the political establishment. According to Abu Zayd, tyranny becomes possible when theologians manipulate and monopolize the right to interpret the Qur'an. He distinguished between the authority of the text and its interpretation, which he thought should always be historicized, adapted, updated, and regenerated. In his *Mafhum al-Nas: Dirasa fi 'ulum al-Quran* [The concept of the text: A study of the Quranic sciences] published in Cairo in 1990, he argued that the Quran is both revelation and a piece of literature and thus a cultural product that is reflective of the linguistic and cultural codes of the time and place in which the texts appeared, in order for it to be understandable

---

[65] Hatina and Schumann, *Arab Liberal Thought after 1967*, pp. 30–31. A number of liberal manifestos were written. The Jordanian Shakir al-Nabulsi wrote his manifesto in 2004 (*man hum al-libiraliyun al-arab al-judud wa ma huwa khitabuhum*, and the Tunisian 'Afif al-Akhdar wrote *al-Mithaq al-'Aqlani* in 2007 (see Hatina and Schumann, *Arab Liberal Thought*, p. 31). Although liberals' concerns have changed and are more focused on questions of authoritarian rule and citizens' freedoms than those of the nineteenth century, they all agree that Arab liberal discourse and the liberal movement is not a new phenomenon, but has roots in the classical period (eighteenth to early twentieth century). This reference to previous liberals serves to provide historical depth and continuity. For instance, Faraj Fuda points to Ahmad Lutfi al-Sayyid (died in 1963) and Taha Husayn (died in 1971) as his mentors (Fuda, *al-Irhab*, 1988 and Fuda, *Hiwar Hawla al-'Almana*, 1986), judge Muhammad Sa'id al-Ashmawi is endorsed by Tawfiq Hakim (dies 1987) in his book, *Ususl al-Shari'a*, Cairo, (1996), and the Syrian writer Saadallah Wannous asserted intellectual continuity and authenticity in a periodical he helped found in the early 1990s (see later in this chapter).

in the seventh century AD. The challenge, he argued, was to continue the hermeneutical decoding in order to differentiate between those messages that were intended for the time of the Prophet and the receivers of the Quran at the time, and those normative messages that are meant to be universal and timeless. This is not an easy task, he explained, as it requires historicizing the Quran, as well as removing layers of added commentaries and dogmatic and political interference. Human knowledge, he argued, is always interpretative and thus relative. In so arguing, Abu Zayd validated and asserted the inevitability of the existence of plural meanings and metaphorical possibilities woven within the Quran, thus advancing a liberal view of truth. Abu Zayd was also critical of Imam Shafie's elevation of the Sunna, arguing that the Sunna is not divine, nor a source of legislation as the corpus contains too many contradictions within it.[66] Abu Zayd thus disputed the theological foundations Islamic scholars relied on to regulate society, and in so doing he disputed more than these scholars' legitimacy and dominance, but their monistic systems of governance as well. In making his arguments, Abu Zayd referred to liberal medieval exegetical authorities within the Islamic Sunni tradition such as the Mu'tazila, Ibn Arabi, and Averroes among others.[67] And unlike other critics such as Fouda, Abu Zayd was a student of Islamic Studies having earned a Ph.D. in Islamic Studies from Cairo University, and so he was especially convincing and intellectually threatening; he could not be dismissed by the oft-used "what does he know."

Abu Zaid was also directly critical politically. He saw the struggle between the Muslim Brotherhood and the regime as a fight over who has the right to present a monolithic narrative and claim absolute sovereignty within Egyptian society. To him as for other liberals, no one claiming a right to sovereignty is to be trusted. He wrote,

These tensions one witnesses between the regime, its institutions, and the full array of religious factions and streams are not an ideological struggle about differences in ideas or beliefs. It is a struggle around the rightful ownership of divine sovereignty, with regards to the management of society. It is about who is speaking in the name of its divine sovereignty and is therefore protected by its legitimacy. It is a struggle between political forces that hold similar ideas about power, control, and authority.[68]

---

[66] Pierre Roshdy Loza, "The Case of Abu Zayd and the Reactions It Prompted from Egyptian Society" (Georgetown University: Masters' Thesis, 2013), pp. 13–14.

[67] Georges Tamer, "Nasr Hamid Abu Zayd," *International Journal of Middle East Studies*, Vol. 43, No. 1 (2011), pp. 193–195.

[68] Nasr Abu Zaid, *Critique of Religious Discourse*, 3rd ed. (Casablanca: Arab Cultural Center, 2007), p. 84, quoted in Loza, "The Case of Abu Zayd," p. 24.

Abu Zayd gave examples from the Nasser and the Sadat eras during which he showed complicity between conservative Islam and the governments which sought divine legitimacy and sovereignty in the name of the people. Thus both the regime and Islamists have used theology instrumentally in order to assert their will. Additionally, he accused the State of using notions of secularism and democracy as empty qualifiers to suppress or to empower different groups when and as needed. Thus overall, violence within society is the result of the violence and ruthlessness of the Egyptian regime.

Abu Zayd's theses are not entirely new since as we saw in Chapter 1, many other liberals have historically made similar arguments about the need for democracy and pluralism in order to put an end to violence, whether by regimes or society. It is the popularity of his work and its direct message that angered Islamists and regime officials. An opportunity to silence him showed itself as Abu Zayd was applying to be promoted to full professor at Cairo University. An Arabic linguistics professor who was a member of the ruling party's Religious Affairs Committee and a prominent TV preacher accused Abu Zayd of disdaining the Islamic faith and rejected his promotion as a result.[69] He also publicly denounced Abu Zayd's work. By that time, the culture of repression and censorship in the form of laws had become fully institutionalized even on university campuses.[70]

Things escalated quickly; voices from within al-Azhar "recommended confiscating his books and barring Abu Zayd from teaching at academic institutions in order to protect the faith of Muslim students."[71] He also received death threats and a group of professors at al-Azhar university issued a joint statement calling for his execution. Articles appeared in the official press accusing him of apostasy, and finally a group of Islamists sued Abu Zayd in court for apostasy. The Court of Appeal judge and his fellow jurists read his work and declared Abu Zayd an apostate in 1996.[72]

---

[69] Navid Kermani, "From revelation to interpretation: Nasr Hamid Abu Zayd and the literary study of the Quran," in Suha Taji-Farouki (ed.), *Modern Muslim Intellectuals and the Quran* (Oxford University Press, 2004), p. 170.

[70] For instance in 1972, law 49 stipulated that promotions are to be approved by regime-appointed permanent committees and by the Supreme Council of Higher Education. And in 1977, State security services were allowed on university campus.

[71] Muhammad Abu Samra, "Liberal Critics, 'Ulama' and the Debate on Islam in the Contemporary Arab World," in Meir Hatina (ed.), *Guardians of Faith in Modern Times: "Ulama" in the Middle East* (Leiden, Boston: Brill, 2009), p. 280. See also, George Sfeir, "Basic Freedoms in a Fractured Legal Culture: Egypt and the Case of Nasr Hamid Abu Zayd," *Middle East Journal*, Vol. 53, No. 2 (1998), p. 414.

[72] For more on this, see Caryle Murphy, *Passion for Islam: Shaping the Modern Middle East the Egyptian Experience* (New York, London: Scribner, 2002), pp. 203–206.

The ruling stated that Abu Zayd is a threat to national security and that his attacks on Islam are attacks on the State. Then Abu Zayd's marriage was nullified based on an Egyptian law that a Muslim woman cannot be married to a non-Muslim man. The State appeared entirely absent throughout the ordeal and Abu Zayd and his wife ended up having to leave the country to stay together.

Abu Zayd's supporters included liberal journalists and authors who decried the factional politics of the Islamists and the radical implications of the case, and who asserted that the public outcry following the judges' decision demonstrated Egyptians' support for freedom of expression and their civil rights. The academic committee at Cairo University fought the decision against Abu Zayd by eventually promoting him to full professor. The committee wrote:

...we have reached the following conclusion: [Abu Zayd's] prodigious academic efforts demonstrate that he is a researcher well-rooted in his academic field, well-read in our Islamic intellectual traditions, and with a knowledge of all its many branches ... He has not rested on the laurels of his in-depth knowledge of his field, but has taken a forthright, critical position ... In sum he is a free thinker, aspiring only to the truth. If there is something urgent about his style, it stems from the urgency of the crisis which the contemporary Arab-Islamic World is witnessing and the necessity to honestly identify the ills of this world ... Academic research should be allowed to participate in current debates and to present solutions to current dilemmas by allowing researchers to investigate and interpret as far as possible.[73]

Fouda and Abu Zayd were not Egypt's first liberal thinkers and activists but they were probably two of the most influential liberals in Egypt and the Arab World more broadly at a time when liberal ideas were silenced and banned. Further, their work helps to illustrate the ongoing dynamism and adaptations of liberals in Egypt during the 1960–1990 period, as well as their broader public engagement and influence beyond simply rarefied salons of the elites. Other liberal thinkers and writers such as Sayyid al-Qimni, Muhammad Sa'id al-'Ashmawi, Naguib Mahfouz, and Tawfiq al-Hakim, among many other activists, thinkers, writers, journalists, film-makers, and artists, have done equally impactful work. They have challenged patriarchy and autocracy, and advocated for gender equality, for pluralism and for freedom of expression and action, and for individual rights and liberties. Certainly, more works should be dedicated to the analysis of their work through a liberal lens.

[73] Cited by the Center for Human Rights Legal Aid, *Freedom of Academic Research* (Cairo: September 1996), www.wluml.org/node/262

Together, the liberals pushed back against what they viewed as undue power mostly from below, peacefully, focusing on looking inward, on teaching, writing, and on cultural production to challenge essentialist and monolithic ways and to shatter illiberal claims about authenticity and Truth. The 1980s and 1990s saw Egyptian intellectuals and activists, accompanied by numerous civil society and human rights groups, becoming increasingly critical of Islamist radicals and of an authoritarian State that had everything to lose. And while the laws were stipulated in such a manner as to restrict their reach, and court trials were used against them to destroy their reputation, stop them from sharing their ideas and from producing work altogether, liberals continued to advance liberal conceptualization of rights and freedoms and the political system that could support them, and to have their voice heard in all of Egypt and the Arab World. Indeed, if anything, harassment emboldened activists and intellectuals, brought them together, and in some cases, actually helped to promote their work.[74]

Syria: The Rise of Civil Activism

The 1960 to the 1990s were equally, if not more, ominous times for Syria's political liberalism. The liberal era of notable politicians had come to an end in the late 1950s–early 1960s. The liberal parties of Syria's liberal oligarchy such as the National Bloc and the People's Party were initially contested and then abolished, and their leaders such as Ibrahim Hananu, Jamil Mardam Bey, Hashim al-Atassi, Faris al-Khuri, and Shukri al-Quwatli were isolated and delegitimized. Indeed, the 1954 parliamentary elections gave a few, albeit important, seats to a number of socialist and communist parties, signaling the rise in popularity of leftist ideals in their focus on anti-imperialism, pan-Arabism, egalitarianism, and state-led economic development.

A duality of power emerged between the parliament, still dominated by the liberals, and the officer corps, which tended to be rather illiberal and more left-leaning than the Syrian oligarchy. The liberals at the time had failed to understand and address the needs of the rising working and peasant classes. Union with Nasser's Egypt in 1958 sealed the deal in its promotion of a more populist and radical form of nationalism and of repressive laws, and the Syrian liberal oligarchy could no longer recapture the State. This was the end of Syria's young and fragile liberal institutions and system of governance. As stated earlier, the new focus

---

[74] Abu Samra, "Liberal Critics, 'Ulama' and the Debate on Islam," p. 278.

was now on unifying forces instead of pluralism, achieving Arab unification and identity instead of diversity and freedom, and planning the economy in order to address issues of rapid urbanization, population growth, alienation, and economic malaise. Populists argued that a democratic system could not truly be representative without the achievement of economic justice first, and that freedom meant also freedom from exploitation and imperialism.[75]

New laws that were issued reflected the changes in political focus. Law No. 93 was legislated on associations and private societies in 1958 during Syria's union with Egypt (1958–1961), allowing the Ministry of Social Affairs and Labor (MoSAL) to control the registration of all civil society associations and giving jurisdiction to intervene in the internal governance and day-to-day operations of any association as well as to oversee its ties and cooperation with the international community. Under the law, associations were to notify the ministry of their meetings and activities well in advance, and representatives of the ministry have the right to attend meetings.[76] The idea behind it was that the State should not only monitor non-governmental groups, but also guide their work. Another regulation was article 59 of the newly promulgated 1962 Constitution, which included a provision that granted the president the right to govern by presidential decrees, thereby granting the president increased powers at the expense of parliament. In 1969, legislative decree 224 amended Law No. 93, increasing the State's ability to interfere in the work and organization of civil society groups, to merge associations that do similar types of work, to dissolve associations, and to refuse to register groups based on security issues, claims, or disapproval of their leaders' background.[77]

With these changes, the 1960s ushered in an era of increasing autocracy that the liberals had failed to adequately prepare for. And this process accelerated with the Ba'thist coup d'état of 1963, which catapulted into power a particularly autocratic group of army officers who were frustrated with what they perceived as bourgeois politics.[78] These ideologically driven army officers did what Nasser had done in Egypt, which was to get rid of any opposition actors including the liberal and leftist

---

[75] For more on this, see Hanna Batatu, *Syria's Peasantry, the Descendants of Its Lesser Rural Notables, and Their Politics* (Princeton, NJ: Princeton University Press, 1999).

[76] Human Rights Watch (HRW), *No Room to Breathe: State Repression of Human Rights Activism in Syria* (October 2007), pp. 1–4.

[77] 'Ala' Ramadan and Yasin al-Suweiha, Muqarabat 'an al-mujtama' al-madani al-Suri, Al-Jumhuriya.net (October 15, 2020), www.aljumhuriya.net; See also HRW, *No Room to Breathe*, pp. 18–20, www.hrw.org/reports/2007/syria1007/3.htm

[78] Hinnebusch, "Calculated Decompression as a Substitute for Democratization: Syria," p. 225.

politicians and intellectuals who believed in competing in and working through parliament. They also declared a state of emergency, which gave the State the right to place "restrictions on freedoms of individuals with respect to meetings, residence, travel and passage in specific places or at particular times; to preventatively arrest anyone suspected of endangering public security and order; to authorize investigation of persons and places; and to delegate any person to perform any of these tasks."[79]

But this significant disregard of rights by the State also gave birth to Syrian liberal activism from below. And while the 1970s saw the culmination of the autocratic trend, including the closing down of any forum, syndicate, or café that allowed people to exchange their ideas freely,[80] and the harassment and imprisonment of pro-democracy activists and thinkers, it also witnessed the determined rise of liberal activist voices as well as their adoption of innovative methods to challenge tyranny – driven by a realization that they needed to connect with the public masses. It would become gradually clear to most in Syria that the right to express oneself and to dissent were no longer ideals for intellectuals to champion in order to achieve a better life, but fundamental necessities to fight for in order to topple the totalitarian and violent state and live in peace.

"The command of free life and of democracy" was still felt, tells us writer Khairi al-Zahabi.[81] And so one of the first attempts to revive the liberal order included members of the Lawyers' Bar Association, who in 1976 formed a human rights committee (Freedom and Human Rights Committee) to hold the State concretely accountable by publishing details about abuses of citizens' rights, and calling for a return to the rule of law and constitutionalism. Between 1978 and 1980, all of Syria's leftist, centrist, and right-wing leaders joined the movement. Judges, university professors, and religious leaders were denouncing political abuses of power. Even workers and army officers, who were the regime's basis of support, would join in.[82] The goal of these diverse forces was no longer to capture the State but to defend citizens' rights and recreate a liberal democratic system of rule.[83] People even started expressing their yearning for the ideals and "bourgeois democracy" of the 1940s and 1950s.[84]

---

[79] Cited HRW, *No Room to Breathe*, p. 15, www.hrw.org/reports/2007/syria1007/3.htm.
[80] Nasser, "Khairi al-Zahabi."
[81] Ibid.
[82] Michel Seurat, *Syrie, l'Etat de barbarie* (Paris: Presses Universitaires de France, Kindle edition 2015), chapitre 3.
[83] Ibid, p. 1015.
[84] Ibid, p. 1039.

The Lawyers' Bar Association and its human rights committee drafted a public document demanding the lifting of the state of emergency (in place since 1963) and requesting that the government respect the separation of powers and the independence of the judiciary, and that it abolish special courts such as the Supreme State Security Court (SSSC), which was established in order to prosecute defiant citizens who challenged the status quo. In addition to these constitutional measures, they demanded the release of political prisoners as part of a comprehensive move toward freedom, plurality, and human rights in Syria. Other professional organizations such as the Doctors Association, the Engineers Association, and the Pharmacists Association followed suit and signed the document as well as participated in a mass one-day strike in March 1980 to push their demands. Liberal notions that were no longer expressed at the State level due to the victory of the socialist forces, such as constitutionalism, parliamentarianism, and individual freedoms (see conclusion of Chapter 1), were thus resurfacing at the societal level. Political and intellectual leaders began to think that the distinction between the left and the right didn't matter if a liberal framework for political rule was not reinstated.[85]

The late 1970s also saw the rise of many writers, journalists, artists, and intellectuals turned political activists.[86] This was the case of writer Michel Kilo, who would become one of the most prominent activists in Syria. Kilo would be asked to express his opinion at a conference of the Arab Writers Union of Syria held in 1979 about how to proceed at the political level. Like Sadat, the Asad regime's aim in this kind of conference was not to improve freedoms but to expand the membership of the National Progressive Front (a grouping of parties permitted by the regime) in order to solidify its legitimacy. Instead of accommodating the State, Kilo and other influential intellectuals, such as writer Mamduh 'Adwan, gave speeches openly challenging the regime's narrative about the external and internal threat and accusing the State of disenfranchising Syrians over 17 years of autocratic rule. Parts of the speeches were recorded on thousands of cassettes and distributed all over Syria.[87]

[85] See the work of leftist thinkers like Ilyas Murqus and Yasin al-Hafez, who in the 1970s began to argue that doctrinaire rigidity should be shunned and that the political reality in the region requires one to look beyond ideology in order to integrate practices and ideas that liberate the individual and allow for diversity. Murqus argued that no one ideology is correct and that pluralism is essential to create a harmonious society.

[86] It was considered an uprising by some such as prominent Syrian journalist Ibrahim Hamidi. See Alan George, Syria: Neither Bread nor Freedom (London and New York: Zed Books, 2003), p. 34.

[87] See Seurat, Syrie, p. 1080; "Michel Kilo Yatakalam athna' mu'tamar itihad al-kutab al-arab 'am 1979," www.youtube.com/watch?v=Hx9rxdNPqwE

During the conference, Kilo addressed his audience with determination and audacity. He stated that he believed Syria was on the right path once, notwithstanding the few mistakes that could have been easily fixed. The "conspiracy" (al-mu'amara) he explained, started with the dismissal or elimination (isqat) of a long period of "freedoms" (huriyat) and "liberalism" (al-liberaliya), with the dismissal of the achievements (injazat) of Syrians in the face of the Ottoman and French occupiers – referring to the liberal era – and when Syrian citizens lost their rights and freedoms and millions of people were dragged into accepting a nondemocratic framework of governance (itar ghayr dimucrati).

Prominent writer Mamduh 'Adwan was equally forthright. He stated that the people are the victims of the regime's lies (dahiya li-kizb al-anzima). "Governments that lie are governments that are afraid their people will see them for who they are," he asserted. He lamented the loss of democracy and freedoms in the name of fighting American imperialism and interference when "not one American spy was found in Syria."[88] Kilo and Adwan agreed that the "external threat" (meaning the Israeli and American imperial projects in the region) was being used by the State to manipulate the public and they asserted that opposing Israeli and American interference in the region with words and on the radio does not mean actually resisting them in reality.[89] This was a clear attack on the nationalistic claims and narrative of the regime as the true resistor to Israel and the United States.

The regime felt itself to be under serious threat, and retaliated swiftly. Hundreds of army officers associated with the democratic opposition were arrested or dismissed from their positions. Then, all professional unions and associations were dissolved and replaced under Ba'th party rule and oversight, with government-appointed leaderships. The regime also responded ruthlessly toward the entire elected executive committee of the Lawyers' association by dismissing it, dissolving the human rights committee, and arresting a number of its most prominent members including its president, Haitham al-Maleh. Al-Maleh had been a well-known judge and activist since the end of the 1950s.[90] He was dismissed from his position by the Syrian authorities because of his public opposition to emergency laws imposed in 1963 and to the regime's suspending

---

[88] Mamduh 'Adwan athna' *mu'tamar itihad al-kutab al-'arab*, 1979, www.youtube.com/watch?v=ZbldbHuSgv8&feature=emb_logo

[89] Michel Kilo yatakalam athna' mu'tamar itihad al-kuttab al-'arab 'am 1979, https://youtu.be/Hx9rxdNPqwE

[90] Maleh would become the president of the Human Rights Association in Syria in the early 2000s.

of citizens' freedoms and constitutional rights.[91] The March 1980 strike led to Maleh's imprisonment for six years (1980–1986).[92]

Another gathering, the National Democratic Gathering (*al-tajammu' al-watani al-dimucrati* – NDG) was created in 1979 as an umbrella organization intended to counter the power of the regime-led National Progressive Front and united Nasserist, socialist, and communist leaders such as Jamal al-Atassi and Riad al-Turk. These leaders asserted in their meetings that democracy, political pluralism, and freedom of expression were pillars for the creation of a sound political system.[93] Indeed, they had realized sometime in the 1970s that a focus on freedoms and liberties was of utmost importance if Syria was to ever emerge from dictatorship.[94] And so the NDG put aside their ideological differences and defended civil freedoms and the right to express one's opinion within a pluralist and democratic setting.[95]

One of the leaders of the NDG, Riad al-Turk, would become known as the "Mandela of Syria."[96] Al-Turk was detained as a prisoner of conscience from 1980 to 1998 because of his engagement and activism against the authoritarian State, his refusal to become part of the ruling coalition, and more importantly because of his willingness to work with other parties and activists including the Syrian Muslim Brothers in order to reinstate parliamentarianism in Syria. Al-Turk had established the Syrian Communist Party's Political Bureau (SCPPB) in 1973 to separate his work from that of the Communist Party leader, Bakdash, who had merged the Syrian Communist Party with a coalition of organizations allied with the ruling Ba'th party (the National Progressive Front). The SCPPB was very critical of the Ba'th regime's dictatorship at a time when both Syria's Muslim Brotherhood and

---

[91] Sharif Abdel Kouddous, "A Lifetime of Resistance in Syria," *The Nation* (September 1, 2011).

[92] HRW, *No Room to Breathe*, p. 10.

[93] For a look at their more recent political and economic program issued in December 2001 in Arabic, see mafhoum.com/press2/77taj.htm. To read about the shift from socialism and communism toward liberalism in the 1970s and 1980s, see Manfred Sing, "Arab Post-Marxists after Disillusionment: Between Liberal Newspeak and Revolution Reloaded," in Hatina and Schumann, *Arab Liberal Thought after 1967*, pp. 152–153.

[94] See the work of Marxist thinker, Yasin al-Hafez (1931–1978). This work considers these activists as part of a "modern liberalism," which promotes ideals of social liberalism, positive freedom, a managed economy, social responsibility, and a welfare system. While they could be considered "social democrats," their decision (whether momentary or not) to focus on establishing freedoms and on the fundamental nature of human rights instead of egalitarianism and collectivism, in addition to their distrust of authority, places them closer to modern liberalism than to socialism.

[95] Indeed, someone like Riad Turk, who was the founder of a communist party in the 1980s, would join a liberal alliance in the 2000s and would turn his party, renamed the Democratic People's Party, into a liberal one.

[96] Although a few other political prisoners have also been called that, such as Khalid al-Ukla, who spent 27 years in prison.

the liberal intelligentsia were also rebelling against the State. At the time, al-Turk perceived the rebellious activity including the Muslim Brothers' activity as part of a nation-wide popular rebellion of the Syrian people revolting against the repressive State; but his views contradicted the official narrative, which portrayed the rebellion as Islamist terrorism.

The consequences of his outspoken challenge and the potential alliance between these diverse political forces and the fear it generated within the regime were dire for all involved, and particularly for al-Turk. He was held without charge or trial, mostly incommunicado, in the Military Interrogation Branch (*Fir' al-Tahqiq al-'Askari*) in Damascus, and was kept in solitary confinement from 1980 to 1998, a period in which he was tortured and deprived of medical treatment. His wife, Asma al-Faisal (1931–2018), one of the first medical doctors in the city of Homs, was also arrested and held for a few years because of her own work with the SCPPB, as well as with the Syrian Women's League (founded in 1948) and the Syrian Red Crescent Organization (founded in 1942).[97] Riad al-Turk was only released in May 1998 under an amnesty declared by the late President Hafez al-Asad before an official visit to France.[98]

Thousands of political prisoners, from all ideological leanings, were arrested, some never to be seen again. Michel Kilo for example was arrested shortly after his speech – discussed above – from 1980 to 1983, accused of leaking information against the interests of the Ba'thist State, and tortured so badly that he almost died. Kilo went on to become a prominent journalist, a prolific writer, and a political thinker writing in several Arabic newspapers such as An-Nahar, al-Quds al-Arabi, and As-Safir. He has asserted himself as a master of bottom-up politics, and a key element in the formation of almost all the liberal political initiatives in Syria since 1979 (as will be seen in the sections in Chapter 2 and in Chapters 3 and 4).[99] In that role, he has committed to challenging

---

[97] "Riad al-Turk: The Old Man of the Syrian Opposition," *Fanack.com* (October 23, 2018), https://fanack.com/syria/faces/riad-al-turk/?gclid=EAIaIQobChMIvLT98-GX5wIVELbICh10TgIlEAAYASAAEgJ89_D_BwE; "Syrian Opposition Figure Asmaal-FaisalDiesinCanada,"*EnabBaladi*,(January8,2018),https://english.enabaladi.net/archives/2018/01/syrian-opposition-figure-asma-al-faisal-dies-canada/amp/

[98] Amnesty International, *Smothering Freedom of Expression: The Detention of Peaceful Critics* (June 6, 2002), pp. 4–8, www.refworld.org/docid/3cff2aa74.html

[99] Kilo would become a central figure in the writing of the Statement of the 99 in 2000, the same year he helped form with Fayez Sara and other activists the Committees to Revive Civil Society in Syria (a civil society group), then the writing of the Damascus Declaration (DD) of 2005, and the Beirut-Damascus Declaration in 2013. He then helped establish the National Coordination Commission (NCC) and the Democratic Forum (the liberal bloc). See "Who's Who: Michel Kilo," *The Syrian Observer* (September 27, 2013), https://syrianobserver.com/EN/who/34536/whos_who_michel_kilo.html

the Syrian regime for the past 40 years and has proclaimed in his many diagnoses that the Ba'thist regime has created a social, economic, and political environment that is incapable of providing solutions to Syria's problems, that in its disenfranchising structure it has not only failed but also lost all legitimacy in the eyes of its constituents. The only reason the regime has survived, explains Kilo, is related to its use of an extensive network of security apparatuses and draconian security solutions learnt from countries such as the Democratic Republic of Germany (the former East Germany) and North Korea.[100] But, Kilo argues, the Syrian regime has relied on "neutralizing" the middle class through co-optation and assimilation, thinking that disallowing it an independent role would guarantee the regime's survival.[101] And yet this strategy has failed, despite some appearances to the contrary, because it requires that those who are co-opted and advantaged ignore the disadvantaged social milieu in which they live.[102] In his attempts to deny the regime total control of the public stage, Kilo has asserted for years that Arab intellectuals have a very important role to play in order to advance liberal notions and to curb the political culture of authoritarianism, arguing that intellectuals can affirm people's rights and power by separating "the cultural field in all its forms from the dominant Arab politics in order to build a cultural field which is independent and resistant to it (i.e., to politics)."[103]

Like many Syrian activists and intellectuals, Kilo was once considered a leftist who then turned his focus toward questions of political participation and civil rights and individual freedoms. Indeed, as stated earlier, the 1970s, 1980s, and, certainly, the 1990s witnessed a shift away from dogmatic commitment to ideology and toward a more critical stance in which the focus was no longer on how to achieve a monolithic set of principles, but rather on how to allow for plurality and the establishment of the necessary freedoms that safeguard diversity, thus recognizing the

---

[100] Michel Kilo, "Syria ... the road to where?," *Contemporary Arab Affairs*, Vol. 4, No. 4 (2011), pp. 432–433, https://doi.org/10.1080/17550912.2011.630884; Radwan Ziadeh, *Power and Policy in Syria: Intelligence Services, Foreign Relations and Democracy in the Middle East* (London: I.B. Tauris, 2012).

[101] Salam Kawakibi explains this strategy in *Syrie: malgré la débâcle militaire, la renaissance de la société civile*, Carep Paris, (October 2020), www.carep-paris.org/wp-content/uploads/2020/10/Syrie_malgre_la_debacle_militaire_la-renaissance_de_la_societe-civile_Salam_Kawakibi.pdf

[102] Kilo, "Syria," p. 434.

[103] See: Michel Kilo, "Shahadat: Mishel Kilo," *al-Nahj* 40 (1995), p. 118; quote cited in Manfred Sing, "Arab Post-Marxists after Disillusionment: Between Liberal Newspeak and Revolution Reloaded," in Hatina and Schumann (eds.), *Arab Liberal Thought after 1967: Old Dilemmas, New Perceptions* (New York: Palgrave Macmillan, 2015), p. 164.

need for the establishment of a political liberal framework.[104] We see then that many of Syria's leftist activists break with communist and Marxist principles and switch to struggling against totalitarianism, with some preferring to be perceived as social democrats and others as leftist liberals. Indeed, Yasin al-Hafez (1931–1978), a Marxist theorist, had asserted the need for Arab leftists to integrate liberal notions within the political consciousness.[105] The shift was pressing and vital, "often literally to preserve life" explains Kassab, "a real need to secure some level of physical and moral integrity in the face of pervasive power."[106]

The results of the late 1970s and early 1980s battle against the Syrian regime were horrific for most activists who had demanded political pluralism, civil freedoms, and the rule of law. Notwithstanding this violent reality, the dream of political change continued, mostly in secret throughout the 1980s, but also expressed very clearly through art and theater, as will be discussed hereinafter. Toward the end of the decade, the unraveling of the Eastern Bloc and the Soviet Union – which was a patron of the Syrian regime – gave a push to Syria's liberal forces.

In 1989, a number of liberals including Kamal al-Labwani and Aktham Nu'aissa (or Naisse) formed a new human rights group, the Committees for the Defense of Democratic Freedoms and Human rights in Syria (CDF) [lijan al-difa' 'an huquq al-insan fi suriya]. The CDF operated secretly in the country and openly and actively in Europe, mainly France and Germany. In April 1990, the Committee started publishing a bulletin, *Sawt al-Demoocratiya* (Voice of Democracy) that was illegally distributed within Syria and that reported on human rights abuses as well

---

[104] Joe Stork writes about Hani Shukrallah, one of the founders of the EOHR in 1985, "For him the global developments of the 1970s and 1980s led to an 'epistemological break with dogmatic leftist thinking. I [Shukrallah] started to see how democracy and human rights were essential for human emancipation …'" (Stork 2013, p. 113). Another activist, Muhammad al-Sayyid Sa'id, explains, "To be frank, most of us were not really Nasserists or Marxists any more. We had these roots but we no longer defined ourselves that way." (Stork 2013, pp. 114–115). Indeed Muhammad al-Sayed Sa'id who had founded the Cairo Institute for Human Rights Studies, which aimed to create a social setting for democracy and human rights considered himself a left-leaning liberal.

[105] See Abd al-Razak Eid, "al-nukhab al-suriya wa taraf al-ikhtiar bayn al-dimucratiya wa al-libraliya!" *Shafaf al-Sharq al-Awsat* (August 5, 2005), www.metransparent.com/old/texts/abdelrazak_eid/abdelrazak_eid_syrian_elite_democracy_andliberalism.htm; Yasin had once described his position toward Nasserism "as ranging between support and critique, hope and despair." He argued that "an attempt to build socialism without a rational and modern basis would only result in the reproduction of a traditional society behind a socialist facade, a mixture of backwardness and socialism." Cited in Manfred Sing, "Arab Post-Marxists after Disillusionment," p. 158.

[106] Elizabeth S. Kassab, "The Arab Quest for Freedom and Dignity: Have Arab Thinkers Been Part of It?" *Middle East Topics and Arguments*, Vol. 1 (May 1, 2013), p. 28, https://meta-journal.net/article/download/1038/988/

as discussed issues of civil freedoms and democracy. On December 10, 1991, the CDF issued a statement commemorating the 43rd anniversary of the Universal Declaration of Human Rights, calling for free elections, and criticizing a referendum held on December 2, 1991, that approved Hafez al-Asad's reelection to the presidency with 99.98% of the vote.[107]

This defiance did not go unnoticed by the regime's leaders and the various elements of the security apparatus. According to the regime, not only were activists members of an illegal organization but they disturbed public confidence in the political authorities and challenged the regime at a time when the regime was finally feeling in control of its regional environment following the American intervention against Saddam Hussein in Iraq.[108] The State thus arrested hundreds of critics from the CDF in late 1991 and early 1992. And in March 1992, an exceptional security court sentenced ten of those activists, including lawyer and human rights activist Aktham Nu'aissa, to prison terms ranging from five to ten years.[109] Those who were charged faced accusations of "criminal offenses such as 'opposing any of the goals of the [Ba'thist] Revolution,' 'publishing false information with the aim of causing disorder and shaking the confidence of the people in the aims of the Revolution,' and membership in secret organizations 'created to change the economic or social structure of the state or the fundamental fabric of society'."[110] The severity of the regime's repressiveness is underlined by the fact that family members would also be harassed and at times detained (including children) without charge in order to exert further pressure on the activists.[111]

---

[107] HRW, *No Room to Breathe*, p. 8, www.hrw.org/report/2007/10/16/no-room-breathe/ state-repression-human-rights-activism-syria)

[108] The Iraqi and Syrian regimes were not on good terms at the time. The Syrian regime aided in the intervention and was rewarded generously by its Gulf counterparts, thus enhancing its regional position and standing.

[109] HRW, *No Room to Breathe*, pp. 8–9.
   For more background on CDF and the trial of the activists, see: Middle East Watch, *Syria Unmasked: The Suppression of Human Rights by the Asad Regime* (New Haven: Yale University Press, 1991), pp. 85–88; Middle East Watch, *Syria Human rights Workers on Trial*, Vol. 4, No. 5 (March 1992), pp. 3–4.

[110] HRW, *No Room to Breathe*, p. 9.

[111] The case of leftist activist Abd al-Aziz al-Khayyir demonstrates this trend. See a conversation with Abd al-Aziz al-Khayyir on DayPressNews (July 20, 2013), www .youtube.com/watch?v=BIOe6nwupsQ; Sada al-muwatana: watha'iqi 'an al-munadel Abd al-Aziz al-Khayyir, www.youtube.com/watch?v=JDcHOeSPWSk; Amnesty International, *Smothering Freedom of Expression: The Detention of Peaceful Critics* (June 6, 2002), pp. 8–9, www.refworld.org/docid/3cff2aa74.html. 'Abd al-'Aziz al-Khayyir's family members including his brother, sister, and cousin were arrested and detained to exert pressure on him. His wife, Muna Saqr al-Ahmed, was also detained without charge or trial in connection with the PCA from August 1987 until December 1991. During his underground years, al-Khayyir helped publish

The lengthy sentences were intended to punish those who continued to dream about the possibility of inducing political liberalization by reporting on and exposing political abuses, but also to deter future dissenters.[112] When liberalizing work could not be done within Syria, it was done by Syrians living overseas, mainly France, who would represent the liberals "on the inside" (*fi al-dakhil*) and the democrats in general abroad, who would write and report on the situation of political and human rights abuses, of political fraud and illegal acts, and would contact international human rights organizations in order to help fellow activists. Thus, while most English and French-speaking academics and journalists were asserting the stability of these regimes, activists on the inside and outside were attempting to reveal their weaknesses.

Political activists and journalists were not alone. Syrian writers, artists, and even liberal Islamic leaders[113] joined in the quest to advance liberal ideals and mindsets and to try to induce change, despite the very high levels of political repression witnessed in the country. The repression was so severe that the 1970s and 1980s would also witness the migration of liberal activism and resistance in Syria from the political to the cultural, literary, and academic fields, a reengagement and a reorientation that was aimed at expressing as widely as possible ideas that the State had effectively silenced within the political realm. And though the State would continue to supervise and interfere when it perceived

three important journals: Al-Shiyu'i (The Communist), "the Red Flag" (Al-Raya al-Hamra'), and "The People's Call" (Al-Nida' al-Sha'bi). The *People's Call* became a very popular newspaper in Syria throughout the 1980s. He also wrote the Black Book, a manuscript reporting and detailing the regime's abuses of power and torture methods. Following their arrest in February 1992, Abd al-Aziz al-Khayyir and his colleagues were held in incommunicado detention for about three months, first in Firi' Filastin (Palestine Detention Centre) and Far' al-tahqiq al-'askari (the Military Interrogation Branch) where they underwent interrogation and torture. On April 14, 1992, 'Abd al-'Aziz al-Khayyir was transferred to Sednaya prison on the outskirts of Damascus where he was held until 2005. Abd al-Aziz al-Khayyir was eventually tried in August 1995 and sentenced to 22 years' imprisonment (the longest sentence known to have been handed down thus far by the SSSC) on charges of membership of the PCA and for working against the socialist regime and endangering its stability and security. He was not released with the other members of the PCA who were released in December 2001 as part of a presidential amnesty. Al-Khayyir was released in 2005 and he almost immediately returned to his activism. He helped found the National Coordination Committee for Democratic Change (Hai'at al-tansiq al-wataniya li-quwa al-taghyir al-dimucrati) in July 2011, made up of dozens of pro-democracy leftist parties, and dozens of independents. He was recaptured in 2012 and no one knows if he is at present dead or alive.

[112] Human Rights Watch/Middle East, *Syria: The Price of Dissent*, Vol. 7, No. 4 (July 1995), www.hrw.org/reports/1995/Syria.htm.

[113] See section on Shaykh Jawdat Said.

a direct threat to the official storyline, the cultural field was nonetheless perceived as less menacing and so was relatively less restricted. Allowing some limited degree of openness was also one way to monitor criticism of the regime, and maybe even to allow a safety valve to vent emotions whether on the part of the artists or the audience. Important for this book is that while artists and writers did not openly declare their defiance (and so were less menacing), the stories and ideas they communicated were dissecting the official storyline and in many ways undermining it. Indeed, the culture of liberalism was slowly spreading in Syria – and in the region overall – through these cultural works, to the extent that the regime soon had to adapt its official storyline in an attempt to address the intellectuals' critique and to assert a process of political liberalization as early as the start of the 1990s.[114]

One of these intellectuals, Saadallah Wannous (1941–1997), a journalist and a playwright, was a force to be reckoned with in the critical movement. His plays are still performed in the Arab World and Europe and his work is read and studied all over the world.[115] Like Kilo who argued for politicizing culture in order to advance democratic ideals, Wannous believed in theater as a place for political activity. In his critique of the dominant (authoritarian) political project in the region, which preached an identity and politics focused on unity and conformity over individuality, Wannous wrote, "As we have envisioned the group with one face and one temper and negated exception and individualism, we have forgotten that it is exception and individualism that turn a group into a human force, not the accumulation of empty numbers and objects."[116] Wannous objected to the accumulation of power not just at the political level, but at the socioeconomic level as well. He revolted against tyranny and social rigidity, shattering taboos, revealing the contradictions of religious leaders, and fighting for human rights and human dignity for all including for homosexuals – a topic that most Arab liberals have avoided. He also decried the Zionist project in Palestine as one of the fiercest forms of world imperialism and aggressive colonialism, yet

---

[114] American intervention in the region is often cited to explain the changes most of the Arab regimes undertook. This work argues that a change to public discourse and policies would have been entirely unnecessary had activists and intellectuals not been pushing for change and sowing the seeds of political liberalism from within. For more on political liberalization and democratization in the region, see Bahgat Korany, Rex Brynen and Paul Noble (eds.), *Political Liberalization and Democratization in the Arab World*, Vol. 1 (Boulder, CO: Lynne Rienner, 1998).

[115] See Asaad Al-Saleh, "Approaching Sa'dallah Wannus' Drama: The Manifestos of a New Arab Theater," *Alif: Journal of Comparative Poetics*, Vol. 39 (2019).

[116] Cited in Sing, "Arab Post-Marxists after Disillusionment," p. 165.

he asked his readers and audience to look in the mirror, to rethink their own ways and mindsets, and to face the reality that their humiliation and defeat is the product of their own hands.[117]

In one of his plays, "*Haflat Samar min ajl Khamsa Huzeiran*" (A Soiree for the 5th of June – translated into English by Roger Allen), Wannous presents the opening night of a play "*Safir al-Arwah*" [the Whistle of the Souls] that never starts. The acting spectators (actors playing the role of the spectators) waiting for "Safir al-Arwah" to begin start shouting sarcastically "Have the actors lost their roles," and "is this an imperialist conspiracy?" The director finally appears to explain why the play hasn't started yet. In his explanation, Wannous complicates the national story that most Syrians and Arabs adhere to, and presents his own understanding and the many layers to war, heroism, shame, inadequacy and honor, and to ideology and patriotism. He explains how villagers had to flee their homes because they were abandoned and confused, and how they were then humiliated as refugees, and how soldiers were unprepared, deserted, and unaware of what was going on around them. The acting spectators to whom the director is offering this explanation then become part of the conversation as they start interfering in his story, asking questions, and voicing their opinions of what happened and should have happened during the war, how villagers and soldiers should have faced the major aggression. Finally, one spectator claims that one should look at oneself in the mirror, explaining that we (Syrians and Arabs overall) are, "...images [that] have been erased in the name of national interest ... year after year, questioning, seeing, and thinking were regarded as punishable crimes in the face of a national interest that was defended in dark dungeons. What is left in a picture in which the tongue, the eyes, and the ears are erased?"[118] Another spectator intervenes saying, "our mistake was to ask for weapons to fight, not for our eyes, not for our tongues, not for our right to think, not for our right to exist with identifiable features. [An] [e]rased picture we remained, incapacitated and defeated." The play ends with an official ordering his men to arrest everyone, including those who haven't spoken.[119] Wannous, like other activists and writers who were active in the 1970s and 1980s, asserted that the main mistake in the attempt at nation-building was the disenfranchisement of the public and the suppression of pluralism and diversity in the name of achieving rapid modernization and independence. Overall, Wannous demanded a focus on the political in every act.

---

[117] Kassab, *Contemporary Arab Thought*, pp. 48–50.
[118] Translated in Kassab, *Contemporary Arab Thought*, pp. 52–53.
[119] Kassab, *Contemporary Arab Thought*, p. 53.

In his "masrah al-tasyis," [politicizing theater], Wannous hoped to reawaken citizens' sense of self and of their rights.[120] Kassab explains that Wannous perceived theater as a place for people to enhance their critical faculties and to develop authentic awareness within an environment that forbids critical and progressive thinking. It is thus a place to mobilize that awareness in order to challenge tyranny and empower oneself. Theater effectively becomes then a stage of practical resistance. But resistance, according to Wannous, can only ensue if the public is engaged in forming their own understanding and critical view of their environment after they have contemplated the story and its relevance in their own lives.[121] Wannous held that Arab theater and art should be organic but not separate and isolated from other traditions, "Authentic theater has to be local, but not exclusively or necessarily in a geographical sense."[122] This need to connect with other cultures and ideas is typical of the discourse of most liberals, who have argued that being authentically Arab or local does not mean limiting oneself to one's heritage and one's knowledge, but also drawing from other cultures in order to address local problems and engage one's specific malaise.

In 1978, Wanous wrote an article that he published in *As-Safir* newspaper, "Ana al-Janaza wa al-mushayi'un ma'an" [I am the Funeral and the Mourners at the Same Time], in which he lamented the citizen's lack of rights. He wrote, "My life has neared its end and I still dream of saying 'No.' I wanted, and I want to say 'No' to the 'Yes' citizen, to the prison-homeland, to the modernization of the methods of torture and domestication, to the official discourse, to the visas for Arab countries, to the fragmentation and the division, to the referenda of 99.99 percent, to the balloon celebrations, to the wars that strengthen the police, to the victories which offer the leadership of the Arabs to the oil princes, that increase the gains of the businessmen, and lead to the agreements of Camp David...."[123] Wannous' critique of the inability to publically counter the dominant discourse, to simply declare one's opinion out loud, is in all of his works.

Showcasing the liberals' history and intellectual contribution in the region became Wannous' new project at the end of his life. When he and other Syrian writers launched the magazine *Qadaya wa Shahadat* in 1990, they dedicated its first edition to examining the work of Taha Hussein

---

[120] Sa'dallah Wannous, *Bayanat limasrah arabi jadid* (Beirut: dar al-fikr al-jadid, 1988)
[121] Kassab, *Contemporary Arab Thought*, pp. 53–54.
[122] Ibid, p. 55.
[123] Translated by Kassab, *Contemporary Arab Thought*, pp. 56–57. See also Syrian director Omar Amiralay's film about the life of Saadallah Wannous, "wa hunak ashia' kathira kan yumken an yatahadath 'anha al-mar'" [There are so many things still to say], released in 1997 and aired on al-Jazeera then.

(see Chapter 1).[124] Their concern was to establish some continuity with the liberal intellectuals of the *Nahda* period, to recognize, renew, and continue their liberal heritage. Indeed, Wannous was once a Marxist who turned into a liberal like many thinkers within Syria (see above) who witnessed the morbidity of dictatorship. In one of Wannous' letters to the Egyptian writer 'Abla al-Ruwaini, he lamented his initial illiteracy in political liberalism, by which he meant having liberal freedoms in order to contribute to the fate of his nation.[125] Wannous' work appeared in most countries in the Arabic-speaking region, inspired many, and provoked much debate.

He was not alone. In the 1970s and 1980s, art and literature would become paths through which Syrian liberals impacted their social and political environment, denounced abuses, and inspired others to seek freedom. Many have contributed to these paths: names such as Zakaria Tamer (1931), who helped found the Syrian Arab Writers Union in 1968, and poet and writer Muhammad al-Maghut (1934–2006), who stayed in Syria until his death in 2006. Both denounced the regions' authoritarian regimes, monolithic thought, religious radicalism, and repression, and the characters in their works resisted oppression and longed for freedom and rule of law. These authors' dark humor decries *istibdad* and reveals the dogmatism, idiocy, physical brutality, and psychological violence of those in power in the region. They showed how regimes have turned citizens into mere subjects through brutality and oppression. In Muhammad al-Maghut's words, Zakaria Tamer's work contrasted with that of Charles Darwin: one showing how humans developed from monkeys, and the other showing how humans could be manipulated into becoming monkeys under repression.[126] While Wannous believed that hope was never lost, Tamer presented an un-sanitized, blunt, and often offensive reality that was truly devoid of hope and in which humans lost their humanity because they lacked their basic rights. Tamer would leave Syria for the UK in 1981, but one hope he still had over 30 years after leaving was "to sit in a Damascus café and swear at the top of my voice at all the Syrian officials without feeling intimidated or fearing arrest."[127]

In the televised and very popular play *Kasak ya Watan* (1979), Muhammad al-Maghut also presented citizens who have become helpless in the

---

[124] Qadaya wa shahadat, No. 1 (Spring 1990).
[125] See 'Abla al-Ruwaini, *Haka al-ta'er saadallah wanus* (Cairo: Dar Meret, 2005)
[126] See "A summary of What Happened to Mohammed al-Mahmoudi," and "Tigers on the Tenth Day."
[127] Ziad Majed, "A Dialogue with Zakaria Tamer" (translated by Syrian Translators group), Ziad Majed's Blog, https://freesyriantranslators.net/2012/07/22/a-dialogue-with-zakaria-tamer-2/

face of State oppression and tyranny, although not numbed by it. In Maghut's works, the torture chamber is a constant during which there is assertion of power and an attempt to silence those who protest the regime's arbitrary ways and disregard for the law and who long for freedom. In another one of his plays, *Day'at Tishrin* (The Village of Tishrin, 1974), one of the villagers, Nayif, is arrested and tortured for complaining about the shortages of food. The village has plenty of food, he is told; it is all in the house of the village leader. Another villager is also taken to the torture chamber, not because he has objected to anything, but precisely because he said nothing. The interrogator tells him: "Here is the danger. Here is plotting more serious than Nayif's. Nayif spoke and we know what is in his mind. But you said nothing and we don't know what you are up to."[128] In both Maghut and Wannus' works, they reveal how natural it is to have an opinion, and yet how this right is considered transgression under dictatorship.

In his famous poem, *al-Qatl* [The Killing], Maghut writes mainly about his own incarceration at the Mezzeh prison in 1955. He writes, "Put your stone foot on my heart, sir...here is the tyrant's chariot, pushed forward by the wind and here we advance as a sword that infiltrates a skull. How miserable I am, to hell this homeland that inhabits my heart..." [author's translation][129] Muhammad al-Maghut became a poet during his time in jail that began in 1955.[130] He was subjected to torture, and confessed to have cried and screamed from pain and sadness. Al-Maghut never recovered from his time in prison (he was arrested again in 1961) and said in an interview that he never recovered from the torture, "that he lost security in jail, and learned the meaning of fear."[131]

Repression impacted Syrian intellectuals profoundly. Yet while repression halted the direct political activism against the State, it certainly did not stop Syrians from producing critical work aimed at revealing and denouncing the mechanisms and absurdity of repression, as well as asserting human freedoms and rights. In the words of al-Maghut, "[f]ear is the lack of freedom."[132] In other words, these writers and activists' work reflected the people's grievances, but it also shaped the popular understanding of local

---

[128] See Lisa Wedeen, *Ambiguities of Domination: Politics, Rhetoric, and Symbols in Contemporary Syria* (Chicago and London: University of Chicago Press, 1999), pp. 93–55.

[129] As recited by al-Maghut on the program Adab al-Sujun, "Muhammad al-Maghut," *Al-Jazeera* (April 10, 2006). For more on Muhammad al-Maghut's work, see: Muhammad al-Maghut, al-a'mal al-shi'riya (Damascus: Dar al-Mada, 2006); Lu'ay Adam, Watan fi Watan: Muhammad al-Maghut (Damascus: Dar al-Mada, 2001).

[130] Adab al-Sujun, "Muhammad al-Maghut."

[131] Sami Moubayed, "Farewell Mohammad al-Maghut," *Mideast views* (April 3, 2006), www.mideastviews.com/articleview.php?art=104

[132] Adab al-Sujun, "Muhammad al-Maghut."

and regional events as well as the perception and reaction to oppression, helped to mobilize citizens against injustice and despotism, and mirrored their emotions and needs during an often dark and difficult time. Their work has been especially impactful within the region as a result of appearing in popular newspapers and periodicals, and because it was turned into plays, documentaries, television programs, and films.[133]

Even a few religious shaykhs turned to liberal interpretations in order to challenge authoritarianism whether at the social or political level. This was the case of Islamic leader Jawdat Said. Said is one of Syria's most dedicated thinkers to the quest of freedom and individual rights. He is a prominent Islamic scholar and philosopher who is considered the father of nonviolence in the Arab World. Born in 1931 in Syria's Golan Heights, in the town of Quneytra, Said studied Arabic literature at Cairo's al-Azhar University before returning to Syria (then the United Arab Republic) in the late 1950s. While working as an Arabic language teacher in Damascus, he was repeatedly transferred, persecuted, and imprisoned a few times between 1964 and 1973 for his intellectual activism against *istibdad* (tyranny or despotism), and he was finally barred from teaching in the late 1960s without the right of objection.[134] He returned to near his hometown of Quneytra in 1973, where he continued his work on reinterpreting Islam.

According to Said, Islam is a peaceful and liberal religion. He explains that in the Quranic version of the story of Cain and Abel, Abel says to his jealous brother: "If thou dost stretch thy hand against me, to slay me, it is not for me to stretch my hand against thee to slay thee, for I do fear God, the cherisher of the worlds" (Quran 5:28). Thus, Said concludes, according to the account in the Quran, "the first murder in history is accompanied by the first act of nonviolence, a refusal to kill, even in self-defense, through mindfulness of a God who stands far above partisan conflict."[135] It is upon this that Jawdat Said bases his theory of nonviolence and in this that he sees the spirit of Islam.[136]

---

[133] Other liberalizing attempts were undertaken by the intellectuals through publishing houses and TV programs. In 1998, Dar al-Fikr, a publishing house based in Damascus began publishing a series entitled "Dialogues for a New Century," which pits ideologically opposed intellectuals against one another other in the context of a single volume. The secular writer and Damascus Spring activist, Abd al-Razzaq Eid, and the Islamist activist, Muhammad Abd al-Jabbar, faced off on the theme of "Democracy, between Secularism and Islam." A female Islamist activist, Heba Raouf Ezzat, and the secular feminist, Nawal Sa'dawi, took on the issues of "Women, Religion and Ethics." See Browers, *Political Ideology in the Arab World*, pp. 77–78.

[134] Author's communication with Shaykh Jawdat Said.

[135] Michael Nagler, "Lamp in the Storm," *Yes Magazine* (July 30, 2012), www.yesmagazine.org/peace-justice/syria-lamp-in-the-storm

[136] In this section about Jawdat Said, English translations of his work and of Quranic verses is by Said, unless otherwise noted.

Jawdat Said's interpretation of the Quran challenges the traditional and orthodox hermeneutical readings in that it sees the Quran as essentially a text about peace, individual freedom, democracy, and rationality.[137] Theoretically and methodologically, Said places himself in the tradition of Arab and Islamic reformers such as Abd al-Rahman al-Kawakibi, and the mystic poet and philosopher Muhammad Iqbal, and the Moroccan philosopher Mohammed Abed al-Jabri. Said has written 12 books and been interviewed many times on Arab and European television, and has made many appearances and presentations throughout the Arab World and Europe. He has also captured the imagination of many Arabic-speaking individuals because of his pioneering views and his defiance of monolithic and radical streams of Islam through a response firmly rooted in theory and scholarship.[138] For thousands in the Arab region, Said's work embodies the hope and kindness that are all too often eclipsed by the more sensational and frightening discourse of orthodox Islamism.

Like 'Ali 'Abd al-Raziq, Jawdat Said sees a dynamic relationship between humans and the divine text. He contends that the Quran, while immutable and absolute, can only reveal itself through time and through our changing reality (since God is always in the act of creation) and, more importantly, our evolving understanding and appropriation of our reality as humans. Thus the meaning of the text is not merely hidden within it, rather it is through a constant rereading and reinterpretation of the text that humanity discovers God's message.[139] This communication between the text and humans based on our understanding of our empirical world is one of the essential parts of Said's philosophy since, as he asserts, a proper understanding of the Quran can only come about gradually in conjunction with our study of objective reality.[140] This, in

---

137 Author's communication with Shaykh Jawdat Said.

138 His books include *Mazhab ibn adam al-awal* [which he refers to it in English as The Doctrine of Adam's Better (or First) Son] (1966): *Mushkilat al-'unf fi al-'amal al-siyasi; Iqra' wa rabika al-akram* (1988); *Al-din wa al-qanun: ru'ya qur'aniya* (1998); *Kun ka-ibn adam* (1996); *lima haza al-ru'b kuluh mina al-islam wa keyfa bada'a al-khawf?* [Why Is Such Dread from Islam (publisher's proposed translation)] (2006). I have opted to quote Said directly in many instances in this section since there is very little work in English about him and thus it gives an opportunity for readers to get a first-hand glimpse of the way he discusses and examines issues.

139 "Interview with Jawdat Sa'eed," *Current Islamic Issues* (April 1998), www.jawdatsaid .net/en/index.php?title=Current_Islamic_Issues

140 Jawdat Said, *Mazhab ibn Adam al-awal: mushkilat al-'unf fi al-'amal al-siyasi*, 5th ed. (Beirut: Dar al-Fikr, 1993), pp. 13–14. The 5th edition is available online at www .jawdatsaid.net/index.php?title=الطبعةالخامسة_آدم_ابن_منهب_مقدمة. Because the edition does not show page numbers, it is assumed that the first page following the cover page is page (1) and pagination follows forward.

turn, allows Said to assert a number of liberal values that he believes the Quran promotes: first, that for humanity to discover the universal meaning of the divine text and to "know" God, we need to rely on the use of our endowed rational faculty; this is the only way for humanity to discover the laws (*sunan*) of the universe surrounding us.[141] An understanding of the Quran thus involves a learning process, even scientific and technological "growth."[142] A Muslim thus never is but is always in the process of becoming, and similarly the interpretations of the words of God are never final and thus never absolute regardless of who articulates them. In other words, the Quran is absolute and eternal, but its interpretation is always contingent and shifting, depending on humans' overall ability and willingness to critically engage with the changing universe around us.[143] Consequently, Said's second liberal assertion is in the way he connects religiosity and spirituality to human knowledge and makes them *contingent* on epistemological investigation as well as rational, scientific enquiry.[144] Third, Said asserts that dogma is to be shunned. He explains that medieval clerics have attempted to confine Muslims in the world and words of the fathers' (*al-aba'* and *al-aba'iya*).[145] The problem of the orthodox mind, he explains, is that it believes itself to have already answered all questions. Said writes, "A dogmatic mind is that of a person who, when the objective circumstances call for a change in attitude... fails to make that change."[146] He calls on Muslims and Islamic clerics to free themselves of the dictates and rituals of their forefathers, to stop raising leaders above their human place, and to accept their fallibility.[147]

Fourth and related to the previous points is Said's conceptualization of *individuality*, which is determinedly liberal. Previous reformists, he explains, have been keen on safeguarding society from the ills of disunity and degeneration (*inhilal*), so much so that in an attempt to create order they produced a uniform world with established ways of behaving and thinking for all. Here, Said announces his most liberal idea: that

[141] For more on Said's thoughts on rationality and the necessity for continuous scientific enquiry for the achievement of Good, see Jawdat Said, *Iqra' wa rabika al-akram*, Abhath fi sunan taghyir al-nafs wa al-mujtama' (Damascus, 1988); and Jawdat Said's talk in Bir Ajam (November 24, 2006), available at, www.youtube.com/watch?v=9VUN6Cj2B5o

[142] "Interview with Jawdat Sa'eed," *Current Islamic Issues*.

[143] Jawdat Said, *Mazhab ibn Adam al-awal*, pp. 6–7, 11.

[144] Jawdat Said, "Law kan al-din bi al-'aql," *Al-Majala* (date n.d.), www.jawdatsaid.net/index.php?title=بالعقل_الدين_كان_لو

[145] Jawdat Said, *Iqra' wa rabika al-akram*, pp. 17–18 (page numbers are not available, and so it is assumed that the first page of the book is page (1) and so forth).

[146] "Interview with Jawdat Sa'eed," *Current Islamic Issues*.

[147] Ibid.

orthodox jurists and clerics forgot that the destiny (*masir*) of peoples depends more on the value of the individual than on order, and that societies that are too orderly crush the individual, who benefits from all the fruits of collective thinking and yet loses his or her soul. Thus only a strong sense of our individuality can safeguard us from degeneration and *zulm* (injustice) as only it can allow us to craft innovative solutions to our present problems.[148] Fifth, Said reasserts Muslims' right to democratic rule and the rule of law. He explains that the Quran opposes *ikrah* (coercion) and favors *rushd* (rationality, maturity): "There is no coercion in religion: *rushd* (moral and intellectual maturity) stands out as clearly distinct from *ghay* (domination, wickedness): who-ever rejects *taghut* (tyranny) and believes in God, has grasped the most secure handhold that never breaks loose. And God hears And knows all things. (Surah 2 Al Baqarah: 256)"[149] He explains, not only equality and choice (which are the outcome of his principle of noncoercion) are the most important principles within the Quran, but indeed that pluralism and democratic rule are the logical practical outcomes of these concepts. Indeed, for Said, *rushd* and *la-ikrah* are positive and mature values that lead a society to democracy.[150] The word "*taghoot*" (tyranny), he tells us, is explained by orthodox clerics as "evil," "Satan," or "the idols." And yet: "No one is held up in the Qur'an as the prototype of *taghut* more than Pharaoh; not any name – apart from that of Allah – is mentioned in the Qur'an more often than that of Moses, the man who stood in the face of Pharaoh; and that in the greatest civilization of the ancient world. The Quranic Pharaoh thus represents the tyrant and all that which an oppressor says and does, while Moses is the exemplary human who challenges the tyrant and who leads people away from their 'submissive state'." Said then argues, "It must be revealing that the story of Moses and Pharaoh has been repeated in the Qur'an more than any other story."[151]

And so, the "upright condition" according to Jawdat Said, is one in which humans' freedoms of thought, belief, and expression are safeguarded, and in which the protection of these rights is applied in the same way to everyone, whether believer or not.[152] Here, Said proclaims what he calls the universal and inclusive message of Islam, that the good can only be known through difference, and through constant human

---

[148] Jawdat, *Mazhab ibn Adam al-awal*, p. 7.

[149] For more on *rushd* and *ikrah*, see: Jawdat Said, *Kun ka-ibn adam* (Damascus, 1996), chapter 1, especially section on the prophets and freedom of expression (al-anbiya' wa hiriyat al-tafkir).

[150] Said, "Al-la 'inf huwa al-la ikrah."

[151] Ibid; see also Said, *Mazhab ibn Adam al-awal*, pp. 32–33.

[152] For more on freedom of expression, see Said, *Mazhab ibn Adam al-awal*, pp. 32–33.

exchange. He writes, "In difference we deepen the right"[153] [author's translation]. He then praises "Westerners" for creating democratic political systems that allow for the transfer of rule without any sort of physical violence, which safeguard a person's right to her opinion.[154] Said concludes that the old paradigms of obedience, worship, and power seeking are creating "a perpetual, glaring violation of the principles of human rights and hence giving capital and justification to the small dictators of the developing world."[155] He explains that only once the entire world becomes liberal democratic does the institution of war (*mu'asasat al-harb*) end and international justice can be achieved.[156] Said's work on nonviolence has acted as a guidepost for Muslim activists calling for civil and human rights in the region. His first book, *Mazhab ibn Adam al-awal*, published in 1966, has sold thousands of copies, and has subsequently gone on to have five further editions.

Together, Said and other Syrian liberals pushed back the repressive State from below. Just like their Egyptian counterparts, they did so peacefully, focusing on reexamining the self, on teaching, writing, and cultural production. In so doing they challenged essentialist and monolithic claims, and asserted people's right to choose for themselves and to experience their individuality. In the 1970s and 1980s Syrians had less space to act than their Egyptian counterparts, and yet they still managed to advance liberal conceptualization of rights and for democracy, and to express their yearning for individual freedoms and rights.

The 1990s: The Era of Hope, Defiance, and the Use of the Media to Propagate Liberal Ideas

The 1990s would become the decade of hope in Syria and Egypt, even though at the political level, the autocrats appear on top of their games. It is then that Arab liberals started to make use of the popularity of television programs to propagate their ideas. Even prior to the 1990s – for instance, in 1986 a debate was held between Shaykhs Muhammad al-Ghazali and Yusuf al-Qaradawi, two religious 'ulama', and liberal philosopher Fouad Zakariya. And as we saw earlier in this chapter, another debate was held in 1991 between Shaykh al-Ghazali and the Islamic thinker Muhammad 'Imara versus two liberal critics, Faraj Fuda and the modernist shaykh Muhammad Khalafalla. Both of these debates were

---

[153] Said, *Mazhab ibn Adam al-awal*, pp. 12–13.
[154] "Interview with Jawdat Sa'eed," *Current Islamic Issues*.
[155] Said, "The Role of Religious Actors in Peace Building."
[156] Author's communication with Jawdat Said, 2017.

widely viewed and discussed all over the Arab World;[157] but such debates remained rare because they took place on national television, a medium that was heavily controlled by the regime.

This would change as the 1990s progressed, with liberals increasingly taking advantage of new avenues to express and disseminate their ideas. They thus went from having to rely on print culture and national television to using the new information outlets such as satellite channels as well as online forums, which, in turn, revolutionized and magnified their ability to reach out to citizens. More particularly, the rise of media outlets such as mbc and LBC, in addition to relatively independent news channels such as al-Jazeera and al-Arabiya, although themselves hardly liberal, allowed for the creation of a political and social environment with increased diversity, pluralism, and allowed the liberals to express their ideas and their demands for civil rights. Liberals also started appearing on and participating in an increasing number of debates that pitted them against traditionalists, conservatives, and regime sycophants. For example, "Al-itijah al-mu'akis," a very popular program on al-Jazeera, hosted several televised debates, such as that between Muhammad al-Khuli, a professor of Islamic fiqh at al-Azhar university, and Muhammad Arkoun, a professor at the Sorbonne and a prominent liberal critic. And 'Ali Jum'a, the mufti of Egypt, appeared on a two-hour Egyptian TV program with 'Abd al-Mu'ti Hijazi, a poet and liberal critic.[158] Further, Ayman Nour, an Egyptian liberal (see Chapter 3), appeared on Al-Jazeera numerous times such as on the program "fi al-'umuq" [in depth], and focused on defining and discussing Arab liberalism as well as promoting it while also revealing the problem of what he calls "al-liberaliyun al-maghshushun" [The fake liberals] who, according to him, claim to be liberal but are not consistently committed to liberal ideals.[159]

Lebanese newspapers in which Syrian intellectuals express themselves more freely, and European based pan-Arab newspapers such as al-Sharq al-Awsat and al-Quds, also came to be discussed on the satellite channels, with sections of the news solely concerned with summarizing their content to the audience. This further contributed to the opening up of intellectual and political space, an opening up that liberals could legitimately claim to have helped stimulate and which they also made ample use of. And so, liberals were finally able to discuss and debate openly and directly with their audiences notions of freedom, equality, social justice,

[157] Abu Samra, "Liberal Critics," p. 270.
[158] Ibid.
[159] Fi al-'umq, "Al-liberaliyun al-arab wa al-dimucratiya," *al-Jazeera* (May 12, 2014), www.youtube.com/watch?v=U_K_w7meM9E

women's rights, and human rights more generally, as well as to have a more direct impact on Arab public discourse and thus on political culture overall. Even Islamists would debate their ideas, and in many ways more liberal interpretations of Islam increasingly appeared on the ideological scene. Indeed, as Abu Samra explains,

In coping with the liberal accusations, 'ulama' are driven into a "foreign land"; they are obliged to adapt to the liberal critics' discourse and adopt aspects of their cultural terminology too. Presenting the tolerant aspects of Islam, promoting the status and rights of women, equality between non-Muslims and Muslims, and freedom of thought and religion are in part a response to liberal criticism. This applies equally to the attempts to present the shari'a as a flexible and dynamic legal system and reinterpret some of its rules to counter internal and external accusations against calls for the application of Islamic law.[160]

The 1990s would certainly see the diminution of the culture of fear with the issuing of one of the first independent statements signed by intellectuals in Syria since the 1970s. In 1991, Syrian intellectuals demanded that the State respects the wishes of its people in not taking part in the American-led coalition against Iraq. Another statement would be written by cinematographs, producers, movie directors, and script writers in 1999 denouncing the corruption and inefficiency of the public institution responsible for making movies in the country, and asking for reforms and, more importantly for this book, independence from the State. In a bold move, the signatories of the statement requested that the State cease its political interference in and censorship of their work. Very soon after its release, another statement, "bayan al-muthaqafin li-da'm al-sinema'yyin" (The manifesto of the intellectuals in support of film makers) prepared by academic and activist Hassan Abbas[161] and signed by a number of Syrian intellectuals, was published in the Lebanese press (due to the refusal of Syria's official newspapers to publish it).[162] The statement was meant to support the efforts and reiterate the demands of the directors, producers, and writers and an attempt to show esprit de corps at a time when Syria's civil society was considered inexistent by most observers.[163] In 1999, Hassan Abbas and feminist activist Nawal Yazji opened Syria's first forum in Yazji's home. The goal was to create a space for dialogue between intellectuals, hence its name, the

---

[160] Abu Samra, "Liberal Critics," p. 271.
[161] Hassan Abbas would later become the godfather of a movement for citizenship culture and awareness in Syria.
[162] Wael al-Sawwah, "Hassan 'Abbas wa Rabi' Dimashq: al-quwwa al-na'ima," in Fayez Sara (ed.), *Hassan Abbas bi-'uyun mu'asira* (Partners: November 2020), pp. 25–27.
[163] Al-Sawwah, "Hassan 'Abbas," p. 26.

Forum of Cultural Dialogue, but also to reinstate civil society and soften people's fears of assembling.

Of course, the 1990s also saw ruling coalitions fight back; they adopted measures to counter and postpone meaningful structural adjustments, co-opted both business and intellectual elites by engaging in a selective economic liberalization, and forged partnerships with rising business people in order to cement their position in power. But co-optation meant that a few groups started to accumulate the benefits of the wealth created by the selective economic liberalization without the promised trickle-down effect to the majority of the populace, thus breeding a growing resentment and disillusionment on the part of the disenfranchised public masses. Aware of the upsurge of nongovernmental groups and of the rising awareness among the people, the 1990s also saw many regimes in the region promise that some form of political liberalization would come soon.

The space created, no matter how small, emboldened civil society. An increasing number of human rights organizations emerged, taking on some of the roles abandoned by the States such as safeguarding of women's rights and aid to the poor. These groupings became able to work and organize together as they were no longer as effectively atomized. And thus this new environment of selective economic and political liberalization allowed liberals to grow more aware of one another and to even interact and work together.

Conclusion

The authoritarianism that dominated in Egypt and Syria from the 1960s through to the 1990s forced the liberals, whether consciously or unconsciously, into a new strategy that involved recalibrating their direct methods in an attempt to continue existing and having a voice. They thus turned from focusing on social and political change from above to inducing change and propagating liberal views from below and at the cultural and grassroots levels. Their paternalistic tone also changed as they had to rethink their relationship with the public. And so they turned toward social activism; nongovernmental institutions, which they founded; issues of human including women's rights; and cinema, art, and literature driven by a belief that a bottom-up approach is not just the only possible way but a necessary long-term strategy for awakening a democratic order. In so doing, the liberals were able to exist and to continue to work in the midst of some of the harshest autocratic settings, hidden in plain sight, while also, I argue, helping to foster an environment in which liberalism could continue to exist, to speak, and to be nurtured despite its apparent entanglement within authoritarianism. In other words, the liberal continued to emerge and reemerge in the midst of the autocratic, causing fluctuating configurations of authoritarianism and of rights.

Whether one looks at Egypt or Syria, or even other countries in the region such as Saudi Arabia, we see during this period the survival and even the rise of liberal networks and organizations which in their focus on social rights also managed to train, teach, speak, write, monitor, and promote liberal values, perspectives, and worldviews. And so, despite the fact that the official regimes' narratives remained dominant, liberals were able to speak up and to build on common Arab narratives and mores, embedding and reasserting fundamental liberal values such as pro-democracy and freedom of speech via academic work, art, theater, comedy, film, and human rights organizations, as well as through some media outlets and other published works. Their discourse, in turn, reached many people, with some of the concepts being internalized to the extent that regimes soon felt that they had to meet the challenge by claiming to be in the process of politically liberalizing. This was the case in Egypt under Sadat and Mubarak, as well as in Syria in the 1980s and 1990s.[164] Even Communist and Marxist activists started either switching to liberalism or working within a liberal logic and advocating for a liberal framework to guide political changes. What this underlines then is the wider impact of liberalism in this period, and its contribution to the rise in the 1990s of a greater culture of human and citizens' rights. This contribution has been all too frequently passed over, with much greater attention given to the dominant authoritarian context and to illiberal elements in the region such as political Islam; yet, it is an important one that is the fruit of much effort from a variety of individuals working in multiple domains, and it has had a larger influence than is often acknowledged.

[164] Stork, "Three Decades of Human Rights," pp. 113–114.

3   The 2000s
The No Longer Politically Quiet and Secret
Activism and the More Visible Buildup

This chapter discusses the phase spanning from the 2000s until the start of the Arab Spring in 2011, a period that saw a liberal renewal and revitalization. It pays particular attention to how activists and communities have come together in pursuit of shared liberal notions and goals, and how they have impacted political conduct and affairs.

In hindsight, the 1980s and 1990s saw a deepening loss of regime legitimacy in the region, with the old nationalist populist bargains in Egypt and Syria no longer being viable. States could no longer provide for the public masses in return for their acquiescence and obedience. Critiques that had turned inward provided renewed ideas about what a nation, a community and a *muwaten* (citizen) are or should be; and visions that had been suppressed for decades on the political scene re-emerged in books, art, theatre, the printed press, on the internet, and on Satellite television.[1] Intellectuals as well as activists began to think beyond the simplistic yet pervasive categories of so-called "Islamic," "leftist," and "progressive" values in their attempts to re-appropriate, make sense of, and reclaim liberal values. They engaged in debates about citizenship and pluralism stressing issues of civil rights and political freedoms and individuals' right to self-rule. Even leftist thinkers who lost faith in the contentions of the radical era and became disillusioned with authoritarian politics turned to a "liberal-ish" agenda that emphasized liberal rights and freedoms and criticized State logic and monopoly over power and the economy.[2]

This intellectual revival in many ways accelerated in the 2000s, with a general move away from what is considered "dogmatic thinking" or

---

[1] Roel Meijer, "Liberalism in the Middle East and the Issue of Citizenship Rights," in Hatina and Schumann (eds.), *Arab Liberal Thought after 1967*, p. 71.

[2] Different groups understood the extent of freedom differently, thus some would focus on women and minorities rights as part of a commitment to individual freedoms, and as we will see hereinafter, a few would defend LGBT rights. See section on "Societal Liberalism" for more on this.

"ideological thinking."[3] This decade thus witnessed the rise of liberal assertions that change is inevitable, intrinsic to life, and even desirable, and that essentialist, absolutist, and monolithic views are the reasons for the region's socioeconomic and political predicaments. This in turn led different parties and groups to move from perceiving themselves as representing the entire nation, to realizing that they represent only one political camp within the nation.[4] Many political leaders joined their intellectual counterparts in asserting a culture of diversity and of openness, and abandoning their paternalistic methods. The public masses, initially mere recipients of rights in the liberal Arab discourse, became part of the struggle for rights. The Internet was increasingly used to propagate critical messages that were not allowed to be directly expressed otherwise, thus facilitating outreach.

The methodological and ideological fluidity that characterized this period was driven by an essentially liberal environment and rationale that are crucial to understanding the complexity of the realities and ways of thinking that dominated the political scene. More specifically, while some of these ideas were already being asserted in the 1980s and 1990s (as was discussed in the previous chapter), they increasingly lost their subtle or restrained nature and were in full flower during the 2000s.

The States' attempt to control the pace and type of change initially meant a partial opening of the political sphere.[5] While this partial opening was intended as an adaptation ultimately aimed at enhancing the powers and dominance of the State, the discourse used to appease the public utilized concepts such as constitutionalism, separation of powers, freedom of speech, and rule of law. This signaled the depth of changes that were on the table, and showed that States comprehended that certain liberal ideas and practices had become expected by a majority of the populace. The result was that the entire region witnessed a transformation in its political foundations. At his inaugural speech in 2000, for instance, Bashar al-Asad charted a new course for Syria by calling for "democracy [that] is specific to Syria [and] that takes its roots from

---

[3] Elizabeth Suzanne Kassab explains that ideology in this sense means, "a set of ready-made ideas that one adopts dogmatically and is ready to impose on others, even by force." Kassab, *Contemporary Arab Thought: Cultural Critique in Comparative Perspective* (New York: Columbia University Press, 2010), p. 345.

[4] Christoph Schumann, "The 'Failure' of Radical Nationalism and the 'Silence' of Liberal Thought in the Arab World," in Schumann (ed.), *Nationalism and Liberal Thought in the Arab East: Ideology and Practice* (London and New York: Routledge, 2010), p. 179.

[5] See Steven Heydemann, *Upgrading Authoritarianism in the Arab World* (Analysis Paper No. 13, Saban Center for Middle East Policy at the Brookings Institution, 2007).

its history and respects its society,"[6] causing one senior official to state that Hafez al-Asad took power by putting his rivals in jail while Bashar used concepts of democracy and anti-corruption to reach the same goal.[7] Certainly, regimes hoped that promises of liberalization would appease spirits and deflect the need for immediate and transformative action.

And yet, as explained above, this adaptation of the dictators' discourse reflects the changes in the political culture and the citizens' yearnings. Their discourse and concessions, no matter how diluted and small, reveal the strength of this re-emergent liberal culture that had managed to blossom through subtle and concealed negotiations between the regimes and the people.

The expectations of this re-emergent political culture were summarized during the Arab Reform Conference held in Egypt from March 12 to 14, 2004, at the Bibliotheca Alexandrina, and that united both government officials and civil society activists. In the final statement of the conference, "Arab Reform Issues: Vision and Implementation," organizers and activists, namely, the Arab Academy for Science and Technology, the Arab Business Council, the Arab Women's Organization, the Economic Research Forum, and the Arab Organization for Human Rights, asserted that Arab societies "have the maturity and historical experience" to contribute to a "common human civilization," and are capable of taking charge of their affairs while interacting fully with the outside world in accordance with a list of priorities including the implementation of "concrete and genuine democratic systems." The participants agreed that,

Democracy refers to a system where freedom is [a] paramount value that ensures actual sovereignty of the people and government by the people through political pluralism, leading to transfer of power. Democracy is based on respect of all rights for all the people, including freedom of thought and expression, and the right to organize under the umbrella of effective political institutions, with an elected legislature, an independent judiciary, a government that is subject to both constitutional and public accountability, and political parties of different intellectual and ideological orientations. This genuine [i.e. liberal] democracy requires guaranteed freedom of expression in all its forms, topmost among which is freedom of the press, and audiovisual and electronic media. It calls for adopting free, regular, centralized and decentralized elections to guarantee transfer of power and the rule of the people. It also requires the highest possible level of decentralization that

---

[6] David W. Lesch, *The New Lion of Damascus: Bashar al-Asad and Modern Syria* (New Haven and London: Yale University Press, 2005), p. 82.

[7] Lesch, *The New Lion of Damascus*, p. 80.

would allow greater self-expression by local communities, unleashing their creative potentials for cultural contributions to human development in all fields. This is closely linked to achieving the highest level of transparency in public life, to stamping out corruption within the framework of establishing good governance and support for human rights provided according to international agreements. The rights of women, children and minorities, the protection of the fundamental rights of those charged with criminal offences and the humane treatment of citizens are on top of the list. All this is in keeping with accepted practices in those societies that have preceded us on the road to democratic development.[8]

The participants then concluded that the implementation of this reform vision was the responsibility of both governments and civil society.[9] Importantly as well, President Hosni Mubarak of Egypt asserted at the conference that reform should only come from within the region if it is to be effective and representative, thus reiterating Bashar al-Asad's assertions about democracy (see above). Other government officials and leaders furthermore emphasized that not only were they committed to the promotion of democracy but that they already had taken measures towards its advancement.

One could argue that States were forced into these promises for a number of reasons not necessarily linked to a pro-democratic and liberal yearning from within. It is important to state here that the majority of the States could no longer contain the contradictions inherent in their populist authoritarian model, particularly the growing economic aspirations of the State co-opted elite, who wished to increase their wealth by ways of internal and external investments while still restricting others from doing so. Thus, attempts at integration into the global economy might well have played an important role in their concessions to opening up. Economic problems certainly played a significant role in forcing the States to concede on certain issues, as exacerbated inequalities intensified the people's realization that the main problem was their State. And yet, the type and content of these State concessions to their people are clear indicators of the increasingly liberal points of reference that governed and guided them from within their countries. That is, the changes and new configurations that were promised invoked liberties, individualism and democracy, as opposed to pan-Arabism, workers' rights and State-led development.

---

[8] Text of the conference available at http://al-bab.com/albab-orig/albab/arab/docs/ reform/alex2004.htm
[9] Text of the conference available at http://al-bab.com/albab-orig/albab/arab/docs/ reform/alex2004.htm

It is within this economic, intellectual and political context that the protagonists of Arab liberalism re-emerged to the surface. Also significant is that the 2000s witnessed a crucial transformation in approach and maturity. Liberals returned to politics and their overall new focus turned to creating bridges with other currents and parties, empowering citizens, working on the streets instead of in headquarters (Egypt), and establishing open forums that anyone could attend (Syria). This new conciliatory (towards the other opposition) and more direct approach aimed to inspire citizens, to remain attentive to their needs but also to educate them on how rights could impact their everyday life so that they lead the change for rights themselves.

The following pages show how liberal leaders contested the system of power in the 2000s in Egypt and Syria and spearheaded the drive for political rupture with the existing order in favor of liberal democracy.

"Something Is Happening in Egypt!"

While the popular discourse in the 1980s and 1990s focused on issues of human rights and non-governmental organizations, artistic creation, and television appearances aimed at disseminating liberal ideas, the 2000s were the decade in which liberal politics saw a resurgence.[10] Thus, new political parties and civil society groupings emerged in Egypt, most notably the Ghad party the Egyptian Movement for Change (*al-haraka al-masriya li al-taghyir*), which came to be known as the Kifaya movement, Youth for Change, and the April 6 movement. Civil society became increasingly assertive and vital, as well as more politically vocal and active. In opposition to the resilient efforts of the State to upgrade its authoritarian formula, we see the rise of political leaders, of writers and artists, advocacy groups, and human rights groups such as the Egyptian Initiative for Human Rights (EIHR), the Nadeem Center for the Management and Rehabilitation of Victims of Violence, and the Hisham Mubarak Law Center (HMLC), who used the media, the Internet, street mobilization, and strategic litigation to expand the small functional and ideological space that they were allowed in an attempt to advance liberal

---

[10] This is not to say that artists, writers, novelists, playwrights, professionals, and intellectuals in general didn't play an important role. They continued to play an important role in cultivating liberal notions and critiquing the cultural and political status quo and some would eventually be forced into exile because of their social activism and intellectual work against their States. It is important to note here that the increasing openness to liberal ideas including as a result of the ground work and efforts done by liberals (described in the previous chapters) meant that liberalism became active in the political sphere again, hence the focus of this chapter.

norms of freedom and rights and revive the liberal culture that once existed in Egypt.[11] The following sections detail some of this liberal and liberalizing activity in Egypt.

Ayman Nour of al-Ghad Party challenges Mubarak

Al-Ghad Liberal Party (Hizb al-Ghad al-liberali) or Tomorrow Party was founded by Ayman Nour and Wael Nawara in 2001 and granted legal recognition and status from the State's Parties Licensing Committee in 2004 following three years of rejections and multiple court battles.[12] Ayman Nour was not a new political activist; he had been an active member of the New Wafd Party (see Chapters 1 and 2) since the late 1970s, and a member of parliament since 1995. He considers himself to be a modern liberal and is critical of the regime's neo-liberal policies, including remaining committed to the need for the public sector and the welfare state to uphold the middle class, considered a linchpin for liberal organizing and democratic safeguarding by modern liberals in general. He has advocated for a plethora of political, economic, and social reforms that aim to advance human rights, and reinstate civil freedoms and a pluralistic and democratic system of rule.

His work is innovative because it has targeted specific people and mechanisms of oppression. In the late 1980s, he authored a number of reports about police torture against detainees that he published in al-Wafd's newspaper. These reports were at the heart of a memorable clash between Al-Wafd Party representatives and the Minister of Interior during a 1987 parliamentary session.[13] In 1995, he also established a non-governmental organization called the Nour Cultural Center in order to directly communicate with and galvanize the public.

While quite active in Egypt's political sphere and parliament, the New Wafd became marred with leadership challenges and problems of inconsistency in the 1980s and 1990s, hence Ayman Nour's decision to leave the party and create al-Ghad in 2001. The Ghad Party philosophy

[11] Heba Morayef, "Reexamining Human Rights Change in Egypt," *Middle East Report* 274 (Spring 2015), pp. 9–13.

[12] The Parties Committee had to certify that a party's platform does not contradict Islamic Law or the ideals of the 1952 Revolution, and that it presents an agenda that is different from the agenda of other existing parties. See Tamara Cofman Wittes, "The 2005 Egyptian Elections: How Free? How Important?" *Brookings* (August 24, 2005), www.brookings.edu/research/the-2005-egyptian-elections-how-free-how-important/?amp.

[13] "Ghad al-Thawra Party," *Al-Ahram Online* (December 3, 2011), http://english .ahram.org.eg/News/26694.aspx)

was similar to that of the New Wafd in the sense that it also adopted a modern liberal stance marked by calls for democratic rule, civil rights and freedoms, and social justice. It advocated for a secular constitution that would uphold a parliamentary system with well-defined limits on presidential authority and time in power, and the separation of powers as well as the decentralization of political power. It supported the right to free education for all citizens and believed that unemployment and social security programs should be supported by the State and managed by agencies monitored but not run by the State.[14] At the economic level, the party supported limited State intervention in the economy to protect private property. It advocated for public healthcare, as well as protection against monopolistic practices. The Ghad pledged to promote foreign investments, and to support small and medium enterprises as well as workers' rights to organize and to strike.[15]

But a significant difference in approach distinguished al-Ghad since its establishment, that is, it was less paternalistic and elitist than its Wafd counterpart. It was furthermore less willing to compromise and work with the regime than the Wafd leadership. Al-Ghad party also focused on mobilizing the youths and promoted a very effective strategy that saw activists focus on personal agency and direct action within neighborhoods and on street mobilization and campaigning. This strategy was exceptionally appealing to a youth that yearned for more tangible methods and results, and that appreciated the one on one raising of awareness. It also helped in transforming the Egyptian politics and the entire resistance movement by introducing the idea of cooperation between different parties and groups in order to achieve a democratic order.[16] The rationale was that a move away from back-rooms and institutionally permitted dissent through parliament, and from dogmatic and monistic thinking is vital to negotiate and then unravel the complexity of the systems of cultural heritage and political oppression. Furthermore, like other liberal intellectuals, Ayman Nour and Wael Nawara advocated for the need to move beyond exclusionary configurations and the general ideological categories of "Islamic," "leftist," and "progressive." They have supported the creation of an environment that allows for debate, for tolerance and for change. In effect, al-Ghad focused on what united rather than what divided Egyptians, on consensus-creation, inclusiveness and diversity, and on empowering the youth, and thus seemed less ideologically driven than previous liberal

---

14 Ibid.
15 Ibid.
16 "Tashwish al-mu'arada," video posted on Ayman Nour's Facebook page, https://fb.watch/6qOR_iVZQq/

groupings. At the same time, its leaders turned their attention to the shared commitment to comprehensive political reforms between citizens, civil society activists and the State. The three main issues that the party focused on are respect for the value of human rights, pluralism, and social justice.[17] This new inclusive approach and general focus, as well as the focus on direct action, were a success in that they attracted thousands of young activists to join the party, activists that would very quickly become vocal and active actors during the pro-democracy protests of the early to the mid-2000s, as we will see hereinafter.

Ayman Nour's popularity and work soon became a serious problem to a regime that was hoping for a lasting separation between speech and action, particularly since Nour was putting his words into action. In January 2005, the State disregarded Egyptian law and stripped him of his parliamentary immunity, then put him in prison having accused him of forging powers of attorney and some 2,000 signatures to gain the license for his al-Ghad party. But prison did not stop him from writing articles criticizing the regime, and al-Ghad from demanding a new Egyptian constitution. This demand was done against the backdrop of the presidential elections of September 2005. Titled "Tomorrow's Constitution: Their Words are for History and our Words are for the Future," some 209 articles were presented, the aim of which was to introduce the party's liberal platform to the public as well as to call for extensive constitutional and judicial reforms. Nour was released in March 2005, which allowed him to present his candidacy in the presidential elections announced by Mubarak, thus boldly and directly challenging the Mubarak regime. In so doing, he became the first politician to run against the president (later on there would be nine candidates, some of whom were encouraged by the regime's NDP party to present their candidacy). Although Mubarak still won about 88% of the votes in what is considered a rigged election, Nour came in second at 7.6% of the votes.[18] His unexpected ability to capture votes within a context of incredible repression and lack of access to the national broadcast media was so threatening and his defiance so groundbreaking that Nour would be indicted and put back in prison shortly after the release of the elections results. He would stay in prison until 2009 despite much international pressure for his release.[19]

[17] Dina Shehata, "Youth Activism in Egypt," *Arab Reform Initiative* (October 23, 2008), p. 6.
[18] "Nour Vows to Lead Egypt Opposition," *Al-Jazeera* (September 20, 2005), www .aljazeera.com/amp/news/2005/9/20/nour-vows-to-lead-egypt-opposition
[19] "President Bush Visits Prague, Czech Republic, Discusses Freedom" (June 5, 2007), speech available at
https://georgewbush-whitehouse.archives.gov/news/releases/2007/06/20070605-8.html

Nour and the other leaders and members within the Ghad party had made a point about the need for direct action and to not submit to undue power no matter the consequences. Indeed, when the party was established in 2004, its general assembly voted that the party would participate in all elections no matter what.[20] The party also made a point about the obsolescence of the regime in addressing the daily problems faced by citizens, who had no access to the government and no say in governance. Al-Ghad's program suggested that the president suffered a legitimacy deficit because he devoted much of his attention to past events and offered very little practical policies and solutions to Egyptians' actual problems. The program's main focus was to empower the citizens so that they end up leading the change based upon increased rights.

In their usage of new, more direct tactics, al-Ghad had helped create a rupture in the Egyptian political continuum and an abrupt shift in the domestic political balance that no other activists were able to do, a result that was significant even despite the all too-predictable victory of Husni Mubarak.[21] The party also contributed to mass inclusion, consensus creation, direct work, and personal agency increasingly becoming the defining features of the liberal movement in Egypt. The approach was guided by a belief that if allowed to exist freely, liberal notions would become more widespread than they seemed to be under the then-current *istibdadi* situation. Indeed, Nour and other liberals politicians such as Amr Hamzawi, Osama al-Ghazali Harb, Hisham Qasem, Ahmad Said, and Wael Nawara among others believed and continue to believe that the liberal movement is much more popular in Egypt and the Arabic-speaking world than authoritarian regimes allow it to appear on the surface of things. While some argue that this remains very difficult to prove beyond seemingly anecdotal evidence, liberals have become more visible in large numbers with the rise of social media platforms that allowed activists and the public to communicate more freely and directly. One journalist explains,

When I spoke to Wael Nawara, a ... Ghad activist ... he explained why, for him, getting on Facebook was such a big eye-opener. If you look at Egyptian politics on the surface, he said, you might think that the Muslim Brotherhood is the only

[20] Things would change following the imprisonment of Ayman Nour in 2005 and the regime's many attempts to bring down the party. Michele Dunne, "Interview with Wael Nawara, Secretary General of the Ghad," *Carnegie Endowment* (November 3, 2010), http://carnegieendowment.org/sada/41861

[21] Yoram Meital, "The Struggle over Political Order in Egypt: The 2005 Elections," *The Middle East Journal*, Vol. 60, Number 2 (April 2006), pp. 257–279.

alternative to the Mubarak regime. But "Facebook revealed a liberal undercurrent in Egyptian society," Nawara said. "In general, there's this kind of apathy, a sense that there is nothing we can do to change the situation. But with Facebook you realize there are others who think alike and share the same ideals. You can find Islamists there, but it is really dominated by liberal voices."[22]

This realization and the example of al-Ghad contributed to the emergence of other liberal parties such as the Democratic Front (*al-Gabha al-Dimucratiya*). The Front was established in May 2007 by Yahia al-Gamal and Osama al-Ghazali Harb, a law professor who was once part of the NDP. The party sought separation of powers, constitutionalism, rule of law, human rights, civil freedoms, as well as internationally recognized human rights. Like the Ghad Party, and while still being committed to the creation of a secular political order and opposing the use of religion to achieve political gains, al-Gabha maintains that everyone, including Islamists, have the right to participate in Egyptian politics and to shape political outcomes, although this would only be possible within a political system that ensures all have the right to participate.[23] This ability to compromise and to accept that liberal change is a necessarily gradual and organic process that distinguishes these new parties from the regime co-opted parties (even those who claim to espouse a liberal agenda) who have posited the Islamists, not the regime, as their main enemy (more on this in Chapter 4). Thus, the ability and willingness to accept others, including illiberal others, and coordinate with different activists and groupings in order to achieve a liberal political order became the *modus operandi* of the liberal movement in Egypt, one that allowed it to disseminate its ideas as well as to empower activists. Liberals began coordinating with others, notably with other movements that also struggled against despotism in the mid-2000s such as the Kifaya group.

Kifaya or Egyptian Movement for Change, was groundbreaking in that it was the first grouping to call for Mubarak's resignation in addition to demands for liberalization and democratization. The Kifaya movement was a byproduct of the idea that resistance to authoritarianism has to be collective, above dogmatic narrow-mindedness, and direct if it is to be effective; Kifaya leaders thus agreed with al-Ghad party at the time that a movement has to be inclusive and take to the streets instead of staying in its headquarters.

[22] Samantha M. Shapiro, "Revolution Facebook-Style," *The New York Times Magazine* (January 22, 2009), www.nytimes.com/2009/01/25/magazine/25bloggers-t.html
[23] "Egypt Elections: Democratic Front Party," *Carnegie Endowment* (September 20, 2011), http://egyptelections-carnegieendowment.org/2011/09/20/al-ghabha-al-dimuqrati-the-democratic-front-party

While Kifaya officially emerged in 2005, its origins go back to the left-ist, liberal, and Islamic university student movements of the 1970s, to the 1990s civil society activists, and to the committees that spread through-out Egypt from university campuses in support of the second Palestinian Intifada of October 2000.[24] These latter committees involved a new gen-eration of ideologically diverse activists and intellectuals, including a col-lection of 20 NGOs and independent activists who in 2003 formed the backbone of Egypt's anti-Iraq war movement and fueled one of Egypt's biggest demonstrations on March 20, 2003.[25] About 10,000 protestors took to the streets that day in March to protest the American interven-tion in Iraq, breaking the firmly observed rules of unlawful street pro-tests. Importantly for this work, these protestors were not only protesting the American-led war on Iraqis but also the fact that this war took place with their government's blessings and without their approval. Indeed, they viewed their own regime and the American administration as well as the Israeli State equally dismissive and oppressive toward the Arab people.[26] Their collective activism and bold defiance did not go unno-ticed by the regime and hundreds of participants were rounded up and put in prison in the following days.[27]

Before long, Kifaya and other embryonic groups would move beyond foreign policy concerns and issue-specific protests. In so doing, it would bring yet another fresh tool to the battle against the regime as it made use of its technologically savvy members who employed online content, SMS messages, and high tech encrypting to assemble, disseminate their messages, and document abuses of power by the police and government officials. From 2004 to 2008, the movement organized a series of pro-tests that attracted thousands including Workers and Youth for Change, Women for Democracy, and Journalists for Change among others.[28] These new activists were also from diverse ideological orientations and parties, namely leftists, Nasserists, liberals and Islamists, but they even-tually all agreed on the need to focus on domestic issues in order to bring about liberal democracy and civil and political freedoms.

[24] Manar Shorbagy, "Understanding Kefaya: The New Politics in Egypt," *Arab Studies Quarterly* Vol. 29, No. 1 (Winter 2007), pp. 39–60.
[25] Negar Azimi, "Egypt's Youth Have Had Enough," *OpenDemocracy.net* (August 31, 2005), www.opendemocracy.net/en/enough_2794jsp/; Rabab el-Mahdi, "Egypt: A Decade of Ruptures," in Lina Khatib and Ellen Lust (eds.), *Taking to the Streets: The Transformation of Arab Activism* (Washington: Johns Hopkins University Press, 2014), p. 54.
[26] Azimi, "Egypt's Youth." See also Sadiki Larbi, "Popular Uprisings and Arab Democratization," *International Journal of Middle East Studies* 32, 1 (2000), pp. 71–95.
[27] Azimi, "Egypt's Youth."
[28] Rabab el-Mahdi, "Enough: Egypt's Quest for Democracy," *Comparative Political Studies*, 44, 5 (June 2009); El-Mahdi, "Egypt," p. 55.

In August 2004, the activists signed a Declaration to the Nation (August 7, 2004) which criticized the regime's response to the United States' meddling within the region.[29] In September of the same year, they presented their platform explaining that the only way to deal with the dangers of the American intervention in the region was by replacing the dictatorial regimes that were upheld by American administrations and that have sanctioned American actions in return. The platform described how despotism aggravates the national calamity faced by Egyptians.[30] In so doing, these activists replicated the late nineteenth century liberal assertions that occupation, backwardness (*inhitat*) and corruption (*fasad*) were the results of political tyranny (*istibdad*), and that one solution to the Arab predicament was the replacement of absolute rulers with representative governments. The Kifaya activists proclaimed, "we believe that there is no way to rescue Egypt except in the actual replacing of its government."[31] This belief was clearly stated in their liberal influenced long-term vision entitled "A Project for Democratic Change in Egypt – toward a New Socio-Political Contract," in which they called for an end to unchecked power and the restoration of political freedoms and civil liberties (more on this hereinafter).[32]

On May 5, 2005, Egyptians were called to join the protest movement and to demand independent elections and a new constitution, thus joining the Ghad Party in its calls for constitutional reforms. In a formidable show of togetherness, the protesters took to the streets in 14 cities to object to the authority of President Mubarak and his plans to assume a fifth presidential term at the 7th of September elections.[33] It was in September 2004 that the Kifaya movement was officially founded as a historic amalgam of some 300 individuals – belonging to different existing political parties as well as independent political forces – such as Ayman Nour, George Ishaq (communist), Abu al-Ala Madi (moderate Islam), and Abd al-Halim Qindil (Nasserite), and so liberals as well as communists, socialists and Nasserites, all united in a desire to see the end of authoritarianism in Egypt.[34] "Kifaya," meaning "enough" in Arabic, was a most fitting slogan

[29] Meital, "The Struggle over Political Order," p. 267.
[30] Shorbagy, "Understanding Kefaya," p. 47.
[31] Quoted in Meital, "The Struggle over Political Order," p. 268.
[32] Shorbagy, "Understanding Kefaya," p. 49.
[33] Meital, "The Struggle over Political Order," p. 268. See also Khalil al-Anany, "Egypt's Democratization: Reality or Mirage?" *Open Democracy* (May 9, 2005), www .opendemocracy.net/en/article_2491jsp/
[34] Ahmad Ali Mukheylef, "Dawr Harakat Kifaya fo Amaliyat al-tagyir al-siyasi fi Misr 'am 2011," *Majalat Buhuth al-Sharq al-Awsat*, N. 45 (March 2020), pp. 144–145.

to express the overall mood of the movement: kifaya to injustice, kifaya to poverty, kifaya to corruption, to the lack of freedoms and dignity, and kifaya to emergency laws and one-party rule.[35] These activists and intellectuals were not looking for reforms (islah); they were looking for change and rupture (taghyir), and a "new social-political contract."[36]

As mentioned above, in order to achieve the change they wanted, they presented a list of major demands as part of a new social contract that is effectively liberal democratic: rotation of power, limits on terms in office, the holding of direct and democratic presidential elections, limits on the powers of the executive, accountability, constitutionalism, and responsible government, independence of the judiciary and separation of powers, the removal of restrictions on the formation of political parties and newspapers, the respect of individual and civic rights and freedoms, the respect of citizens' equality under the law and equality of opportunity for all, and the release of the thousands of political prisoners the regime held unlawfully. Economically, the movement demanded a system in which both the State and the private sector worked together to combat corruption and achieve industrial and technological parity with more advanced nations, and a better life for Egyptians.[37] The end to authoritarianism was the common thread (parliamentarianism, separation of powers, rule of law) and citizens' civic rights and dignity was the goal.[38] The movement expressed its demands clearly, boldly and peacefully: no to the re-election of Husni Mubarak, as well as to his plans to transfer his powers to his son Gamal Mubarak.[39]

These demands reformulated the object of discontent, no longer seen as the Islamists or American imperialism, but the regime itself. They also broke with many of the taboos that had characterized public life in Egypt since the rise of Nasser to power: "First the protestors focused on domestic as opposed to foreign policy issues. Second, they staged popular demonstrations in public areas without official permission, thereby challenging a long-standing ban on popular demonstrations outside

---

[35] Mukheylef, "Dawr Harakat Kifaya," pp. 148–149.

[36] Ibid. p. 153.

[37] Ibid., pp. 153–155; Mona El-Ghobashy, "Egypt Looks Ahead to a Portentous Year," *Middle East Report* (February 2, 2005).

[38] For more on this, see Ahmad B. Shaaban, *Raffat al-farasha, Kifaya: al-Mady wa al-Mustaqbal* (Cairo: Kefaya Publications, 2006); George Caten "Harakat Kefaya al-misriya tatajawaz al-ahzab al-aydiyologiya," *al-Hiwar al-Mutamaden*, No. 1238 (June 24, 2005).

[39] El-Ghobashy, "Egypt Looks Ahead to a Portentous Year"; "'Kifaya' in Egypt," *The Washington Post*, March 15, 2005, p. A22, www.washingtonpost.com/wp-dyn/articles/A35379-2005Mar14.html.

university campuses. Third, they [chanted] slogans that directly attacked the president and the security establishment, [thereby] also challenging a long-standing taboo against directly criticizing these 'sovereign' institutions."[40] Kifaya thus shattered the barrier of fear and embedded the democratic right to criticize and demonstrate peacefully in the imaginary of most Egyptians, especially the youth.

The organizational skills, boldness, endogenous nature, and popularity of the movement compelled the regime to respond to the pressure with some compromise. This was a local movement focusing on domestic issues and employing homegrown methods that could not simply be dismissed for its affiliations with Western groups or for its Western funding, as was done with other NGOs.[41] Of course, international and American pressures to democratize might have played a role in Mubarak's decision to compromise, but these pressures were in line with and reflective of the demands of domestic actors and would have been insignificant, even non-existent, had there not been serious and mounting domestic demands for liberalizing change from within.

And so in a seismic shift, Mubarak announced in February 2005 an amendment to Section 76 of the Constitution that would authorize other candidates to run for president. He stated that this change emanated from "my full conviction of the need to consolidate efforts for more freedom and democracy."[42] Eighty-three percent of those Egyptians who voted in the referendum on the constitutional amendments agreed with Mubarak that it was time. Indeed, surveys showed that a considerable majority supported democracy in Egypt in the 2000s.[43] The constitutional amendment stated that the electoral process would allow more than one candidate to contend for the presidency of Egypt, that elections would be general, free, and secret, thus transferring the authority to choose a president from the members of Parliament to the citizenry.[44] The process was finalized in July 2005, giving Egyptians the right to choose a candidate in the coming presidential elections to be held that September rather than having to answer "yes" or "no" in a staged presidential referendum.

---

[40] Shehata, "Youth Activism in Egypt," p. 5.
[41] Indeed the movement had agreed to refuse any foreign funding in order to avoid being labeled a foreign-manipulated movement.
[42] Neil MacFarquhar, "Mubarak Pushes Egypt to Allow Freer Elections," *The New York Times* (February 27, 2005), p.1.
[43] By 2010, about 80% of Egyptians supported democratic rule. See Mark Tessler and Amaney Jamal, "Citizen Attitudes in Selected Arab Countries about Whether Democracy is the Best Form of Government," *Arab Barometer Project*, 2010, www.arabbarometer.org
[44] Meital, "The Struggle over Political Order," p. 264.

Another incremental but important reform concerned the laws governing the formation of political parties. The Egyptian parliament amended the Parties Law by removing and softening restrictions such as the requirement that party platforms conform to Islamic law and a socialist agenda and to have a distinct platform from other, already-existing parties. For instance, party platforms now needed only to represent a "new addition" to political life. The composition of the Parties Committee also expanded to include independent public figures.[45] These changes could be considered minor compared to the many barriers to democracy and civic freedoms Egyptians continued to face, including an environment of intimidation and lack of freedom of speech and association with emergency laws that confronted candidates and parties to be considered legal or to be allowed to continue working once approved. Indeed, a majority within the Kifaya movement would end up considering the constitutional reforms offered by the Mubarak regime as insufficient. As a result, the movement called for boycotting the presidential elections, demanding better mechanisms that show real transfer of power to the citizens, as well as shifts toward unconstrained pluralism.[46]

Notwithstanding these barriers and the many regime attempts that would follow to dilute and counter reforms, the Kifaya movement and al-Ghad party were able to help bring about important liberalizing changes, not to the political structure since these reforms were manipulated and diluted by the regime, but to the political culture, by publicly asserting liberal and democratic rights and by forcing the State to negotiate and implement symbolically significant changes influenced by these demands, thus heralding a new political phase for Egypt.

This new political phase saw the right to protest, which had been banned for so long outside university campuses, practiced by many groups and currents within society, thus dynamically linking these groups' members and uniting their efforts at change.[47] The result is that street protests would become more numerous and protestors more vocal in the following years.[48] Overall, activists felt emboldened and effective. They knew that liberalization would inevitably follow a long, multi-tiered and multi-dimensional process, but at the same time there was a sense that the silence and the fear of taking to the streets and demanding political change were shattered.[49] Kifaya would also inspire a number of

---

[45] Wittes, "The 2005 Egyptian Elections: How Free? How Important?"
[46] Opposition candidates are required to have the written support of around 300 members from elected bodies that were essentially part of the National Democratic Party (NDP). In practice, very few candidates were eligible to take part in the presidential elections.
[47] Mukheylef, "Dawr Harakat Kifaya," p. 156.
[48] Azimi, "Egypt's Youth."
[49] Al-Anani, "Egypt's Democratisation."

groups such as the March 9 Movement and Artists for Change, Doctors for Change, and Pharmacists for Change, thus deepening democratic practices and taking away power from the State-led syndicates that controlled these groups.

One very important arm of the Kifaya movement was a group of young men and women called "Youth for Change" (*shabab min agl al-taghyeer*). These activists personified politics from below and direct engagement with the public. They met at coffee shops, in university halls and cafes, unions and syndicates. They targeted working-class neighborhoods such as Shoubra and Sayeda Zeinab. They visited public squares and parks and went on public mini-buses in which they engaged the public and then hopped off to avoid the police.[50] They created mini-exhibitions, undertook street theatre and distributed flyers. Their strategy was thus more imaginative and pro-active than that of their older counterparts, driven by one unifying concern: to demonstrate to Egyptians that daily problems are directly linked to failure of the State to provide for human rights, to liberalize and democratize.[51]

Later on, Youth for Change would withdraw from Kifaya and the movement would be weakened in general due to divisions between its liberal and Islamist components. But the impact of these groups is not to be dismissed. Kifaya effectively united many political organizations and their leaders under the banner of political liberalization, as opposed to regional and economic concerns. Indeed, while the constitutional amendments were considered insufficient, they were still the outcome of the adamant and persistent activism from within.[52]

Other members of Kifaya, such as Asmaa Mahfouz, who would later on receive the Sakharov prize for freedom of thought for helping spark the Egyptian revolution, Ahmad Maher, who in 2011 would appear in the award winning documentary How to start a revolution,[53] Esraa' Abdel Fattah, Ahmed Salah, Ahmad Douma and Muhammad Adel, all of whom had worked with Kifaya since 2005 and been imprisoned for their activism, would become the co-founders of a very important movement, the April 6 Youth Movement. Founded in March 2008 initially as an Egyptian Facebook group and event "April 6th: A General Strike for the People of Egypt," the April 6 Youth Movement would go on to play an important role in the Egyptian revolution of 2011 that toppled

---

[50] Azimi, "Egypt's Youth."
[51] Ibid. See also el-Mahdi, "Egypt: A Decade of Ruptures," p. 56.
[52] For more on this, see Gene Sharp, *From Dictatorship to Democracy*, pp. 17–21.
[53] British documentary, *How to Start a Revolution*, directed by Ruaridh Arrow, www .howtostartarevolution.org/about

Mubarak.[54] Here we see the impact of blogging and online networking on Egyptian politics. Beginning in 2005, there was a significant increase in the number of websites and blogs and social media, in both Arabic and English, dealing with the political struggles in the entire region. Often anonymous authors and reporters discussed abuses of human rights, regime repression, ways to change, and plans for protests. Thus, the websites and blogs allowed activists and the public to communicate freely and transparently, and more importantly to organize. The April 6 Youth Movement was originally established to support a textile workers' strike in the industrial city of Mahalla – a 2008 event that proved a revolutionary moment in the mobilization of activists from all movements including Kifaya. As the protests and police violence escalated into a nationwide strike, the Facebook group gained momentum and eventually coalesced into the political movement known as the April 6 Youth Movement. The regime's attacks on the group on Egyptian State television would end up increasing the movement's popularity. But it was the group's ability to connect with other experienced activists,[55] as well as to use the online environment that proved the most effective in its mobilization, as 100,000 Facebook users joined the online group to express their solidarity with the workers.[56]

The April 6 Youth Movement activists would be harassed by the police and the security forces, with several injured and killed; and in a determined show of force by the State, the movement's co-founder Ahmed Maher would end up being arrested and tortured in 2008. But he and his fellow activists were determined to pursue their demands for democratic change and social justice. Muhammad Adel for example joined a training program organized by the Center for Applied Non-Violent Action and Strategies (CANVAS), a Center founded by the Otpor youth movement, which had spearheaded the uprising that brought down Serbian leader Slobodan Milosevic. The activists were well informed and strategic. Furthermore, the regime could not effectively dismantle the movement's online network – due to some of the activists' technological expertise – and thus the network managed to escape the authorities' control.[57]

[54] Essam Fadl, "Asharq Al-Awsat talks to Egypt's April 6 Youth Movement founder Ahmed Maher," *Asharq al-Awsat*, February 10, 2011, www.aawsat.com/english/news .asp?section=3&id=24109

[55] For instance, meetings and training sessions of the April 6 Youth Movement took place in the Hisham Mubarak Law Center.

[56] "April 6 Youth Movement," *Carnegie Endowment* (September 22, 2010), https://carnegieendowment.org/2010/09/22/april-6-youth-movement-pub-54918

[57] Samantha M. Shapiro, "Revolution, Facebook-Style," *The New York Times* Magazine (January 22, 2009), www.nytimes.com/2009/01/25/magazine/25bloggers-t.html

Meanwhile, the human rights and advocacy community were also challenging the authoritarian structure from below throughout the 2000s. Groups such as the Egyptian Initiative for Personal Rights (EIPR), the Nadeem Center for the Management and Rehabilitation of Victims of Violence, and the Hisham Mubarak Law Center (HLMC), as well as prominent human rights lawyers such as Nabil al-Hilaly and Gamal Abdel Aziz, would make use of the independent media and the Internet as well as strategic litigation to expand the small functional and ideological space they were allowed, in an attempt to chip away at the regime's power, to challenge the constitutionality of emergency law and administrative detentions, and to advance notions of tolerance, pluralism, freedom of expression, and equality.[58] For instance and more specifically, since its foundation in 2002, EIPR has fought to protect Egyptians' rights to freedom of religion and belief, as well as to the "individual's personal freedom," which they argue is "protected under the Egyptian Constitution and defined in scope by the Supreme Constitutional Court as 'what is closest to the personality, inseparably linked with the human self, within the sphere of his life's aspects and his personal choices in their most minute orientations and in their noblest goals'."[59] EIPR makes a point that it protects issues of freedom of religion and opinion, not from the perspective of collective minority rights, but from the perspective of the individual's right to self-determination, thus asserting a liberal perspective on rights. Both EIPR and HLMC have issued press releases and launched international campaigns in order to expose the Egyptian State's violations of rights it claims to adhere to, thus reminding Egyptians of their rights under the law as well as expanding their understanding of these rights. In a similar manner to Egypt's artists and intellectuals, these organizations have also exposed the direct connections and illiberal ways shared between the State, namely the State Security Intelligence and the Ministry of the Interior, and religious leaders in their attempts to stifle freedoms.[60] By 2008, routine practices of abuse and disregard for Egypt's penal code and constitution are documented, reported in press releases, and brought to the Supreme Court as well the

---

[58] Heba Morayef, "Reexamining Human Rights Change in Egypt," *Middle East Report* 274 (Spring 2015), pp. 9–13.

[59] EIPR, *Freedom of Belief and the Arrests of shi'a Muslim in Egypt* (August 2004), available on EIPR.org, https://eipr.org/en/publications/freedom-belief-and-arrests-shia-muslims-egypt

[60] See for instance, press release issued July 4, 2005, in which the EIPR calls for the immediate release of a citizen in detention because of his "theological research", https://eipr.org/en/press/2005/07/detainee-goes-hunger-strike-after-two-years%E2%80%99-imprisonment-writing-unpublished

Public Prosecutor with the demand that human and individual rights are respected. Overall, the strategy is to reconnect and empower the public so that they could collectively hold the government to account and thereby contribute to liberal change.

In April 2009, the real estate tax collectors formed the first State independent union since the rise of Nasser to power, which showed that the attempts to challenge the institutional and autocratic basis of State corporatism from below were working.[61] Already prominent Egyptian artists were joining the movement and giving it a push. These included internationally renowned actor and human rights activist Khaled Abol Naga, who would eventually be denied membership in the Egyptian Actors Syndicate for his dissent (see next chapter), actors Basma Ahmad and Najla Fathi, and directors Ali Badrakhan and Yousry Nasrallah.[62] In 2010, these artists as well as activists from Kifaya, Youth for Change, and the April 6 Movement and others including the al-Ghad Party would join the National Association for Change, a group that was founded by Mohammad el-Baradei, another liberal leader, who returned to Egypt from abroad in February 2010. The activists and political leaders helped Baradei to collect signatures for his seven-point petition for political change, helping him garner about 1 Million signatures. The el-Baradei National Association for Change followed suit in its commitment to an all-inclusive platform, beginning with the aim of reshaping the electoral process so that Egyptians of all political affiliations including Islamists could be represented.[63] The consensus was that opposition to the regime should be expressed through a broad coalition in order to effectively push for constitutional reforms and political change.

The spark that set things off was the June 2010 sharing on Facebook by Ayman Nour of the image of the deformed face of a young man by the name of Khalid Said, who had been brutally beaten up and killed by two police officers in Alexandria. The horrific image was then shared by Wael Ghonim, a Google executive and an online activist who was part of the Egyptian liberal opposition movement, even though he was working in Abu Dhabi (UAE) at the time.[64] Ghonim and other activists from

---

[61] El-Mahdi, "Egypt," p. 59.

[62] See for instance, "Najlaa Fathi tarfud taqdim dawr walidat khalid said: Azhab ila midan al-tahrir mutakhafiya" *Elfann* (March 13, 2012), elfann.com/news/show/1010465; Najlaa Fathallah, "Yusri Nasrallah: 'amr sakhif' tahwil al-fan li-khidmat al-siyasa," *Alrai Media* (October 7, 2007), www.alraimedia.com/article/419252

[63] Dina Shehata, *Islamists and Secularists in Egypt: Opposition, Conflict and Cooperation* (London and New York: Routledge, 2009).

[64] Ghonim was imprisoned on the January 27, 2011, at his return to Egypt to take part in the revolution.

the National Association for Change created an Arabic Facebook page called "We are all Khalid Said."[65] Ghonim writes, "It was a horrifying photo showing the distorted face of a man in his twenties. There was a big pool of blood behind his head, which rested on a chunk of marble... his jaw was seemingly dislocated.... The image was so gruesome that I wondered if he had been wounded in war."[66] The image sparked outrage and increased levels of cyber-activism.[67] Ayman Nour and other activists reported that Said was punished because he planned on posting a video on YouTube that showed corrupt police officers dealing drugs.[68] On the activists' Facebook Page, postings were all action-oriented, inviting people to react, to work together, and to take to the streets as one. One observer explains that postings were "crafted to inspire followers to believe that, despite decades of Mubarak rule, things can in fact change."[69]

It was finally in January 2011 that these youth witnessed the full impact of all the mobilization and all the work that had been done over the previous years, as we will see in the next chapter. Meanwhile, ideas about collective movement and the possibility for liberal change were spreading and propagating on Arab satellite television and news networks and social media platforms like never before.

Syria Witnesses a Political Spring

Syria in the 1990s had become known as the epitome of "Middle East exceptionalism" in the sense that it had witnessed the least political liberalization throughout the 1980s and 1990s. And yet as the previous chapter showed, although liberal ideas were stifled by an authoritarian regime that was "peculiarly resistant to political liberalization,"[70] they never really disappeared and continued their work underground and at the cultural level.

---

[65] El-Mahdi, "Egypt," p. 64.

[66] Wael Ghonim, Revolution 2.0: The power of the people is greater than the people in power. A memoir (New York: Houghton Mifflin Harcourt, 2012), p. 58.

[67] Kara Alaimo, "How the Facebook Arabic Page 'We Are All Khaled Said' Helped Promote the Egyptian Revolution," Social Media + Society (July-December 2015), p. 1.

[68] See video "Tashwih al-Mu'arada," available on Ayman Nour's Facebook Page at https://fbwatch/5g65DJX-pM/

[69] Alaimo, "How the Facebook Arabic Page," p. 6.

[70] Raymond A. Hinnebusch, "Calculated Decompression as a Substitute for Democratization: Syria," in Bahgat Korany, Rex Brynen and Paul Noble (eds.), Political Liberalization and Democratization in the Arab World (Vol. 2): Comparative Experiences (Boulder, CO: Lynne Rienner, 1998), p. 225.

The death of Hafez al-Asad in June 2000 and the rise of his son Bashar to power were hoped by liberal intellectuals and civil rights activists to be the start of democratization and liberalization in the country. And indeed, Bashar al-Asad's inaugural speech promised political reforms, modernization, accountability and transparency, vowing the dawn of a new era, and recognizing the people's aspirations for and expectations of political liberalization. Much would change in the 2000s. A civil society of intellectuals and thinkers reappeared, hoping to make the most of the perceived opening in the autocratic system in order to force political change. This was what would become known as the Damascus Spring.

The result was that the activists who had just been released after years in prison and those who had just returned from their self-imposed exile resumed mobilization and work. These activities remained illegal, and yet this time they felt able to mobilize openly. Their goal was to revive the pluralist and liberal environment that once existed in Syria, through the creation of new organizations to uphold civil society and defend human rights, and by propagating democratic concepts by holding open meetings and gatherings at thinkers' and activists' own houses. Thus, hundreds of salons or forums and discussion groups were established all over the country, the most prominent of which were the Riad Seif Forum (the National Dialogue Forum), the Jamal al-Atassi Forum (representative of the National Democratic Gathering), and al-Kawakibi Forum for democratic dialogue. These salons emerged illegally on the Damascene and Aleppine scenes and in other cities such as Lattaquieh, Tartus and Qamishli, 'illegally' in the sense that they did not acquire the necessary permits to function; but they were surprisingly influential, so much so that they soon became too much to handle for the regime. The salons saw members discuss the potential for political reform and democratization in the country. But the main idea of most meetings – which were attended by hundreds of Syrians at a time, especially many youths, as in the case of Egypt – was to empower and educate the public so that society could "restore itself."[71] By 2001, about 21 informal associations and civic movements had formed, holding weekly meetings and lectures.

Thus liberal intellectuals such as businessman and member of parliament Riad Seif, one of Syria's most daring liberals, economist 'Aref Dalila, thinker Abdul Razzaq Eid, and Kamal al-Labwani, a physician and founder of the Democratic Liberal Gathering, spiritual leaders such as Jawdat Said, and academics and activists such as Najati Tayara,

---

[71] Alan George, *Syria: Neither Bread nor Freedom* (London: Zed Books, 2003), p. 33.

Hassan Abbas[72], Salam Kawakibi (the grandson of Abdul-Rahman Kawakibi)[73], and Suheir al-Atassi were some of the most influential activists in a movement uniting thousands of intellectuals, artists, actors,[74] journalists, professors, and activists, all pressing for the government to end emergency laws and to uphold the constitution, which guarantees pluralism and civil and political freedoms.[75]

Riad Seif was the first, following the death of Hafez al-Asad, to establish the National Dialogue Forum at the end of August 2000, and began holding weekly meetings and public lectures.[76] His intention was clear from the outset: transforming the forum into a larger organization called "the Friends of Civil Society," (*ansar al-mujtama' al-madani*), in addition to creating a new party called the Social Peace Party (*hizb al-salam al-ijtima'i*).[77] Other liberals such as Fayez Sara, Michel Kilo and Abdul Razzaq Eid created the Committees for the Revival of Civil Society, which would end up drafting an important document in Syria's political life in the early 2000s. Both Kilo and 'Eid helped establish some of the most liberal forums in Syria, and 'Eid delivered one of the Jamal al-Atassi forum's first lectures in March 2011, entitled "The Culture of Fear." Three hundred people attended that lecture, including Ba'thists who were there in the spirit of open dialogue.[78] These activists' main

[72] See previous chapter for more on Hassan Abbas. Abbas was a professor and a researcher at the French Institute of Damascus, and the founder of the Syrian Citizenship League, an initiative to help explain what it means to be a "true citizen" and to foster a culture of dialogue and respect, which he considered essential to resist the autocratic State.

[73] Salam Kawakibi is one of the relentless and hidden activists in Syria who dedicated his life to raising awareness about rights and freedom. Inspired by his grandfather, Abdul-Rahman Kawakibi, he has made use of his position at the French Institute of Aleppo to provide a stage for other activists and thinkers in an attempt to help produce gradual rupture with the existing political culture by spreading values of citizenship, freedom, and pluralism. He has been constantly harassed, summoned, and threatened by agents of the Syrian *mukhabarat*, and finally decided to leave for France in 2007 in order to avoid imminent arrest. Author's communication with Salam Kawakibi in 2019, and then in 2021.

[74] As stated earlier in this work, actors and directors have played a very important role in critiquing and challenging the regime in Syria. Some of the names that come to mind are Mar Amiralay, Jamal Suleiman, Hatem al-'Ali, May Skaf, Fares al-Helou, Khalid Taja, and Yam Mashhadi. Some of these artists' work will be discussed in Chapter 4 of this work.

[75] Volker Perthes, *Syria under Bashar al-Asad: Modernization and the Limits of Change* (London and New York: Routledge), p. 15.

[76] As we have seen in Chapter 2, Hassan Abbas and Yazji had already established a forum at the end of 1999.

[77] Eyal Zisser, *Commanding Syria: Bashar al-Asad and the First Years in Power* (London and New York: I.B.Tauris, 2007), p. 81; Perthes, *Syria under Bashar*, p. 16.

[78] "Al-Atasi Forum and the Culture of Fear," *Arabic News* (March 13, 2001), www.arabicnews.com/ansub/daily/day/010313/2001031316.html.

concern was to reconnect and empower the public so that they could all hold the government to account and thereby contribute to change.[79]

The Committees for the Defense of Democratic and Human Rights in Syria (CDF), founded in 1989, also revived its work in September 2000, and its activities became more public. In an interview published by Human Rights Watch with one of its founders, the activist reported the conscious decision to organize openly; as he explained, "most of us [activists] were released by then, and we held a meeting in September 2000. We decided that our work will become more public, and we published the names of our members."[80] The State seemed to respond favorably to all this activity as the information minister announced that the emergency law was no longer in force on 29 January 2001.[81]

An important activist who resumed work at his release was judge Haytham al-Maleh. Al-Maleh had spent seven years in jail for his pro-democracy work within the Freedom and Human Rights Committee of the Syrian Lawyers Union (see Chapter 2). At his release, he co-founded the Organization for Human Rights in Syria in July 2001, and was awarded the Dutch Geuzen Medal (named after Dutch resistance fighters against the Nazis) for "his brave struggle for human rights" in 2006.[82] He also presided over the Human Rights Association in Syria (HRAS, *Jam'iyyat Huquq al-Insan fi Suria*), which was founded in July 2001 and was represented by other former activists and leftist intellectuals who had also spent years in jail in the 1980s such as Salim Kheirbek (13 years in jail), Ahmad Fayez al-Fawaz (15 years in jail) and Aktham Nu'aissa (9 years) (see previous chapter).[83]

The movement held seminars and lectures, and issued reports, studies, and statements with the aim of educating the public, as well as demanding that the State reinstate freedoms, namely freedom of expression, freedom of the press and freedom to assemble, and requesting

---

[79] It is important to re-state here that these activists are all considered liberal in this work because they are focused on advancing liberal values and seeking the establishment of a liberal political framework. And so, as stated earlier, although Michel Kilo might have once been perceived as a socialist and Turk was once a communist, their activism would transform over the years such that they began pressing for pluralism, individual freedoms, liberal democracy and respect for liberal understandings of human rights rather than socialist and communist notions and systems of rule (see Chapter 2 for more on this).

[80] HRW, *No Room to Breathe*, p. 10.

[81] Karim Atassi, *Syria, the Strength of an Idea: The Constitutional Architectures of Its Political Regimes*, translated from French by Christopher Sutcliffe (Cambridge University Press, 2018), p. 357.

[82] HRW, *No Room to Breathe*, p. 11.

[83] Ibid., p. 10.

the creation of a pluralistic political system, respect for liberal human rights, as well as the independence of the judiciary and the rule of law, especially by the State. Expressing opinions about the need for political change and writing openly about political issues in general was perceived as so timely that even Ba'thist newspapers engaged in the conversation. For instance, Mahmud Salama, the editor in chief of the government newspaper, al-Thawra (the Revolution), wrote an editorial asserting that political change had just started and that national consensus could not be achieved by means of a monist and unilateral official discourse, but by political, economic, and cultural pluralism.[84] And in July-August 2000, Riad al-Turk and philosopher Antun Maqdisi wrote open letters asserting that it was time for Syrians to become actual citizens of their country, to enjoy their rights and freedoms, and to live with dignity and peace.[85]

On September 27, 2000, 99 thinkers and activists including Antun Maqdisi, Michel Kilo, Fayez Sara and Jawdat Said to name but a few put down their demands in a very short but powerful and symbolically important manifesto, the Manifesto of the 99, which was published in the Lebanese press.[86] The document begins with the following preamble:

Democracy and human rights today constitute a common humanitarian language...And even if some countries use these to promote their policies and interests, interaction among peoples need not result in domination ... It was permitted to our people in the past, and it will be permitted to them in the future, to be influenced by the experiences of others, and to add their own contribution, thereby developing their own distinctiveness without being closed-in on themselves.[87]

The document thus summarized in few words the dialectic between the illiberal and liberal forces in the region, as well as an implicit assertion that the liberals have an established past and are here to stay. Then it went on to request the abolition of martial law and of special courts; "the release of all political prisoners and prisoners of conscience, the return without fear of prosecution of all political exiles, the establishment of a law-abiding State, the granting of freedoms, and the recognition of

---

[84] Salama would be fired from his position soon thereafter. Perthes, Syria under Bashar, p. 19.

[85] Maqdisi was removed from his ministerial job at the Ministry of Culture right after the publication of his letter in al-Hayat newspaper. Wael al-Sawwah, "Hassan 'Abbas wa Rabi' Dimashq: al-quwwa al-na'ima," in Fayez Sara (ed.), Hassan Abbas bi-'uyun mu'asira, (Partners: November 2020), p. 29.

[86] As mentioned earlier, most of Syria's intellectuals and activists write and publish in the much freer Lebanese Press.

[87] Translated in Alan George, Syria: Neither Bread nor Freedom (London and New York: Zed Books, 2003), p. 178.

political and ideological pluralism, the right to organize, freedom of the press, speech and expression, and the release of public life from supervision."[88] The document also demanded the resumption of the right to form political parties and to have independent civil organizations.[89] The conclusion of the document notes that economic, judicial and administrative reforms are incomplete without political reform. It is important to emphasize that this was not a revolutionary document, indeed, these demands had been expressed throughout the 1970s and to a lesser degree in the 1980s. One difference though was its directness, clarity and brevity, and most importantly the attention and interest it received from the public, so much so that Lebanese newspapers which published the document were censored in Syria, and the Syrian media and press completely ignored it.

Despite this censorship, there was suddenly a feeling that the era of authoritarianism was receding into the past, like a nightmare disappearing in the rearview mirror. The regime did not comment on the Statement, but it also did not arrest the signatories. It even seemed to concede to some of their demands by releasing members of the Muslim Brotherhood and the Communist Action Party (CAP) shortly after the statement was published.[90] The regime officials also started attending civil society meetings and even engaged in discussions that criticized the regime.

A few months later, Seif established an independent parliamentary bloc that included 21 independent members of parliament. The bloc was not recognized by the president of the People's Assembly, but this did not stop the members of the group from coordinating their overall activity and their pointed critique during the Assembly discussions.[91] At the same time, 70 lawyers published a document demanding the legalization of political parties, separation of powers and an independent judiciary, and again, respect for the rule of law.[92]

Intellectuals and activists reckoned that they needed to press further for real change, and to show more unity. While in Egypt this could be done through protest movements such as Kifaya, in Syria the space provided by the State was much more restricted. Syrian activists could not form parties (not that Seif and others did not try) and they could

---

[88] Quoted in Ziesser, *Commanding Syria*, pp. 83–84.
[89] Middle East Intelligence Bulletin, *Statement by 99 Syrian Intellectuals*, Vol. 2, N. 9 (October 5, 2000), www.meforum.org/meib/articles/0010_sdoc0927.htm; see also in George, *Syria: Neither Bread nor Freedom*, pp. 178–181.
[90] Jonas Bergan Draege, "The Formation of Syrian Opposition Coalitions as Two Level Games," *Middle East Journal*, 70, 2 (Spring 2016), pp. 192–193.
[91] Ziesser, *Commanding Syria*, p. 83.
[92] Perthes, *Syria under Bashar*, p. 16.

not initiate large protest movements (again, not that they did not try); but they could form civil society groups, and they could publish documents that they could disseminate more broadly. And so they mobilized around a founding document, the "Basic Document of the Committees for the Revival of Civil Society" known as the "Statement of the 1000" (referring to the number of individuals who signed it) that was issued in January 2001. This document was lengthier and more detailed than the Manifesto of the 99, certainly more direct in naming the culprits and the crimes. It accused the State of marginalizing civil society, which had existed in Syria before "revolutionary legitimacy" trumped "constitutional legitimacy," in the name of insuring stability and security. It said that this marginalization of civil society led to the deterioration and reduction of the meaning of citizenry. The document also accused the regime of distributing Syria's wealth to opportunists and loyalists of the regime, thus creating a feudal system – supposedly what the regime had sought to put an end to when it first came to power in the 1960s – in which citizens were treated like herd animals.

One of the most liberal elements in the document refers to "tyranny." Tyranny, the document stated, could be overcome through dialogue and respect of freedoms and rights, and "the consequences of coups against political democracy in the name of socialism are plain."[93] Again, this was not a revolutionary document if one looks back at the demands for liberty and rights that activists expressed from the 1970s to the 1990s, and not even by nineteenth century standards (see Chapter 1). But it was revolutionary in the sense that it dared to re-articulate these demands and to accuse the State of betraying its own promises, and to frame them within the context of years of repression and imprisonment and forced exile that activists had faced in Syria. The document not only called for political reforms, a clean environment and the abolition of legal discrimination against women, it also denied the regime's self-proclaimed achievements: its commitment to socialism and economic egalitarianism, to patriotism, and its ability to repel Israeli aggressions. Thus, the regime's entire legitimacy was being questioned.

Shortly afterwards, 16 of the signatories, including Shaykh Jawdat Sa'id, Riad Seif, Michel Kilo, Abdul Razzaq Eid, Arif Dalila, as well as renowned leftist professor Sadiq Jalal al-Azm, announced the first meeting of the Committees for the Revival of Civil Society. The aim of this organization was to coordinate and link "all the committees and forums that have begun to function throughout Syria with the goal of

---

[93] Quoted in George, *Syria*, p. 44.

establishing a civil society in Syria in response to the problems of this country."[94]

In April 2001, Michel Kilo and Abdul Razzaq Eid and other colleagues at the Committees for the Revival of Civil Society issued yet another statement that undermined the regime's overall arguments about the activists' recklessness, inability to respond to the needs of the masses, and failure to recognize the dangers that Israel presents to Syrians. "Towards a National Social Contract in Syria" asserted their commitment to the Palestinian cause and the recapturing of annexed lands, but it also emphasized the citizens' role in the national project, and demanded that citizens be treated as free actors with dignity, which can only be achieved through a democratic and transparent environment. The document was published in Lebanese newspapers (relied on by Syrians to read uncensored news) and comprised nine points, including a reminder of the declaration of rights in the Syrian Constitution and of Syria's commitments to universal human rights, an assertion that Syrians have the right to choose their political, social and economic system, and that dialogue and consensus are the only ways to settle disputes and avoid violence.[95] The writers added, "Democracy, which embraces transparency, political and media pluralism, civil society, the rule of law, separation of authorities and free elections held under independent supervision, is a necessary condition for the success of economic reform"[96] (which was claimed to be the priority of the regime). In this environment, even Syria's Muslim Brothers, in forced exile since the early 1980s, expressed their commitment to democracy and pluralism.

Unlike the Mubarak regime of Egypt, the Asad regime was much less willing to negotiate or to even feign interest in entertaining these demands. This was a harbinger then of the coming end of Bashar al-Asad's brief period of tolerance. No one had imagined the amount of criticism that would be hurled at the regime and activism that would be unleashed with only a little bit of political openness. It emphasized that the culture of fear, which governed Syrians' lives for so many years, was not as successful as it was believed to be in tamping down dissent. As reformers and liberals seemed to appear out of nowhere, the regime began to rapidly put in place its counter-attack. Already in September 2000, the editor of an official newspaper, *Tishreen*, argued that the activists were only a minority seeking publicity and fame and power, while most in Syria were struggling too and thus more worried about making a

---

[94] Quoted in Ziesser, *Commanding Syria*, p. 85.
[95] Atassi, *Syria*, p. 362.
[96] George, *Syria*, pp. 52–53.

living. He accused the activists and intellectuals of borrowing dated foreign ideas, claiming that the notion of the separation of powers has itself been proven a delusion within Western countries.[97] Thus, activists were accused of importing foreign notions and empowering foreign powers, and more importantly of providing inorganic and unnatural solutions to Arabs, of being a group of imposters and a heedless and self-serving elite, thus reiterating some of the usual accusations liberals faced in the 1940s and 1950s. The defense minister at the time, Mustafa Tlas, also warned that no one was allowed to take power from a regime that acquired it with the barrel of the gun,[98] reminding everyone of the violence that could ensue if activists continued their outreach and defiance.

In January 2001, Syrian Information Minister Adnan Omran declared that civil society is an "American term" that had recently been given "additional meanings" by "groups that seek to become (political) parties."[99] Two main accusations would keep being made in the leadup to the regime's retaliation, that the liberal movement was inspired and helped by American and European powers looking to impose their will on Syrians through the movement, and that the movement was not really a movement, but composed of a vocal and misled minority that would bring disaster onto the country, if not onto the entire region.[100] A month later, Bashar al-Asad expressed his warnings to the civil society movement:

When the consequences of an action affect the stability of the homeland, there are two possibilities: either the perpetrator is a foreign agent acting on behalf of an outside power, or else he is a simple person acting unintentionally. But in both cases a service is being done to the country's enemies, and consequently both are dealt with in a similar fashion, irrespective of their intentions or motives.[101]

The regime's response was not mounted with words only. In February 2001, the State imposed restrictions on the activities of the forums, banning them from operating without acquiring the necessary permits, which in turn meant that most had to close their doors. Still, the most active forums disregarded the new restrictions. This was the case with

---

[97] Ziesser, *Commanding Syria*, p. 84.
[98] Perthes, *Syria under Bashar*, p. 17.
[99] HRW, *No Room to Breathe*, p. 11; George, *Syria*, p. 47; Ziesser, "A False Spring in Damascus," *Orient* 44, n. 1 (2003), pp. 52–60.
[100] For more on the regime's reaction, see Atassi, *Syria*, pp. 358–359.
[101] "Interview with Bashar al-Asad," *Asharq al-Awsat* (February 8, 2001), passage quoted in HRW, *No Room to Breathe*, p. 11. And in Cameron W. Barr, "Syrians Test New Signs of Freedom," *The Christian Science Monitor* (February 13, 2001), www .csmonitor.com/2001/0213/p1s4.html.

Riad Seif's National Dialogue Forum, which pursued its activities and meetings on and off following the governmental ban. This disregard led to 10 activist leaders being arrested following their participation in a seminar led by Seif in September 2001, during which they discussed the need for issuing a call for a civil disobedience campaign.[102] About 500 people had attended the seminar.[103]

Riad Seif and Ma'mun al-Homsi were the first to be punished for their clear defiance. The two members of parliament had their parliamentary immunity removed with no regard to Syrian law, and were taken in by the political security bureau (*al-Amn al-Siyasi*). They were accused of "attempting to change the constitution by illegal means" and "inciting racial and sectarian strife" and were sentenced by the Damascus Criminal Court to five years in jail.[104]

The other eight activists, Riad al-Turk, who accused Bashar al-Asad of being a Stalin-like dictator during a seminar at Jamal al-Atassi forum, Economics Professor 'Aref Dalila[105], activist Walid al-Bunni, Kamal al-Labwani, writer Habib Salih, who had established the Tartus Forum of National Democratic Dialogue[106], Hasan Sa'dun and Habib 'Isa, who are founders of HRAS, and lawyer Fawwaz Tello, who was representing Riad Seif, were all referred to the Supreme State Security Court, which issued prison sentences of between 2 and 10 years.[107] All were sent to the 'Adra prison in Damascus. This prompted thousands of supporters to gather outside the Justice Palace to support them.[108]

'Aref Dalila was the Dean of the Faculty of Economics at Damascus University, and wrote for the satirically political weekly *al-Domari (the lamplighter)*. Like others, he would end up spending years in solitary confinement in the political section of the 'Adra prison having been sentenced in early 2002 by the Supreme State Security Court (SSSC) to 10 years of hard labor. During his interrogation with a political security

[102] HRW, *No Room to Breathe*, p. 10.
[103] Amnesty International, *Syria: Smothering Freedom of Expression*, pp. 4–8.
[104] George, *Syria*, p. 58.
[105] 'Aref Dalilah, is a former dean of the Faculty of Economics of Aleppo University, and a founding member of the Preparatory Committees of the Revival of Civil Society.
[106] Habib Salih, is a writer, businessman, and founder of a discussion forum in Tartus. He was also an active participant in debates organized by the Jamal al-Atassi Forum, and the National Dialogue Forum, and like other activists had accused the authorities of "corruption," "tyranny" and lack of respect for human rights. See Amnesty International, *Syria: Smothering Freedom of Expression*, p. 6.
[107] George, *Syria*, pp. 57–58; Amnesty International, *Syria: Smothering Freedom of Expression: The Detention of Peaceful Critics* (June 6, 2002), MDE 24/007/2002, www.refworld.org/docid/3cff2aa74.html [January 29, 2020]
[108] George, *Syria*, p. 59.

agent, he was beaten and charged with "weakening the national feeling," distributing false news in addition to causing racial and sectarian tensions. These are the same charges that have been used since the late 1970s to detain intellectuals and activists.[109] Other activists who were not arrested were harassed and attacked. In Lattaquieh for instance, Nabil Sulayman, a playwright who had opened a cultural forum, was severely beaten and admitted to hospital.[110] The crackdown was officially justified on the basis that the liberal, anti-socialist, civil society movement was attempting to change the constitution in an unlawful manner, and that it was destabilizing the country and serving the interests of "foreign powers," namely the imperialist West.

Despite the crackdown, and despite many being terrified of being arrested within an increasingly precarious environment, the activists continued their work. *Al-Domari* magazine, which was founded in December 2000 by cartoonist Ali Ferzat and became Syria's first independent publication since the rise of the Ba'th, intensified its critique of the regime and the security apparatus, as well as of the nepotistic and corrupt economic system the regime led. Copies of *al-Domari* sold out, and the magazine soon started publishing twice daily, which was read as a clear threat by the authorities. It was shut down in 2003, prompting its founder Ali Ferzat, an internationally renowned cartoonist, to start publishing it online.[111]

Activists also formed the Arab Organization for Human Rights in Syria (AOHR, *al-Munazama al-'Arabiyya li Huquq al-Insan*) in February 2004.[112] A few months later, in September 2004, former members of CDF split off to form the Syrian Human Rights Organization (*al-Munazama al-Suriyya li Huquq al-Insan*, Swasiah). The year 2004 also saw the emergence and inclusion of Kurdish human rights groups in the Qamishli area.[113] The research center – Damascus Center for Human Rights Studies (*Markaz Dimashq li Dirasat Huquq al-Insan*) was founded in 2005, and the National Organization for Human Rights (NOHR) was founded by a number of former activists in AOHR in February to March 2006.[114]

Syria's equivalent of Nelson Mandela, Riad al-Turk, also reappeared to play a role in the demands for democratic change, as mentioned

---

[109] Dalila started a hunger strike on July 12, 2005, in protest against his solitary confinement and ill-treatment. "Main Case of the Month: Aref Dalila," *English Pen*, www.englishpen.org/campaigns/main-case-of-the-month-september-2006aref-dalila/

[110] Ziesser, *Commanding Syria*, p. 89.

[111] Amnesty International, *Syrian Refugee Crisis by cartoonist Ali Ferzat* (May 18, 2020), www.amnesty.org.uk/syrian-refugee-crisis-cartoonist-ali-ferzat

[112] HRW, *No Room to Breathe*, p. 11.

[113] Ibid., p. 12.

[114] Ibid., p. 12.

earlier.[115] In August 2001, al-Turk appeared on al-Jazeera news channel and reasserted an old idea about the need for transcending dogma and calling on all political factions to unite to liberate Syria. Syrians should stop worrying about the past, he argued, since "the dictator is dead" [al-dictator mat]. His bold simple words and his attempts at unifying the different forces would soon land him in prison again. He was arrested and sentenced to three years in detention, and was also charged with "defying the State and trying to change the constitution by illegal means." Al-Turk was furthermore accused by a number of pro-regime leftists of entirely switching to the liberal [read Western] camp. Prison would not stop him though. He resumed his political activities once again upon his release, renaming the SCPPB the Syrian Democratic People's Gathering (a liberal democratic party) and then stepped down as secretary in 2005. That same year, he signed the Damascus Declaration, a daring statement of unity that was written by Syria's activists and that declared the regime to be "authoritarian, totalitarian and cliquish," and called for democratic reform.

Indeed, the year 2005 would see activists and intellectuals multiply their efforts. That same year, the final declaration of the Ba'thist Tenth Regional Congress indicated that the Ba'th Party was considering a revision of the electoral law for municipal and legislative elections, and the law on political parties. But in practice, reforms were never really pursued and the monist thinking of those in power remained intact. At the same time, the Syrian regime was facing increasing pressure from the international community, namely Europe and the United States, because of Syrian involvement against the American-led coalition in Iraq, mainly related to the regime's toleration of radical Islamists smuggling into Iraq via Syria, and because of the Syrian occupation of Lebanon and the regime's mingling in its politics, most sensationally visible in the assassination of the Lebanese Prime Minister Rafiq al-Hariri in March of 2005, which the Syrian regime was accused of facilitating.

The activists took advantage of the difficult moment the regime was facing mid-decade in order to increase their pressure on it, the result of which was the writing of the Damascus Declaration for Democratic National Change, which was published in October 2005. The Damascus Declaration managed to do something that the regime most feared: unite a very broad platform of activists against it, even broader

---

[115] The reason for considering someone like Turk part of the liberal movement is due to his willingness to transcend dogma and work with other currents, including the Muslim Brothers in order to help establish a liberal democratic framework of rule.

than the one that came together in 2000, including individuals who were part of the Ba'th party. It included the Syrian Democratic People's Party of Riad al-Turk (formerly the Syrian Communist Party – Political Bureau), the National Democratic Gathering, Syria's Muslim Brotherhood, which was in forced exile and had expressed its commitment to democracy and universal human rights (while the Damascus Declaration itself recognized Islam as a religion of ethics and peace and tolerance), as well as Kurdish and Assyrian parties.[116] Overall, some 250 signatories signed the Declaration, agreeing that notwithstanding their ideological differences and their many disagreements on tactics[117], Syria needed to initiate a peaceful transition towards a liberal democratic system of rule. This was a powerful statement not in terms of its content but as a result of the size and ideological diversity of the coalition it represented, which in turn emphasized the willingness of all involved to transcend dogma and to work together through an agreed upon approach for regime change. The peaceful transition that it called for would involve the creation of a National Congress, the election of a Constituent Assembly to prepare a new constitution, and then the holding of free elections for a new government.[118] It was the first time since the late 1970s that such a broad coalition united the forces so publicly and so unambiguously with the aim of initiating a democratic change.

Still, the regime refused to change its methods, and thus initiated further arrests in an attempt to divide the movement. On November 8, 2005, Syrian security forces detained Kamal al-Labwani moments after he had landed in Syria following a two-month trip to Europe and the United States during which he met with foreign government officials, journalists and human rights organizations, and appeared on two Arab television networks.[119]

---

[116] Ferdinand Arslanian, "The Left in the Syrian Uprising," in Hinnebusch and Imady (eds.), *The Syrian Uprising: Domestic Origins and Early Trajectories* (London and New York: Routledge, 2018), p. 293.

[117] Accounts claim there were rifts between the Riad Seif camp and the Michel Kilo camp, with Seif's being more radical or revolutionary than the other. While this may be true at certain levels, it distracts from the actual work and coordination done between the two camps. For more on this, see George, *Syria*, pp. 42–49; Flynt Leverett, *Inheriting Syria: Bashar's Trial by Fire* (Washington: Brookings Institution Press, 2005), pp. 92–93. It is important to note here that when activists withdrew from the Damascus Declaration Coalition, they did so because they felt the coalition was losing its commitment to liberal democracy, not because it was no longer left-leaning.

[118] Atassi, *Syria*, p. 362.

[119] HRW, *No Room to Breathe*, p. 11.

In March 2006, Military Intelligence detained 'Ammar Qurabi, former spokesman for the Arab Organization for Human Rights Syria and one of the founders of the National Organization for Human Rights, for four days upon his return home from Washington, DC, and Paris, where he had attended two conferences on democratic reform and human rights in Syria.[120] He was also banned from traveling. Ammar Qurabi was particularly seen as a threat because he had documented the methods of torture and abuse within prisons, as well as the system of forced disappearances, arbitrary arrests, and unlawful detention and regarding Syria's multi-layered, pervasive security apparatus. He also did research and led information committees in support of political prisoners facing military court trials, and more broadly, fought for the right to a fair trial in Syria and elsewhere in the region. On March 22, 2006, security forces detained Muhammad Najati Tayyara, former vice-president of the Human Rights Association in Syria, for remarks he made at a ceremony on March 12 held to commemorate the second anniversary of clashes in March 2004 between Kurdish demonstrators and security forces in the northern city of Qamishli.[121]

In May 2006, Kilo launched a new platform to unify Syrian and Lebanese dissidents in their quest for political change. The resulting 10-point "Beirut-Damascus Declaration" appeared on Syrian and Lebanese opposition websites and newspapers. It called for the establishment of liberal democratic regimes in Syria and Lebanon, for respect for the rule of law, human rights and citizens' civil freedoms, the release of all political prisoners, including revealing the fate of those who were missing, and for the Syrian government to respect Lebanon's territorial sovereignty. The text was as harsh in its tone and its accusations as was the Damascus Declaration, but it also came at a very bad time for a Syrian regime struggling to maintain its regional standing while also avoiding being punished by the American administration. The report even accused the regime of committing the crime of political assassinations that led to the deaths or wounding of politicians, party members, media personnel, and citizens, and most prominently to the assassination of Rafiq al-Hariri [the former Prime Minister of Lebanon]."[122]

The Declaration coincided with the passing of UN Security Council Resolution 1680, which was backed by France, Britain and the United States and had similar demands to the Beirut-Damascus

---

[120] Ibid., p. 12.
[121] Ibid.
[122] Jonas Bergan Draege, "The Formation of Syrian Opposition Coalitions Two-Level Games," *The Middle East Journal*, 70, 2 (2016), p. 196.

Declaration.[123] The hope was that the pressure from the American Administration under the new President Bush as well as from European powers such as France and the UK and from the UN Security Council Resolution would force Syria to stop the arrests and that the regime would eventually be undermined and toppled by the very strong and insistent pressures from within. Instead, activists saw the worst crackdown on pro-democracy activists since the 1980s, and the regime survived the international pressure and nothing was done about the arrests.[124]

The regime's feeling of victory meant that the signatories of the Beirut-Damascus Declaration were the biggest victims in the ensuing wave of arrests. Michel Kilo was arrested two days after the declaration's release, followed by a broad campaign to target every perceived leader who was left of the dissident community. On May 10, 2007, a Damascus criminal court sentenced Labwani to 12 years in prison including hard labor for "communicating with a foreign country and inciting it to initiate aggression against Syria" because he had met with US officials during his time in the United States.[125] Anwar al-Bunni, a leading human rights lawyer who in March 2006 had opened up a human rights center funded by the EU that was closed weeks later, was charged with inciting sectarian strife and destabilizing the state and treason by accepting foreign money. "Two men wearing civilian clothes dragged al-Bunni away as he was getting into his car outside his home in Damascus."[126] Aktham Nu'aissa, a long-time human rights activist, was arrested as he arrived at the Damascus Airport from Paris. Nidal Darwish, member of the presidential council of the Committees for the Defense of Democratic Liberties and Human Rights in Syria was also arrested. The wave of arrests also targeted 17 government officials who had signed the declaration.[127] Activists who did not want to end up in prison fled the country. This was the case with Salam Kawakibi, who quit his job as head of the French Institute in Aleppo and left for France in 2006.[128]

And yet it is important to note here that not all the efforts to challenge the regime went to waste. The combination of international pressure,

---

[123] Draege, "The Formation of Syrian Opposition," p. 196.
[124] Rhonada Roumani, "Syria Launches Crackdown on Dissent," *The Christian Science Monitor* (May 25, 2006), www.csmonitor.com/2006/0525/p06s01-wome.html
[125] HRW, *No Room to Breathe*, p. 11.
[126] Ibid., p. 12.
[127] "The Beirut-Damascus Declaration," *Free Syria* (July 12, 2006), www.free-syria.com/en/loadarticle.php?articleid=6924
[128] Author's interview with Salam Kawakibi in 2019. Kawakibi was told the French embassy could do very little for him if he gets arrested.

protests on the Lebanese side known as the Cedar Revolution[129], and the activists and intellectuals' work strongly contributed to the withdrawal of Syrian troops from Lebanon and in bringing down the pro-Syria government in that country. Syria would nonetheless manage to maintain its hegemony over Lebanon since Western considerations meant that the pro-democracy movement was isolated. Yet notwithstanding this, 2005–2006 should still be considered a moment of victory for Syrian and Lebanese liberal forces.

The war in Lebanon in July–August 2006 and the nominal victory of Syria's client Hizbullah over Israel, coupled with the victory of Syria's ally Iran in Iraq, put the idea of regime reforms to bed. The Syrian regime was stabilizing at the regional level and did not need to revisit its domestic repression. And yet despite this, activists continued their work. Riad Seif, imprisoned since autumn 2001, was released in January 2006. Shortly afterwards, he was elected President of the Secretariat General of the Damascus Declaration national coalition and held many meetings in his house. In 2007 and 2008, the Damascus Declaration national coalition would manage to hold meetings and open branches throughout Syria, leading to more arrests by the regime including the 78 year-old al-Maleh, who was brought in front of a military court and sentenced to three years in prison.[130]

Notwithstanding these arrests, the Damascus Declaration would become the largest coalition in the Syrian liberal movement when demonstrations spread in Syria in 2011.[131] Surprisingly, between 2008 and 2010, Bashar al-Asad was able to renew Syria's ties with Europe, notably President Sarkozy's France, with the new American Administration under Barack Obama – which sent a new ambassador to Damascus in 2010 – and with the Gulf States, who saw in Syria opportunities for business and investment.[132]

Syria's liberals were once again entirely on their own.[133] Maleh was released at the beginning of 2011 following a general amnesty announced

---

[129] The Cedar Revolution was a pro-democracy movement triggered by the assassination of Prime Minister Rafik al-Hariri. It demanded the end of Syrian interference in Lebanese political affairs and the withdrawal of Syrian troops from Lebanon.

[130] Agencies in Damascus, "Haitham Maleh Jailed for Three Years by Syrian Court," *The Guardian* (July 4, 2010).

[131] Jonas Bergan Draege, "The Formation of Syrian Opposition Coalitions Two-Level Games," *The Middle East Journal*, p. 196.

[132] Atassi, *Syria*, p. 378.

[133] Not that they were not on their own before. Often European diplomats explained to activists that there is very little they can do on their behalf. Author's interview with a number of Syrian activists between 2018 and 2020.

by Bashar al-Asad.[134] Maleh said he was not surprised when the uprising started, "I pushed for this uprising, for this movement, for so many years ... This is the worst regime in the Arab World."[135]

While harassed, imprisoned, and repressed, and ultimately divided and unable to acquire the changes they sought, these forums, activists and organizations challenged the regime, and demonstrated that, despite more than 50 years of autocratic consolidation and political repression in Syria, activists and intellectuals transcended dogma and strove for freedom and formed a liberal movement as soon as they were able to do so by engaging the public, organizing, creating associations, holding public meetings and showing unity. Indeed, whether directly or indirectly, as we will see in the next chapter, these forums and the activists that led them laid the groundwork for those who came during the Syrian Uprising of 2011.

Societal Liberalism?

Some observers have argued that members of these groups and forums and parties and human rights organizations are not all liberals. And yet the project and ideas they are advancing as a collective express political liberal notions and penchants and their work demonstrates a liberal logic, in line with the articulation of liberalism outlined in the introduction to this book. Thus, Browers notes, "[A]nalysis demonstrates that rather than Arab nationalists and socialists becoming more Islamist, or Islamists becoming more Arab nationalist or socialist, a wide variety of ideological groupings are developing a shared store of concepts increasingly dominated by rhetoric traditionally associated with liberalism, and based on notions such as democracy and human rights." But Browers notes that this prevalence of the liberal paradigm and cross-ideological engagement does not necessarily mean increased liberalization within these trends. She writes,

one should not mistake the use of liberal rhetoric for a more categorical transformation toward liberal thought and practice. Rather, what the evidence reveals is something more tenuous: the persistence of those oppositional frames that permit these alliances to take place hinders discussion of various issues– particularly gender and religion, but also other forms of difference– which might contribute to a fuller articulation and more meaningful embrace of liberal and democratic values among the main oppositional forces in the Arab region. While substantive discussion, let alone agreement, on issues of gender and religion has proven nearly impossible in the context of cross-ideological dialogs,

---

[134] From "Haitham el-Maleh," *Carnegie Middle East Center*, https://carnegie-mec.org/syriaincrisis/?fa=48368&lang=en
[135] Kouddous, "A Lifetime of Resistance."

tensions created by the persistence of such issues have contributed toward some liberalization in at least two contexts. The personal relationships and use of liberal concepts fostered in these dialogs has provided space sufficient for development of an oppositional movement that is both cross-ideological and interreligious in the context of Egypt...[136]

It is certain that different members of these broad coalitions would have different views about different issues, especially issues related to religiosity, patriarchy, and gender relations. The fact remains that these groupings are all agreeing on *the priority of* creating a liberal sociopolitical framework in which different points of view can co-exist and compete in the future. This recognition of the need for a liberal framework was not the case for Nasserists and Socialists under Nasser and Sadat, nor the case for most Egyptian Islamists, who have generally shunned the liberals and liberal democracy. This shift of some toward liberal politics and ideology is essential in the sense that the prevailing imagination of the possible political configurations has been transformed.

The problem then lies in how political liberalism can be translated into societal liberalism, meaning how liberalism in the political sphere can be translated into liberal values being practiced in the social sphere. Many argue that the Kifaya movement for instance eventually faltered because of some of its members' inability to agree on social questions related to women's rights, religion and sexuality. One might argue though that other nations and groups have also continuously transformed their discourse, and changes towards more liberties and a more inclusive understanding of freedom and rights was/is also a continuous process in the established liberal democratic world. Even today, liberal societies grapple with questions of marriage and adoption for the LGBTIA2+ community, ultra-radicals remain a problematic current that threatens everything that the liberal West as we understand it stands for, and yet the overall trends have been thus far toward more rather than less liberties. I am not assuming a linear progression toward more liberal practice at the societal levels, the point I am trying to make is simply that this is possible given the political directions the activists have been taking and the focus on individual rights that societal mores become more fluid and shifting in liberal ways.

Conclusion

The 2000s witnessed the vigorous re-emergence of liberal notions and of liberal organization and political activism in the region. This liberalism is

---

[136] Michaelle L. Browers, *Political Ideology in the Arab World: Accommodation and Transformation*, (New York: Cambridge University Press, 2009), pp. 10–11.

a continuation of classical liberalism in the sense that some of its activists refer to the liberal era and its accomplishments, but it is also a renewed version in the sense that it has a new approach and a renewed vision of how change should be achieved. Thus the period saw activists and thinkers making use of human rights groups, of small political openings and legal loopholes, of cultural forums and of intellectual manifestos, of social media and the internet, and of satellite television, to reach out to the public as well as to other activists and like-minded politicians, to draw attention to the fundamental values of freedom and dignity, and to engage in debates about citizenship, individuality, and civil rights. Liberal political leaders integrated the intellectuals' calls to move beyond the simple pervasive categories of so-called "Islamic," "leftist," and "progressive" categories, in an attempt to acknowledge everyone and include political opponents within the nation.

Thus, by the 2000s, liberals and other pro-democracy groups shed their "dogmatic thinking" and asserted the need to coordinate with other groups in order to achieve a liberal democratic environment, which is the aim of most activists. They proclaimed that essentialist and monolithic views and centralized political institutions had catapulted the region into its political and economic crisis, and that a rupture with the extant political order and sociopolitical transformation were sorely needed to get out of the impasse reached. Different parties and groups thus endorsed pluralism and expressed the right to difference. Critique turned inward and engaged with the self instead of looking for outside reasons for failure, which can be seen for instance when Egyptian activists turned from protesting against Israel and the United States to protesting against Mubarak' s rule.

The methodological and ideological fluidity that characterized this period was driven by an essentially liberal rationale or was in line with liberal values even if justified on another basis. And while some of these ideas were already being asserted in the 1980s and 1990s (as was discussed in the previous chapter), they increasingly lost their subtle or restrained nature and were in full flower during the 2000s. In this environment, political activists became united and led by their anti-totalitarian struggle, waiting for the spark of change.

4   2011–2018

Liberalism Out in the Open, the Restitution, and the Loss

> No other goal but the goal of freedom will emancipate you, so hold on to it with everything you do, and never give it up because it alone can end tyranny.
>
> Michel Kilo[1]

Liberals stood at the forefront of the Arab Spring revolutions of 2011, and yet studies on the Arab region and the Arab Spring have tended to ignore their role in the uprisings and the movement in its entirety.[2] Instead, academics, researchers, and analysts have generally focused on the rise of a leaderless movement of alienated youth, generally assuming a lack of ideological content, and focusing on structural, economic, and technological reasons for the onset of the revolutions. The different narratives agree that the groups that showed up at Tahrir Square in Egypt and that thronged the alleys of the old city in Damascus, Darra, Homs, and Hama were not ideologically driven, but rather were loose associations of activists and other disenfranchised citizens driven by a profound malaise with the status quo and who often didn't see eye to eye.

This overall analysis ignores years of liberal and pro-democracy activism against the extant patterns and nature of domination and authority in the region, and the fact that protestors have rallied behind a set of ideas that are consistently and categorically different from the ones rallied behind in the 1950s and 1960s.[3] It also ignores the fact that the protest

---

[1] Michel Kilo's "Commandments to the Syrian People", *Zaman al-Wasl* (19 April 2021). Written a few days before his death in April 2021, as part of his recommendations to the Syrian people.

[2] Revolutions in the sense that they are the result of popular movements that seek to undermine the status quo, to change the nature of authority and its justification, and to transform the entire political system and society as a result. In so doing, the popular movements are a revolutionary process that fuse many people, socioeconomic classes and levels. For more on what the term revolution does and does not imply, see Bjørn Thomassen, "Notes towards an Anthropology of Political Revolutions," *Comparative Studies in Society and History* 54, 3 (2012), pp. 679–706.

[3] Roel Meijer, "Liberalism in the Middle East and the Issue of Citizenship Rights," in Meir Hatina and Christoph Schumann (eds.), *Arab Liberal Thought after 1967: Old Dilemmas, New Perceptions* (New York: Palgrave Macmillan, 2015), p. 66.

movement brought together people from a wide range of backgrounds and socioeconomic groups which, as shown in the previous chapters, became united in their shared fight for freedom and democratic rule.

What is missed in most studies is the deep and consistent transformation and reformulation of the object of discontent. In other words, the protestors' demands no longer reflected the post-colonial discourse with its emphasis on questions of economic egalitarianism, public ownership, rapid industrialization, class conflict and the economically marginalized, and imperialism, even though all of these questions remain concerns of the majority. After all, these regimes had also turned to crony capitalism and adopted neoliberal policies that produced devastating and wide socioeconomic chasms between the haves and the have nots in most societies of the region. One might then think that, instead of focusing on issues of citizens' freedoms and civil rights, the majority of the protestors would object to the end of the Welfare State.[4] Yet this was not the case. One could argue that the protestors' focus on liberal notions emerged naturally from their opposition to the repressive nature of the regime. The liberal movement is certainly organic, as stated throughout this book, and a general disapproval of political repression has certainly driven the overall movement; but disapproval does not explain the consistently liberal nature and direction of the protestors' demands. It is this consistent nature and direction, found across the region, that testifies to the effectiveness of the work that liberal activists and public intellectuals had done in the years preceding the uprisings. Moreover, the fact that millions were willing to face their States despite fear of the regimes' violent security apparatuses so as to openly disseminate the liberal ideas showed that liberalism is vibrant and alive, and that it was hiding in plain sight in youth groups, NGOs, professional associations, on television shows, in theatre, art, at universities and in political forums as well as online discussions, and in literature.

Egypt

The Arab Spring's massive street protests picked up where the three months of demonstrations that took place in Alexandria and Cairo in June 2010 left off. The youth, representing diverse political groups and

---

[4] This is not to say that economic issues were not an integral part of the protestors' concerns, social justice was clearly a main concern voiced by the movement; rather the point is that economic egalitarianism and joining the developed world's post-industrial order were no longer the main concerns, as they were in the 1950s, and that precedence was given to issues of political accountability and pluralism including to achieve greater economic empowerment.

backgrounds, appeared *en force*, continuing the demands of the 2000s. In so doing, they coalesced into what was later dubbed "the Coalition of the Revolutionary Youth", composed of activists from the main political groups who organized the protests of January 2011: "the 6 April Youth Movement and Ayman Nour, the leftist Justice and Freedom Movement, the Dignity or Karama Party (social liberal), the liberal Democratic Front Party (al-Gabha al-Dimucratiya), the Social Democratic Party of Abul Ghar and Amr Hamzawi (leftist-liberal), and the National Association for Change (combining several political parties including representatives of civil society, led by a liberal, Mohammad el-Barade'i, and driven by its young members and a liberal platform)."[5] Even conservative Islamist parties joined in at a later stage, committing to political pluralism and democracy, arguing that these liberal ideas are rooted in Islamic ideals and modalities of piety and social justice. And joining together the protestors was the chant, "The people want the fall of the regime."

Activists and Politicians Went to Work

One of the instigators of these massive street protests in Tahrir Square was a young woman, Asmaa Mahfouz, a 26-year-old business graduate of Cairo University, and a member of the Kifaya movement. Mahfouz posted on Facebook on January 18, 2011, a 4-minute, 36-second video of herself, a video that was quickly reposted to YouTube. In it, she talked calmly and with conviction in an attempt to incite all Egyptians to take to the streets and to protest against the regime: "As long as you say there is no hope, then there will be no hope, but if you go down and take a stand, then there will be hope." She held a sign saying she would go out and protest to try to bring down Mubarak's regime. This was not the first time that a young activist used the Internet as a tool to organize and mobilize, as we have seen in the previous chapters; but her poignant message felt deeply personal and true, and it acted as the spark to trigger rupture with the existing political order. The spirit of her appeal inspired others, who started to post their own videos, holding similar signs to their chests and declaring their intention to take to the streets on January 25, 2011, to demand change.[6] No one knew that it would be

---

[5] Nadine Abdalla, "Youth Movements in the Egyptian Transformation: Strategies and Repertoires of Political Participation," *Mediterranean Politics*, 21:1 (2016), pp. 44–63, https://doi.org/10.1080/13629395.2015.1081445

[6] Mona El-Naggar, "Equal Rights Takes to the Barricades," *New York Times* (February 1, 2011), www.nytimes.com/2011/02/02/world/middleeast/02iht-letter02.html

the start of a new era – yet hundreds of thousands ended up protesting, and ultimately succeeded in toppling the presidency of Hosni Mubarak. Mahfouz said, "I, a girl, am going down to Tahrir Square, and I will stand alone … I will say no to corruption, no to this regime. Come with us and demand your rights."[7] She added, "If you stay home, you deserve all that's being done to you, and you will be guilty before your nation and your people. Go down to the street, send SMSes, post it on the 'Net, make people aware.'"[8]

In Tahrir Square, thousands showed up, with many liberals in the front rows including prominent artists, intellectuals and political leaders such as Wael Nawara and Ayman Nour, and younger activists such as Mahienour el-Masry, Esraa Abdel Fattah[9] and Ahmed Maher, all captured on camera, and by their presence helping to drive others to do the same and thus setting in motion an Egyptian revolution.[10] And in the same vein as the earlier protests, protestors made demands to dismantle the entire political apparatus: first, demanding that Mubarak had to go, then an end to emergency laws, a transitional government to replace the NDP-dominated cabinet and parliament, the holding of new elections, amending the constitution to ensure limits on presidential terms, the institution of an open political process and a political system based on pluralism, civil freedoms, and the rule of law.[11] Importantly, the more conservative groups only joined the protest movement at the end of January 2011[12], making the initial moment truly a liberal one.

---

[7] Orla Guerin, "Revolution a Distant Memory as Egypt Escalates Repression," *BBC* (December 9, 2014), www.bbc.com/news/world-30381292)

[8] Melissa Wall and Sahar el-Zaher, "'I'll Be Waiting for You Guys': A YouTube Call to Action in the Egyptian Revolution," *International Journal of Communication* 5 (2011), www.researchgate.net/publication/298060207_I%27ll_Be_Waiting_for_You_Guys_A_YouTube_Call_to_Action_in_the_Egyptian_Revolution

[9] Esraa Abdel Fattah was a member of al-Ghad Party and as a result of the Kefaya movement. She had also co-founded the Egyptian Democratic Academy, an organization meant to monitor the 2010 parliamentary elections. See Esraa Abdel Fattah, "Loaded Victory: Egypt's Revolution and Where It Stands Post-30 June," in Ronald Meinardus (ed.), *Liberalism in the Arab World – Just a good idea?* (Cairo: Al-Mahrosa for Publishing, 2014), pp. 115–128.

[10] These include pro-democracy actors such as Khaled Abul Naja (or Naga), Amro Waked and Khaled al-Nabawi, who have used their fame to raise awareness about issues of human rights and democratic rule.

[11] Nadine Sika, "Youth Political Engagement in Egypt: From Abstention to Uprising," *British Journal of Middle Eastern Studies*, 39:2 (2012), pp. 181–199.

[12] Gamal M. Selim, "Egypt under SCAF and the Muslim Brotherhood: The Triangle of Counter-Revolution," *Arab Studies Quarterly*, 37:2 (Spring 2015), p. 179.

Mubarak was ousted on February 11, 2011, following twenty years of repression and authoritarianism. Liberals began to imagine what they could achieve next, and people began to think that Mubarak's ousting meant the opening up of the political space. As one observer noted, "Unprecedented opportunity to create a better system of rule presented itself and everyone went to work."[13]

The liberals went to work in order to initiate a democratic restructuring and a more liberal political and economic environment. The first hurdle they met was the takeover of the army during the transitional phase, which the liberals and other activists believed should have been the prerogative of the Revolutionary Youth Coalition. The army won that first battle, and the Coalition of the Revolutionary Youth and human rights groups started thinking of ways to ensure change, including concrete policy recommendations.[14] The Human Rights Community, such as Bahey al-Din Hassan of the Cairo Institute for Human Rights Studies, Ahmad Ragheb of the National Community for Human Rights and Law, and Hossam Bahgat of Egyptian Initiative for Personal Rights (EIPR), focused on policies aimed at reforming the security establishment and freedom of information laws.[15] Morayef explains that activists, "had to run their organizations, oversee the work of lawyers representing victims in the police trials around the country and respond to meeting requests from Government officials, political part[ies], and diplomats, who wanted policy recommendations. They also had to ensure that the new abuses by the police and the military (now running the country) were being documented, all while educating themselves on comparative transition experiences to learn how to deal with a set of issues they had never faced under Mubarak."[16]

Liberal politicians went to work as well. Among them were people like Amr Hamzawi and Ziad al-Eleimy (a close associate of Mohammad ElBaradei, who played a leading role in the Revolutionary Youth Coalition), who joined hands with Muhammad Abu el-Ghar (an ardent secularist and self-proclaimed social liberal) to form the Social Democratic Party (leftist-liberal) in 2011.[17] Then Amr Hamzawi resigned from the Social Democratic Party in April 2011 and formed the Egypt

---

[13] Abdalla, "Youth movements in the Egyptian transformation," pp. 44–63.
[14] Ibid, p. 44
[15] Heba Morayef, "Reexamining Human Rights Change in Egypt," *Middle East Report* 274 (Spring 2015), p. 13.
[16] Morayef, "Reexamining Human Rights Change in Egypt," p. 12.
[17] The Social Democratic Party of el-Ghar and Hazem el-Beblawi would become co-opted by the military by 2015–2016.

Freedom Party in May 2011. Amr Hamzawi would later run for parliament instead of joining the transitional government under the Supreme Council of the Armed Forces (SCAF), and would serve as a member of parliament in 2012 and 2013. In 2011, Ayman Nour established a new party, the Ghad al-Thawra Party (Tomorrow of the Revolution Party), and he planned on running in the 2011–2012 presidential elections only to be stopped by the Presidential Election Commission, under the control of SCAF, who disqualified his candidacy.[18] But this didn't stop him from working with other liberals and Ghad al-Thawra members to unite ranks and gain seats in parliament.

Liberals also created new coalitions that reflected the 2000s trends of inclusion and cross-ideological cooperation, but also atomization. The Democratic Alliance for Egypt was formed in June 2011, consisting initially of 28 political parties. The alliance's main members were the Muslim Brothers, but also al-Wafd, the social liberal Dignity Party (Karama), the liberal Ghad al-Thawra Party, the Egypt Freedom Party of Amr Hamzawi, the Hadara Party, and the liberal Democratic Front Party of Osama el-Ghazali Harb, among others from leftist, Islamist, and liberal backgrounds. In its founding statement, the alliance asserted its commitment to the principles of democracy and civil rights. The alliance emerged to compete for the parliamentary elections of 2011, and one of its main concerns was that ex-regime figures could secure parliamentary seats if there was a lack of coordination between the different pro-democracy parties.[19] The member parties signed a document outlining 21 nonbinding principles that would guide the constitution-drafting efforts following the parliamentary elections. The principles agreed upon included upholding constitutionalism, the rule of law, freedom of expression and belief, the right to form trade unions, the right to education and work, and that Islam would remain the religion of the State and its primary source of legislation.[20] But the alliance would soon be undermined due to disagreements between the liberals and the Islamists over the role of religion in politics. Thus both al-Wafd and the Democratic Front left the alliance soon after the groups' creation, citing major disagreements with the Muslim Brothers. The Wafd opted to stay independent while

[18] Emran El-Badawi, "Conflict and Reconciliation: 'Arab Liberalism' in Syria and Egypt," in Fahmy and Faruqi (eds.), *Egypt and the Contradictions of Liberalism: Illiberal Intelligentsia and the Future of Egyptian Democracy* (London: Oneworld Publications, 2017), p. 298.

[19] Parties and Movements, "Democratic Alliance for Egypt," *Jadaliyya* (November 18, 2011), www.jadaliyya.com/Details/24648

[20] Ibid.

the Democratic Front then joined the Egyptian Bloc, which had a radically secular agenda, insisting on a hardline separation of religion and politics, and was essentially anti-Muslim Brotherhood.[21] Karama Party and Ghad al-Thawra were more willing to compromise on certain principles and electoral lists and continued on within the Democratic Alliance until September 2012, when they realized that the Islamists were reneging on significant liberal promises.

The Egypt Bloc was co-created by a number of liberal figures such as Mohammad Abu al-Ghar who were especially opposed to Egypt's Islamist groups, and thus to the Democratic Alliance for Egypt in principle, and Amr Hamzawi (who had initially joined the Democratic Alliance and then decided to leave). The Bloc initially included 21 groups of liberal and leftist leaning groups such as the Social Democratic Party, the Egypt Freedom Party, the Free Egypt Party, the Popular Socialist Alliance and the National Association for Change, to name a few. Later on, many would defect because of leadership rivalries and an inability to effectively coordinate, leaving only the Social Democratic Party, the Free Egyptian Part and the al-Tagammu' Party remaining in the coalition.

Other broad coalitions of leftists and liberals at the time were the Revolution Continues Alliance (consisting of two socialist and two new liberal parties, namely the Egypt Freedom Party and the Egyptian Current). The coalition was the result of the participation of elements of the Mubarak regime in the Egypt Bloc; the members of this new alliance felt the need to reassert the revolutionary spirit and demands, hence the name.

Liberals then took part in the National Salvation Front (NSF), which at one point included some 30 parties, some which had left the Democratic Alliance and joined the new coalition such as the Democratic Front, the Social Democrats, the Freedom Party, the newly created Congress Party (of Amr Moussa and Ayman Nour)[22], the Free Egyptians Party co-founded by Ahmad Said, the Dignity Party and the Constitution Party (ElBaradei and Nawara). The NSF was formed on November 23, 2012, during a meeting at the Wafd Party headquarters with the purpose of overturning the newly elected President

---

[21] Michele Dunne and Amr Hamzawi "Egypt's Secular Political Parties: A Struggle For Identity And Independence," *Carnegie Endowment* (March 2017), https://carnegieendowment.org/2017/03/31/egypt-s-secular-political-parties-struggle-for-identity-and-independence-pub-68482

[22] Congress Party (Hizb al-Mu'tamar al-Masri) was created in September 2012 by Amr Moussa and included Ghad al-Thawra party.

Mohammad Mursi's illiberal constitutional changes (more on these events hereinafter).[23]

The transitional period (February 2011–June 2012) had already been difficult and disenchanting as SCAF appeared keen to block a genuine liberal democratic transition particularly because it could jeopardize its entrenched economic interests and privileges.[24] The years 2011–2012 would also reveal the liberals' weaknesses and inexperience. More specifically, some self-proclaimed liberals who were actively challenging the autocratic ways of the Sadat and Mubarak regimes turned out to be not so consistently committed to their liberal claims. For instance, a number of activists such as Abu al-Ghar and Saad Eddin Ibrahim (the chair of Ibn Khaldun Center) would betray the liberal cause by joining hands with the military leadership in order to rid Egypt of the Islamists.[25] Emblematic of Egypt's so-called "liberal" landscape, some self-proclaimed liberals would even be accused of having a "fascist nature" no different from that of the radical Islamists.[26] For the "true" and consistent liberals – who are the topic of this book – 2011 and 2012 showed their inexperience in day-to-day politics and their inability to stand together behind one leadership.[27] Others who had more experience, such as Amr Hamzawi, ElBaradei, and Ayman Nour, in addition to a number of younger NGOs' leaders and intellectuals, would find it difficult to navigate the atomized and divided environment. They also found themselves at the mercy of an electoral system that was purposely set up to hinder the chances of those operating outside the traditional party structure.[28] Finally, the liberal majority who had worked for

---

[23] Mursi had announced one day prior to the NSF foundational meeting a number of constitutional amendments that would place legislative and executive powers in the presidency, and that would let the president appoint the new general prosecutor. His statement also announced that the Constituent Assembly – responsible for drafting a new constitution – could not be dissolved by the Judiciary, and that the president's decisions were "final and unchallengeable" until a new constitution had been ratified and new parliamentary elections were held. The declaration was perceived as a power grab that most liberals and secularists felt the need to react to, and react fast and as a group. See: "Egypt's National Salvation," *BBC* (December 10, 2012), www.bbc.com/news/world-middle-east-20667661

[24] Selim, "Egypt under SCAF and the Muslim Brotherhood," p. 180.

[25] Daanish Faruqi and Dalia F. Fahmy, "Egyptian Liberals, from Revolution to Counterrevolution," in Fahmy and Faruqi (eds.), *Egypt and the Contradictions of Liberalism: Illiberal Intelligentsia and the Future of Egyptian Democracy* (London: Oneworld Publications, 2017), pp. 1–17.

[26] Bassem Youssef, "Egypt's Secularists Repeating Islamists' Mistakes," *CNN online* (July 20, 2013), www.cnn.com/2013/07/19/opinion/youssef-egypt-political-upheaval/

[27] See Introductory chapter for a definition of "true" liberal. One commentator stated that this can somewhat be linked to the messiness of social movements in general rather than saying something about the liberals at the time.

[28] Selim, "Egypt under SCAF and the Muslim Brotherhood," p. 181.

years away from the limelight and behind closed doors in order to avoid the repressive hand of the regime could not in a matter of months amass the public recognition required for them to be elected (more on this hereinafter). As Hamzawi and Dunne explained, adding to the difficulty was that parties such as the Social Democratic and Free Egyptians were new parties, "with no track record of election participation and limited organizational assets – unlike the Muslim Brotherhood and Wafd."[29]

The result was that things became very messy very quickly. The many liberal coalitions that appeared and kept shifting and rearranging themselves confused most voters. These coalitions didn't seem to be cohesive enough within the transitioning environment, and they also underlined the actual fragmentation of the liberals at a time when they needed to show unity in order to gain seats and thus have a greater impact. Years of regime "divide and conquer" strategies could not be overcome in a matter of months. The presence of self-proclaimed and inconsistent liberals within these coalitions only complicated matters for those who were fighting against the return or rise of a new autocratic order. The result was voter confusion and an inability to face the mounting challenges of transition and to gain a large amount of seats in parliament.

It is important to underline that no one thought the transition was going to be easy. Indeed, a mere two weeks after the ousting of Mubarak, Egypt witnessed the ascendance of SCAF to executive power. Although the SCAF seemed initially accepting of the democratic game, it did not strongly endorse its liberal components, and did not hesitate to unleash its security forces against those protesting hasty and autocratic decisions that it made in 2011. Indeed, SCAF soon grew clearly anti-liberal and repressive, and lost the trust of the revolutionaries early on. For instance, SCAF was supposed to restore the 1971 liberal constitution with a number of amendments that voters had approved on March 19, 2011; but instead, it issued on March 30 an improvised declaration of 63 articles after consulting a few leaders on an ad hoc basis.[30] The declaration not only ignored the democratic process in its entirety, it also protected SCAF's transitional role as a constitutional actor with lawmaking powers as well as the power to appoint and dismiss ministers until a new president is elected.[31] SCAF

[29] Dunne and Hamzawi, "Egypt's Secular Political Parties."

[30] Nathan J. Brown and Kristen Stilt, "A Haphazard Constitutional Compromise," *Carnegie Endowment for International Peace* (April 11, 2011), https://carnegieendowment.org/2011/04/11/haphazard-constitutional-compromise-pub-43533

[31] The committee that was responsible for drafting the amendments was headed by an Islamist intellectual and judge, Tareq al-Bishri, and a number of professional jurists, including a leading attorney within the Muslim Brotherhood, Subhy Saleh, but none of the liberals. Selim, "Egypt under SCAF and the Muslim Brotherhood," p. 180.

furthermore maintained the requirement that half of the parliamentary deputies be workers and peasants, a requirement that was not only outdated but also worked against the interests of the liberals.[32]

The opaque, unpredictable, and authoritarian way that SCAF dealt with the constitutional issue was revealing for what was to come. SCAF went on to mandate that the next elected parliament be entrusted with drafting the new constitution, which a majority of the liberals objected to, arguing that this created a clear conflict of interest as it would give undue power and influence to the first elected parliament. SCAF also canceled the 64-seat quota allocated to women in the 2010 parliamentary elections, significantly reducing the chances of women being elected to parliament.[33] This was significant because women were and continue to be a major force within the liberal movement. That autumn, the military used violence against the protestors including against a large protest by women in Cairo in October, and then outlined a number of supraconstitutional principles that entrenched the military's repressive power, by giving SCAF influence over the drafting of the constitution as well as power to veto any provision of the new constitution that it deemed to contradict the basic tenets of the Egyptian State.

The Kamal al-Ganzouri government installed by SCAF in December 2011 was also aggressively anti-NGO. This meant that things were bad from the outset even for the civil rights activists who did not necessarily want to join the political system. Prosecutors harassed pro-democracy workers, and questioned staff about their foreign funding and licenses.[34] About 73 democracy groups were also monitored and accused of possible treason, and seven US, German, and Egyptian NGOs were raided on December 29, 2011, by justice ministry inspections teams alongside armed military and police officers, all accused of being foreign players with a foreign (Western) agenda.[35] Groups harassed included the April 6 Movement, Kifaya, the CIHRS, el-Nadim Center for Rehabilitation of Victims of Torture and the Hisham Mubarak Law Center.[36] Their staff were charged on February 5, 2012 with operating without a license, receiving unauthorized foreign funding, engaging in activities prohibited by law such as providing for political training, and violating tax codes

---

[32] Brown and Stilt, "A Haphazard Constitutional Compromise."

[33] Selim, "Egypt under SCAF and the Muslim Brotherhood," p. 182.

[34] Ann M. Lesch, "The Authoritarian State's Power over Civil Society," in Fahmy and Faruqi (eds.), *Egypt and the Contradictions of Liberalism: Illiberal Intelligentsia and the Future of Egyptian Democracy* (London: Oneworld Publications, 2017), p. 136.

[35] Lesch, "The Authoritarian State's Power," pp. 135–137

[36] Selim, "Egypt under SCAF and the Muslim Brotherhood," p. 184.

among other things.[37] EIPR director Hossam Bahgat along with Egyptian Organization for Human Rights' Abu Saeda and other human rights activists and journalists accused the ministry and the army of targeting organizations that were exposing the authorities' abuses.

Also under SCAF, some 12,000 civilians were referred to military courts in the first seven months, with only 7% of them acquitted.[38] Human rights organizations reported that this was larger than the number of those tried under the Mubarak regime's entire tenure.[39]

New waves of protests took place, this time against SCAF, and new rights groups had to emerge to counter the renewed repression; these included No Military Trials of Civilians, the Anti Torture Task Force, and the Front to Defend Egypt's Protestors, all aiming to decry the new abuses of power targeting civilians and human rights activists.[40] Protestors demanded accountability and transparency, in addition to the resignation of the head of SCAF, Field Marshal Tantawi. NGOs such as the Andalus Institute for Tolerance and Anti-Violence Studies and The United Group Law firm campaigned to raise awareness in villages about the electoral system and the role of civil society organizations within a democracy.[41]

Loss of Control

SCAF was not the liberals' only problem, since the Islamists had a clear head start when it came to preparing for elections. That is, they were better prepared in the sense that they had more extensive lists of candidates all over the country that they could rely on, they were better organized with hundreds of established networks of mosques, they were better financed, and they also seemed more cohesive as a group. But more importantly, they were favored by the SCAF, who set up the constitutional drafting campaign and the electoral game in ways that hurt the chances of the liberal forces.[42] This coalition of convenience between SCAF and the Muslim Brothers, while brief, was actively and successfully working against the "true" liberals.

---

[37] Lesch, "The Authoritarian State's Power," p. 138.
[38] Ibid, p. 131.
[39] Lin Noueihed and Alex Warren, *The Battle for the Arab Spring: Revolution, Counterrevolution and the Making of a New Era* (New Haven and London: Yale University Press, 2012), pp. 116–117.
[40] Lesch, "The Authoritarian State's Power," p. 132.
[41] Ibid, p. 133.
[42] Noueihed and Warren, *The Battle for the Arab Spring*, p. 114; Selim, "Egypt under SCAF and the Muslim Brotherhood," p. 182.

Following the first parliamentary elections in 2011, secularists in general, including the liberals, won about 83 seats in the People's Assembly (out of 502). Seven seats went to The Revolution Continues, six seats to the Karama Party, which ran part of the Democratic Alliance coalition, amounting to 15% of the total seats.[43] This was no defeat, but the liberals feared their modest performance was a sign of future and more meaningful setbacks, especially in light of the army's continued manipulation of the system in favor of the repressive and illiberal forces. Hamzawi writes that inexperience and inability to see beyond the elections caused newly established liberal and social democratic parties to see their good performance within parliamentary elections as total defeat. As a result, the Egyptian Bloc refused to accept the results of the elections and hostility reigned in parliament.[44]

The Muslim Brotherhood had initially continued to assert its commitment to the liberalization of the political environment and respect for human and civil rights, hence the preliminary joining together with liberals and leftists in its coalition. But soon enough, for many reasons including finding itself a majority working within a not-so friendly environment, the Brotherhood started reneging on its liberal promises.[45] For instance, the Brotherhood had initially promised not to field a presidential candidate but then it reconsidered its decision claiming it distrusted the secularists, as well as SCAF.[46] Thus, the Muslim Brotherhood announced in April that it would field a candidate in the June 2012 presidential elections, a victory that would give the Islamists power over both the legislative and the executive branches. The announcement was interpreted as showing the Muslim Brotherhood's attempts to take power away from SCAF and to control all State functions, and it prompted the army to interfere.

The army's interference, as explained earlier, was not surprising. The military, which had remained in control of the political environment the entire time of the transition, would repeatedly step in under the pretense of ensuring stability, including making up rules, disqualifying candidates, imposing its will as it saw fit, detaining and killing protestors and civilians, and failing to lift emergency laws throughout

---

[43] Dunne and Hamzawi, "Egypt's Secular Political Parties."

[44] Ibid.

[45] Line Khatib, "Challenges of Representation and Inclusion: A Case Study if Islamic Groups in Transitional Justice," in K. J. Fisher and R. Stewart (eds.), *Transitional Justice and the Arab Spring* (London and New York: Routledge, 2014), pp. 131–145.

[46] Noueihed and Warren, *The Battle for the Arab Spring*, pp. 116–117.

2011.[47] Two days before the second round of presidential elections, on June 14, 2012, Egypt's highest court dissolved the Islamist-dominated People's Assembly under military pressure, thus removing from the Brotherhood its power base in parliament, and boosting the candidacy of the SCAF's candidate, ex-General Ahmad Shafiq, instead. The SCAF also gave itself legislative powers until a new People's Assembly was elected.[48]

In so doing, the army reinvented and reasserted itself as the guardian of the constitutional order, thus turning the military into a sovereign institution over Egyptian politics. These efforts were not unexpected. As mentioned earlier, the military was an integral part of the previous autocratic apparatus, with many entrenched interests and privileges at stake. But the move was a palpable assault on a possible transition towards a liberal democracy. And yet many parties, such as the Wafd and the Free Egyptians, the Democratic Front, as well as some from within the Social Democratic Party, cheered the undermining of the Muslim Brotherhood. Others, who were more clearly and consistently committed to their liberal ideals including the majority of the January 25 revolutionaries (notably leaders such as Hamzawi, Nawara, and Nour), were more worried about the integrity of a nascent democratic system, and denounced the move as a coup from above.[49] Some stated that the decision spelt the end of the revolution and the return to tyranny. El-Baradei declared, "The election of a president in the absence of a constitution and a parliament is the election of a president with powers that not even the most entrenched dictatorships have known."[50]

The presidential elections, now contested between a military-backed candidate who was perceived by many to be an intrinsic part of the Mubarak regime and the Muslim Brotherhood's Muhammad Mursi,

---

[47] See for instance the SCAF supra-constitutional communiqué issued in November 2011, which gave the army autonomy from oversight, declared the army the guardian of constitutional legitimacy and gave SCAF alone the right to discuss matters related to the defense budget. See Yasmine Fathi, "SCAF's Proposal for Constitution 'Abuses Will of the People,' Charge Critics," *Ahram Online* (November 3, 2011), https://english.ahram.org.eg/NewsContent/1/0/25802/Egypt/0/SCAFs-proposal-for-constitution-abuses-will-of-the.aspx. The SCAF withdrew the document following protests on the streets but it continued to act as the de facto ruler of the nation.

[48] SCAF's July 9, 2012, statement giving the military council broad powers in the name of continuity.

[49] See Wael Nawara, "Why General Sisi Should Not Run for President of Egypt," *Al-Monitor* (September 20, 2013), www.al-monitor.com/originals/2013/09/generalsisipresidentelection.html?amp

[50] David Hearst and Abdel-Rahman Hussein, "Egypt's Supreme Court Dissolves Parliament and Outrages Islamists," *The Guardian* (June 14, 2012), amp.theguardian.com/world2012/jun/14/Egypt-parliament-dissolved-supreme-court

would uphold democracy over a return to autocracy by giving power
to Mursi with around 52% of the votes. And so, on June 30, 2012, and
under pressure from the United States to turn power over to the win-
ner of the elections, the SCAF relinquished authority to the first elected
civilian president in Egyptian history, Mohammad Mursi.

This was not the liberal start Egyptian liberals and social democrats
were hoping for. Neither the Muslim Brotherhood nor the military were
committed to the political and socioeconomic transformation the civil
rights activists had risked everything to achieve. The Islamists' ability
to gain control of the legislative as well as the executive branches was
indeed experienced as the return of authoritarian rule. At the same time,
the secularist parties' fragmentation and inability to choose one leader
facilitated if not ensured the ascendancy of Mursi to the presidency.[51]

The Mursi presidency did not make things easier on the liberals.
It began to actively retreat from all previously made promises, and to
antagonize many of its opponents, including SCAF. Between August
and November 2012, the new government issued a number of constitutional decrees and a temporary constitutional declaration (all replacing the previous constitutional amendments passed by SCAF in 2011)
that granted the president far-reaching powers, as well as a say in who
continued the drafting of the constitution if the Administrative Judiciary
Court were to find the current Constituent Assembly (tasked with drafting the constitution) illegitimate. More specifically, the constitutional
decrees consolidated the power of the army and the Ministry of Interior,
and more broadly the power of the executive, namely the president, over
the legislative, including the power to create, promulgate, and object to
legislation.[52] Mursi also issued a decree that made the president and the
upper house, the Shura Council, immune from judicial oversight, and
that let him appoint the new general prosecutor.[53] He had also drafted
bills to monitor and potentially control NGOs, to suppress protests and
restrict freedom of speech, all in the name of the national interest and
the revolution. At the heart of these provisions was the Islamists' fear
that the judiciary would intervene to void the elections, as they had
done with earlier ones.[54] It was also an attempt to counter the expected

---

[51] Dunne and Hamzawi, "Egypt's Secular Political Parties."
[52] Ahmed Aboulenein, "Morsy Assumes Power: Sacks Tantawi and Anan, Reverses
Constitutional Decree and Reshuffles SCAF," *Daily News Egypt* (August 12, 2012),
https://dailynewsegypt.com/2012/08/12/morsy-assumes-power-sacks-tantawi-
and-anan-reverses-constitutional-decree-and-reshufles-scaf/
[53] Dunne and Hamzawi, "Egypt's Secular Political Parties."
[54] Noueihed and Warren, *The Battle for the Arab Spring*, p. 119.

dissolution of the Islamist-dominated Constituent Assembly, which was finalizing the draft of the new constitution to be approved in a referendum on December 15. To the liberals, Mursi's decisions spelled a return to dictatorship.

The November decrees forced the remaining few liberals to resign in vain from the Constituent Assembly and led 25 rights groups to reject the constitutional changes and to file a lawsuit against the draft constitution.[55] Liberals charged the government with violations of freedom of speech, arrests on political grounds and attempts to control the judiciary. As mentioned earlier, el-Baradei, Moussa, and other leaders would form the NSF after a meeting in the headquarters of the Wafd party in Cairo. The NSF united a group of liberal and secularist parties that felt especially concerned by Mursi's presidential decisions.

Liberals also rallied on the streets in the biggest cities, demanding greater diversity in the Constituent Assembly, the annulment of the November decrees and cancelation of the referendum on the draft constitution planned for the 15th of December. They argued that the new government should review its decision to present the constitution to a referendum before the highest court in the land had the chance to review the legality of the assembly drafting it. This was important in the name of democracy and in order to salvage Egypt's democratic transition, explained the spokesperson of the NSF.[56] The street rallies and public meetings amassed strong popular participation, and spelled a new wave of revolutionary activity, which forced the government to repeal some components of the announced changes. The legislative prerogatives were delegated to the sitting Consultative Council and the immunity of presidential decrees and decisions from scrutiny and inquiry including by the public was annulled. However, the new government refused to take back the right to interfere in the judiciary by appointing the new general prosecutor.[57] Furthermore, the government went against the liberals' demands to give the draft of the constitution time to be publicly discussed, and continued its push to hold a referendum on the draft constitution on December 15.

The referendum ended with 63.8% in favor of the army and Islamist-backed constitution and 36.2% against it.[58] But the voter turnout was

---

[55] Lesch, "The Authoritarian State's Power," p. 142.
[56] "Egypt's Morsi Rescinds Controversial Decree," *Aljazeera* (December 9, 2012), www.aljazeera.com/news/2012/12/9/egypts-morsi-rescinds-controversial-decree
[57] Dunne and Hamzawi, "Egypt's Secular Political Parties." Noueihed and Warren, *The Battle for the Arab Spring*, pp. 120–121.
[58] Dunne and Hamzawi, "Egypt's Secular Political Parties."

only 33% of eligible voters, thus casting doubts on the legitimacy of the referendum and the Constitution in its entirety. The document itself was not as authoritarian as some had characterized it to be. For instance, it enshrined the principles of democracy and regular rotation of powers and limited presidential terms to 2 four-year terms, a significant improvement on the 1971 constitution, which allowed an unlimited number of terms for a president once elected. The new constitution declared all citizens equal, although was intentionally and typically vague and failed to make specific provisions on women's rights and minority rights. It enshrined freedom of speech although it also included a provision that protected prophets and individuals from "insults."[59] The new constitution was thus democratic to a certain degree, but illiberal in many ways: It gave the president the right to appoint the heads of independent bodies and regulatory agencies charged with supervising his/her work, to veto laws, and to appoint judges to Egypt's highest court. The constitution also legalized military trials of civilians in the case of offenses against the military. And it created a new government-appointed council to supervise the media and to "observe the values and constructive traditions of society."[60]

The Mursi government's failure to set Egypt on a liberal*ish* path put the entire country on a slippery slope towards instability especially as it antagonized a large part of the population. And while its compromises satisfied some liberal leaders who were relieved to see that the democratic process was safeguarded and looked forward to implementing changes over time, the entire environment seemed prone to reactionary and at times inflexible and rigid politics. Further, a majority of activists and politicians, but also women and Copts (Egypt's Christian minority), viewed the new government's policies and decisions as attempting to impose the Islamists' will over that of other citizens, bringing to the fore fears that the autocratic and monist order was creeping back in.

With so much at stake, millions took to the streets for a second time to call for early elections and support the military coup against Mursi at the end of June 2013. Liberals were again divided between those who supported the military intervention, thinking the constitution could be better drafted to safeguard freedoms and rights, and others who were worried about the integrity of the electoral system, and were more suspicious of the army and wanted the military out of politics as soon as possible.

---

[59] Noueihed and Warren, *The Battle for the Arab Spring*, p. 121.
[60] Selim, "Egypt under SCAF and the Muslim Brotherhood," p. 192.

No matter which side one took, overall, time was conspiring against the liberals and liberalism in general. The complexity and criticality of the situation at the political level denied them the time to think of better strategies to organize, to negotiate as part of an attempt to ensure respect for a liberal environment in which freedoms are safeguarded, and also to come up with a long-term plan instead of getting stuck in a reactionary mode.

At the cultural level, Egypt seemed for a moment to be thriving. Freedom of expression was flourishing on TV shows, in newspapers articles, and on the news in general. Prominent actors such as Khalid al-Nabawi and Amr Waked, and directors Dawud Abd al-Sayed and Khaled Yousef, became vocal about the need to change and endorse liberal democracy. Actor and human rights activist Khaled Abol Naga – who had been an ardent supporter of women's rights and children's rights since the mid-2000s – organized concerts, events, and candle-lit vigils in support of the revolutionaries and their ideas. Bassem Youssef, an equivalent to the American broadcaster Jon Stewart, hosted a satirical news program, *el-Bernameg* (the program), from 2011 to 2014. The show was first broadcast on ONTV, owned by liberal businessman Naghib Swaris, then on CBC. It featured many writers and artists and politicians who spoke freely about their ideas, their work, and their activism. Millions tuned in every week to watch *el-Bernameg*, which had become a huge hit in the entire region, so much so that the show received 200,000,000 hits on its online Youtube channel.

But the show was too popular while also being too critical of the new Mursi leadership as well as of the military regime following the ousting of Mursi. It was indeed representative of a true liberal program, enjoying and aspiring to help shape what it thought was a nascent liberal democratic environment. But the environment would turn out to be not liberal enough, or at least not yet. Youssef was accused of circulating false news, of disrespecting the president, in addition to disrespecting Islam. Youssef appeared in court donning an oversized hat, similar to a hat Mursi had worn during a visit to Pakistan and that Youssef had mocked during his show.[61] He was fined and the case stopped there. Youssef continued to make fun of events and the people behind them, cautioning Egyptians not to return to the security mentality of previous regimes.

---

[61] Joel Gordon, "Egypt's New Liberal Crisis," in Dalia F. Fahmy and Daanish Faruqi (eds.), *Egypt and the Contradictions of Liberalism: Illiberal Intelligentsia and the Future of Egyptian Democracy* (London: Oneworld Publications, 2017), p. 330.

Rise of Military Dictatorship

The Mursi Islamist-dominated government would last in office from June 2012 to July 3, 2013. As explained earlier, Mursi was disappointing to too many who had risked everything to topple autocracy and who yearned for freedom of expression, freedom of action including of assembly, and for their civil rights as citizens. His polarizing and majoritarian attitude and his attempt to interfere in the judiciary gave a green light for the military to continue its interference in order to assert its will. There were some within the April 6 movement who supported this interference, as well as liberals such as Abu al-Ghar, Amr Musa, and ElBaradei himself for a period of time (more on this hereinafter).

Less than a year after the army had removed and arrested Mursi[62], Chief-General Abdel Fattah al-Sisi was elected president (in May 2014). This began a new phase that heralded new lows for Egyptians in general and for Egypt's liberals more specifically. Most secularists (Wafd and Free Egyptians included) and the many parties that emerged post-2011 sided with the new government or remained silent. Some who had joined liberal initiatives and even fought for liberal ideals under the Mubarak regime, such as Abu el-Ghar and Saad Eddin Ibrahim, and even Mubarak's executive director, Dalia Ziada, became part of the For the Love of Egypt Coalition created by General Ehab Saad of the general intelligence services, a coalition that gave significant support and credibility to General Sisi.

Others held fast to their liberal convictions, and thus turned out to be more committed to their ideals than fearful of the Islamists, such as Hamzawi and Ayman Nour. Very soon after the rise of Sisi, el-Baradei, as well as many young activists such as Ahmed Maher and Esraa Abdel Fattah, became targets of the new government.[63] Then in July 2013, Nour publicly refused to support the military's deployment against Mursi and the Muslim Brotherhood. He explained that only liberals and liberalism could save Egypt from tyranny:

I am not a terrorist and [el]Baradei is not a terrorist, but the regime deals with us ... in a more violent way than they do with Islamists. You also have another internal issue that we as liberals, since the March 1954 crisis, have ... with military in government. After January 25 [2011], we were shouting slogans: let the reign of the military fall, well before Sisi came to political life. During

---

[62] David D. Kirkpatrick, "Army Ousts Egypt's President; Morsi Is Taken into Military Custody," *The New York Times* (July 3, 2013), www.nytimes.com/2013/07/04/world/middleeast/egypt.html

[63] Dunne and Hamzawi, "Egypt Secular Parties."

7 July [and the military coup against Mursi], a small number of liberals [supported the coup] ... but they left on the first stop ... The ones still on board that train are not liberal forces. They are the parties allied to Mubarak and some pro-Nasserites, who see similarity between the image of the military under Nasser and the military under Sisi. There is no solution for the crisis going on in Egypt but to have a liberal solution that refuses elimination and believes in the national partnership.[64]

Nour felt compelled to leave the country following a phone conversation with Sisi in July 2013 in which he felt directly threatened. Indeed, Nour became one of the first martyrs of the liberal cause against the military chief Sisi when a lawsuit requesting to rescind his Egyptian citizenship was filed against him. The lawsuit was launched because of his public defiance of the military-instated roadmap that was announced on July 3, 2013.[65]

Nour would not be the only victim. The new Sisi administration launched a massive crackdown on all of the Islamists and the liberals who refused to work within the restrictive confines imposed by the military.[66] This crackdown included intellectuals, journalists, professors, satirists, artists, and actors among others. For instance, both Amro Waked and Khaled Abol Naga had to leave the country.[67] The military regime indeed did not tolerate any liberal or illiberal opposition, and the Sisi government issued a number of draconian laws to control public life. Protest Law 107 was published in November 2013, a law that the elected Mursi government would not have been able to issue. This is because contrary to Mursi, the new military rulers enjoyed the full backing of the security forces. The law stipulates that gatherings of more than ten people require permission from the State, thus giving the Ministry of Interior the tools to control protests and public gatherings, and the police the right to use lethal force, and to imprison demonstrators for up to seven years.[68]

Law 136 was issued on October 27, 2014, and placed most public buildings under the security and protection of the military judiciary, thus controlling as much public space as possible. The thousands of

[64] David Hearst, "Interview with Egyptian Opposition Leader Ayman Nour," *Middle East Eye* (2015), www.middleeasteye.net/news/exclusive-interview-egyptian-opposition-leader-ayman-nour
[65] "Court to consider withdrawing Ayman Nour's Citizenship," *Cairo Post* (January 23, 2014), https://archive.vn/20140131075204/http://thecairopost.com/news/78414/politics/court-to-consider-withdrawing-ayman-nours-citizenship#selection-465.7-469.203
[66] Abdalla, "Youth Movements in the Egyptian Transformation," p. 48.
[67] Both actors would be accused of treason in 2019.
[68] Lesch, "The authoritarian State's Power," p. 148.

protestors who demonstrated in buildings or on roads that were by then under the protection of the military thus faced military trials. Indeed, the prosecutor general shifted 700 cases that dated back to 2013 to military judges. A new law on terrorist activity and entities defined a terrorist group as any group that intends, "to advocate by any means to disturb public order or endanger the safety of the community and its interests, or risk its security, or harm national unity." It defined "terrorist" in extraordinarily broad terms: In addition to language about violence and threats of violence, the law left it to the authorities to decide if actions had harmed "national unity" or the environment or natural resources, or had impeded the work of public officials or the application of the constitution or the laws. A "terrorist" became anyone who supported such an entity – support that could include "providing information" that "impedes the work of public officials"; further, "application of the Constitution" became a potential terrorist offense.[69] This meant that human rights groups as well as journalists, writers, artists, TV hosts and political parties members could all be open to accusations of being terrorists.[70] An additional decree was added in 2015 that shielded the military and police from legal penalties when they used force against prisoners and fining anyone for writing statements that contradicted the official version of events of the military or the police. These new laws supplemented existing Penal Code articles such as 98(f), which prescribed prison and a fine for "exploiting religion" in any manner that "promotes extremist ideologies," "stirs sedition," disparages "any divine religion" and prejudices "national unity."[71]

Tens of thousands of political dissidents were detained. Others were banned from appearing on TV or radio stations, and journalists were banned from writing critical reports about the political apparatus. Outspoken journalists and TV hosts who were critical of the State were forced off air.[72] This became the fate of Bassem Youssef, who was forced to resign following the rise of Sisi to power. The third and last season of the program *el-bernameg* had focused on the military coup, then the new government under Abdel Fattah al-Sisi, and finally General Sisi himself. The show was canceled shortly after the critique of Sisi, and Youssef was accused of slandering the leader of the nation and summoned to court. The court verdict condemned satirical television shows, and accused

---

[69] Joe Stork, "Egypt's Political Prisoners," *Open Democracy* (March 6, 2015), www.hrw .org/news/2015/03/06/egypts-political-prisoners
[70] Lesch, "The Authoritarian State's Power," p. 149.
[71] Stork, "Egypt's Political Prisoners."
[72] Lesch, "The Authoritarian State's Power," pp. 154–155.

Youssef of disturbing public peace and security. Youssef had to tread very carefully but he could not ignore a claim, backed by the Sisi regime, that Egyptian military doctors had found a cure for cancer and for AIDS. In June 2014, he announced that he could no longer stand the intensifying censorship and had to cancel his show.[73] He later had to flee the country, thus becoming one of the many liberal victims of the new military regime.[74]

Hundreds of NGOs also had to close their doors. Further, about 13 new prisons were built.[75] Someone like Belal Fadl, a columnist and a screenwriter, who once wrote, "the government should be proud of its care for the mentally ill: 'Egypt is the only country that allows the mentally challenged to reach decision-making circles'" was blacklisted for writing a column ridiculing the promotion of General Sisi to the rank of field marshal.[76] Blogger and student Karim Ashraf Mohamed al-Banna was given a three-year sentence for a Facebook post that was perceived as promoting atheism.[77]

Thus the renewed repressive environment impacted many dissenters, including all pro-democracy groups and liberal activists. The Sisi government also filed criminal charges against prominent liberal intellectuals and political leaders like Professors Emad Shahin and Amr Hamzawy, who had criticized the military takeover. Liberal activists and the new generation of liberals faced the same fate. April 6 Movement liberal activists such as Ahmad Maher, Ahmad Douma, and Muhammad Adel were found guilty of organizing unauthorized protest in November 2013, and were sentenced to 3 years in prison for violating law 107, among other charges.[78] Others who also protested military trials of civilians, such as Alaa Abdel-Fattah (a prominent opposition activist who has been in and out of jail since the days when Hosni Mubarak was president), activists Yara Salam and Mona Seif (Alaa Abd el- Fattah's sister), Nazly Hussein, and Salma Said, as well as human rights lawyers like Ahmed Heshmat, Mohamed Abdelaziz, and Osama al-Mahdy, and

[73] Gordon, "Egypt's New Liberal Crisis," p. 332.
[74] Interview with Bassem Youssef, "Scaling Free Speech: The Reputation and Replication of AlBernamag," (October 14, 2015), www.youtube.com/watch?v=H0RK-yhZsZQ
[75] Zvi Bar'el, "60,000 Political Prisoners and 1,250 Missing: Welcome to the New Egypt," *Haaretz* (September 11, 2016), www.haaretz.com/middle-east-news/ .premium-60-000-political-prisoners-and-1-250-missing-welcome-to-the-new-egypt-1.5440308
[76] Mayy El-Sheikh, "A Voice of Dissent in Egypt is Muffled but not Silent," *The New York Times* (May 2, 2014), www.nytimes.com/2014/05/03/world/middleeast/an-egyptian-voice-of-dissent-is-muffled-but-not-silenced.html
[77] Stork, "Egypt's Political Prisoners."
[78] Ibid.

journalists such as Ahmad Ragab and Rasha Azab, were all charged with and convicted of violating law 107. Before being charged, Rasha Azab, Mona Seif and Nazly Hussein were beaten up by the police and dumped in the desert.[79]

Ahmad Maher, who had initially supported the military coup against the Mursi government, became vocal about his "stupidity" in supporting the military intervention against the Brotherhood. He realized that the military that he thought would safeguard the revolution was reasserting everything the protestors rose against in January 25, 2011.[80] Emad Shahin was sentenced to death in absentia for conspiring to undermine national security and for espionage. Shahin, a well-known academic and professor of political science, had denounced the military's project of mass political exclusion, and had written about mass killings and mass arrests committed since Sisi's rise to power.[81] The April 6 Youth Movement was finally entirely banned in April 2014, accused of defaming the State.[82]

The 2015 parliamentary elections were rigged. As expected, the pro-Sisi bloc won the majority of seats. The new State declared its intention of focusing on combatting terrorism and curbing Islamism, with little reference to anything else. Repression became official, forceful, and in plain sight. Overall, more than 40,000 were arrested.[83] Egyptians and liberals thus suddenly woke up to a newly powerful, violent, and despotic regime, and saw the State's determination to prevent pluralism and liberal values and practices in every way possible.[84] Even co-opted parties such as the Free Egyptians Party and the Social Democratic Party were divided and weakened through State manipulation. The "security crisis"

---

[79] Sarah El Deeb, "A Sinister Night for 3 Women in Egypt Protest Wave," *Associated Press* (November 28, 2013).

[80] Stork, "Egypt's Political Prisoners."

[81] Emad El-Din Shahin, "Sentenced to Death in Egypt: How I Became Defendant 33 – Yet Another Casualty of the Return to Military Rule," *The Atlantic* (May 19, 2015), www.theatlantic.com/international/archive/2015/05/death-sentence-egypt-emad-shahin/393590/

[82] Leila Fadel, "Examining the Years since Egypt's Arab Spring," *NPR Morning Edition* (February 11, 2015), www.npr.org/2015/02/11/385396424/examining-the-4-years-since-egypts-arab-spring; April 6 movement democratic Front split from April 6 movement, in Spring 2011. Leaders: Tarek Alkholy, Amr Ezz, Yasser Shams Aldden, Selim Alhwary. Both movements banned by an Egyptian court on April 28, 2014. See "We Will Not Be Silenced: April 6, after Court Order Banning Group," *Ahram Online* (April 28, 2014).

[83] Guerin, "Revolution a Distant Memory as Egypt Escalates Repression"; Lesch, "The Authoritarian State's Power," p. 148.

[84] Mohamad Elmasry, "Egypt's Protests: Sisi's Iron Fist Is No longer Enough," *Middle East Eye* (September 30, 2019), www.middleeasteye.net/opinion/egypt-protests-sisi-iron-fist-is-no-longer-enough

claimed by the new political leadership meant that blind obedience was expected from everyone, co-opted or not.

By 2016, all serious opposition parties and groups were banned and opposition media shut down. According to the Arabic Network for Human Rights Information, "nearly 106,000 Egyptians were incarcerated in 504 prisons, over 60,000 of them are political prisoners and detainees. The regime spent $95 million alone on Gamasa General Prison, at a time when Egypt has agreed a $12-billion loan from the International Monetary Fund ... 1,250 people have disappeared in the basements of Egypt's jails, and about whom there is no information ...."[85] The Egyptian Council for Human Rights felt the need to develop a new phone application, iProtect, that allows activists to send text messages alerting their contacts about their whereabouts, and an email with similar information to the Human Rights Council. The application is disguised as a calculator to avoid the scrutiny of police officers checking their cell phone. It is meant to locate arrestees and send lawyers to them before they disappear.[86]

Why the Defeat?

There are a number of reasons why liberals were unable to translate their mobilization into assertive leadership and larger sociopolitical change in line with their goals.[87]

Firstly, liberals failed to present a united front at the institutional or party level, which is not so different from other liberals worldwide, but deadly within the context of a systemic transition away from dictatorship.[88] This could be related to their approach. Indeed, their shift in focus in the 1970s away from the institution of the State and from the paternalistic role of the intellectual and the leader as part of an attempt to engage with and be closer to the people (see Chapters 2 and 3) while also avoiding the repressive State made them vulnerable in an environment that now required assertive, decisive, and recognized leadership. Secondly, the many years of awareness raising by working tacitly, horizontally, and independently in smaller groups – in order to bypass the authoritarian State – impacted upon the liberals' ability to work as a collective within

---

[85] Bar'el, "60,000 Political Prisoners and 1,250 Missing."
[86] Ibid.
[87] Karim Emile Bitar, "The Dilemmas of Arab Liberalism," *Your Middle East* (March 12, 2014), www.yourmiddleeast.com/opinion/the-dilemmas-of-arab-liberalism_22184)
[88] This inability to present a united front is not new, it is symptomatic of the authoritarian context in which the opposition, including the liberals, have to work. For more on this, see Dina Shehata, *Islamists and Secularists in Egypt: Opposition, Conflict, and Cooperation* (Abingdon and New York: Routledge, 2010), pp. 51–82.

a hierarchical structure with clear leadership in order to compete and win elections. Thirdly, as amply discussed earlier, their divisions regarding how to deal with the possible threat of the illiberal Islamists divided their ranks and empowered the illiberal forces. Fourthly, their focus on complex issues such as human rights, tolerance, and separation of powers also weakened their position as political leaders to a people looking for a transition towards freedoms and rights, but also towards concrete stability and security. Certainly the liberals could have spent more time addressing how they planned on providing for stability. Overall, their rational sober messaging failed to stir people's emotions at that specific liminal moment. Fifthly, an added impasse was that the young leaders, so used to working outside formal channels, refused to join established or nascent political parties.[89] Finally, the liberals struggled to recalibrate their methods in a matter of months in order to reclaim their place of impact in the transition and to achieve what was needed in order to recapture the State, namely to create a hierarchical structure that would bring together all liberals in order to showcase a leadership and produce a concrete political program. The result is that both the army and the Islamists were able to undermine the liberals' work.

But the miscarriage of the revolution was not entirely a result of the liberals' failings, far from it. The success of SCAF in bringing back the autocratic order was also the result of regional (from Saudi Arabia and the UAE) and international backing (from Russia) and tacit approval (from the United States and the EU). Indeed, although leaders of powers such as the EU and the United States claim that democracy promotion is an implicit goal of their foreign policy, they also have interests that are often more compelling such as regional stability, trade, and more importantly, a steady energy supply into the international market.[90] It is against the background of this realist logic that a military chief like al-Sisi was "allowed" to violently disregard the revolutionary movement against him and SCAF in 2011–2012, to topple an elected government in 2013, and to reinstate brutal dictatorship in Egypt in 2014.

This failure of Western leadership – and of their top advisors – to uphold democratization is not new, indeed, as we have seen throughout this work, liberal leaders have historically played a negative and at times

---

[89] Dunne and Hamzawi, "Egypt's Secular Political Parties"; And yet youth movements in Egypt had proved capable of framing the issue of regime change effectively, leading ultimately to contention on the streets and the toppling of Mubarak. See: Sika, "Youth Political Engagement in Egypt," pp. 181–199.

[90] Oz Hassan, "Undermining the Transatlantic Democracy Agenda? The Arab Spring and the Saudi Arabia's Counteracting Democracy Strategy," *Democratization* 22:3 (2015), p. 480.

a destructive role when it comes to supporting liberal democratic groups and individuals in the Middle East. It remains significantly more appealing for democratically elected leaders to support autocrats and to rely on their repressive measures to stabilize the Arabic-speaking region, no matter how much the region's liberals and pro-democracy activists suffer or what they say about the destabilizing and far-reaching impact of the autocratic systems in place.

Indeed even the United States and the EU stood by during the pre-Sisi and post-Mubarak transitional phase, emphasizing economic stability and economic liberalization rather than pushing for democracy and human rights.[91] It is within this logic that President Macron invited al-Sisi to France in December 2020 in order to discuss trade liberalization and other geostrategic interests, thus effectively disregarding Sisi's abuses of power at home.[92] This focus on economic liberalization as a means of ultimately promoting political liberalization (consistent with the still-disputed modernization theory) has not really led to democratic transformations and liberalization in the region. If anything, it has inadvertently empowered illiberal regimes, that have instead undertaken only cosmetic changes, as well as turning to other powerful funders when needed. For instance, with Sisi's rise to power, Saudi Arabia was able to replace the United States and the EU as patrons by simply providing more financial assistance to the new despot, while the United States and the EU stood by.[93] Börzel tells us that, "[c]ountervailing democracy promotion is not the same as autocracy promotion. Yet, the outcome of such activities may be still autocracy enhancing."[94] Nowhere is this more palpable than in Egypt and Syria, as we will see in the Syrian section of this chapter.

The Sisi regime and the military establishment in general have especially benefitted from their close ties to their autocratic patrons in Saudi

---

[91] Hassan, "Undermining the Transatlantic Democracy Agenda," pp. 483–484; Danya Greenfield and R. Balfour, *Arab Awakening: Are the US and EU Missing the Challenge?* (Washington, DC: Atlantic Council, 2012), p. 2; Michael Peel, Camilla Hall, and Heba Saleh, "Saudi Arabia and UAE Prop Up Egypt Regime with Offer of $8bn," *Financial Times* (July 10, 2013), https://amp.ft.com/content/7e066bdc-e8a2-11e2-8e9e-00144feabdc0

[92] Macron had to even award Sisi the country's highest award, the Grand Cross of the Legion of Honor, an honor that is given to heads of states who visit France. The award is being challenged by Ghad al-Thawra Party in France's Courts. See: "Macron gave Sisi France's highest award on Paris visit: official," *France 24* (December 10, 2020); and Ghad al-Thawra Facebook Page.

[93] Hassan, "Undermining the Transatlantic Democracy Agenda," p. 485.

[94] T. A. Brözel, "The Noble West and the Dirty Rest? Western Democracy Promoters and Illiberal Regional Powers," *Democratization* 22:3 (2015), p. 524 (pp. 519–535).

Arabia and the United Arab Emirates. The two countries have acted as al-Sisi's main backers against the Mursi government and the Muslim Brothers (perceived as a threatening alternative to the two self-proclaimed religious regimes), and against the homegrown liberal movement that was effectively deemed as threatening to the autocratic regimes in the region more generally. Saudi Arabia and the UAE's financial support has further allowed Sisi to avoid negotiating or compromising with Western powers when it comes to easing repression on pro-democracy activists and allowing for some freedoms within the country.[95]

Finally, Sisi has developed ties with yet another powerful illiberal power, Russia, which has provided his leadership with financial, security, diplomatic, and military support in return for a presence and increasing influence in Egypt. President Putin visited Egypt in 2015 and 2017, and Sisi has visited Moscow three times since 2014, with regular bilateral visits between government officials.[96] Moscow is currently building a nuclear plant in Dabaa city, Russian airplanes and military presence was allowed near the border with Libya, and the Russians have signed arms sales contracts with Egypt totaling about 3.5 billion dollars.[97]

The Arab Spring has indeed revealed not only some of the inexperience of liberals, but also the crisis of liberalism worldwide. The inability of the liberal world leaders to provide meaningful and impactful help and to support Arab liberals in their quest has been confusing and ultimately deadly to many activists and intellectuals within the region, who wonder if the liberal world would ever back them up (a theme that is also pertinent in the Syria section of this chapter).

Hope Is not Dead

The present bleakness, with the revolution a distant memory and the future seemingly hopeless, has devastated most liberals and democrats. And yet these activists and intellectuals are not done yet. Once

---

[95] Hassan, "Undermining the Transatlantic Democracy Agenda?," pp. 479–495; Line Khatib, "Challenges of Representation and Inclusion," pp. 131–145.

[96] Dalia Ghanem Yazbeck and Vasily Kuznetsov, "The 'Comrades' in North-Africa," in Nicu Popescu and Stanislav Secrieru (eds.), *Russia's Return to the Middle East: Building Sandcastles?* (Luxembourg: EU Institute for Security Studies, 2018), p. 74.

[97] Yehia Hamed, "Joe Biden's Administration Should Start Listening to all Egyptians," *Middle East Eye* (November 17, 2020), www.middleeasteye.net/opinion/joe-bidens-administration-should-start-listening-all-egyptians; Roland Dannreuther, "Russia and the Arab Spring: Supporting the Counter-Revolution," *Journal of European Integration* 37:1 (2015), pp. 77–94; Yazbeck and Kuznetsov, "The 'Comrades' in North-Africa," p. 75.

ingrained, the idea is there to stay and to flourish despite the setbacks, says one liberal activist.[98] Activists, like Shahin, think the youth that broke the barrier of fear cannot be intimidated.[99] In the words of Nazly Hussein, "Some died for their dream ... This dream is my compass and until it comes true, I will stay on the streets."[100] Bassem Youssef asserted in 2015, "challenging the status quo ... is happening all over the Arab World. The status quo is not sustainable."[101] Many other liberals agree it is no time for resignation.

Social activism remains one way to resist repression and to maintain hope. Against this background, liberals say that they have so much to learn but that they will continue trying to liberate their country. And while American and European political leaderships seem apathetic to the liberals' pleas in the Arab region, parties and organizations such as ALDE (Alliance of Liberals and Democrats for Europe), the Liberal International, and the German Friedrich Nauman Foundation for Freedom have pledged to increase their support of the Arab liberals.[102] Human rights groups that have survived the Sisi regime such as the EIPR, the Arabic Network of Human Rights Information, the Human Rights Center for the Assistance of Prisoners, and el-Nadeem Center for Rehabilitation of Victims of Violence and Torture (shutdown in 2016) vow to continue working no matter what is hurled at them. Their hope and will become their most precious weapon.

Liberal parties have also continued to oppose the new military dictatorship and they remain active and hopeful. These include the Egypt Freedom Party, the Constitution Party (liberal) and the Dignity Party (social liberal), which together formed the Democratic Current Coalition in 2013. Strong Egypt (liberal Islamic), and Bread and Freedom (Social Democrat – Islamist) have also joined the movement, while the Social Democratic Party joined it later on. They have all continued to work from inside Egypt within the restricted political and social space

---

[98] Interview with author, December 2020.

[99] Fadel, "Examining the Years since Egypt's Arab Spring."; April 6 movement democratic Front split from April 6 movement, in Spring 2011. Leaders: Tarek Alkholy, Amr Ezz, Yasser Shams Aldden, Selim Alhwary. Both movements banned by an Egyptian court on April 28, 2014. See "We Will Not be Silenced: April 6, After Court Order Banning Group," *Ahram Online* (April 28, 2014).

[100] El Deeb, "A Sinister Night for 3 Women in Egypt."

[101] Interview with Bassem Youssef, "Scaling Free Speech: The Reputation and Replication of AlBernamag" (October 14, 2015), www.youtube.com/watch?v=H0RK-yhZsZQ

[102] Koert Debeuf, "From Arab Spring to Arab Revolution: Three years of ALDE Representation in the Arab World," in Ronald Meinardus (ed.), *Liberalism in the Arab World – Just a Good Idea?* (Cairo: Al-Mahrosa for Publishing, 2014), pp. 165–167.

that they have been allowed since 2014. It seems as if they are back to square one in the sense that they have to work on raising their profile and reasserting their narrative and ideals. To do so, they have issued press statements and conference releases that decry abuses of power and human rights, as well as reported on the draconian laws that target civil society activists and citizens. They have also worked with professional syndicates in their struggle against the security services interference. In the House of Representatives, the Civil Democratic Current (Dignity Party, Constitution Party, Socialist Popular Alliance, Freedom Egypt, Popular Current, Bread and Freedom, Socialist Party, Egyptian Social Democratic Party) has mobilized the MPs representing the Socialist Popular Alliance, the Social Democrats, and some independents, to organize an opposition platform in Parliament.[103]

Others who were forced to leave the country are working from outside the system such as the Ghad al-Thawra Party, and the Guardians of the Revolution. Nour explains,

There is no solution for the crisis going on in Egypt but to have a liberal solution that refuses elimination and believes in the national partnership. Thus, there is no exit from this crisis but to have two solutions: developing [nuancing] the voice of the Islamists and development of the behavior of the liberals, and to establish a partnership between the two.[104]

Nour and others within the Ghad Party and el-Baradei's followers proposed to form a shadow government that would encompass multiple political parties in order to ensure representation of the voice of the people.[105]

These liberals turned out to be right in their suspicions of the military, as the ranks of dissidents and human rights defenders who channeled the 2011 revolution have been fractured by mass arrests since 2013.[106] But the crackdown against them, although brutal and meant to stop them

---

[103] Dunne and Hamzawi, "Egypt's Political Secular Parties."

[104] David Hearst, "Interview with Egyptian Opposition Leader Ayman Nour," *Middle East Eye* (2015), www.middleeasteye.net/news/exclusive-interview-egyptian-opposition-leader-ayman-nour

[105] This was not the first time that the proposition for a parallel government was suggested. Al-Ghad Party and the National Association for Change thought of creating a parallel parliament in 2010 in the Ghad Party headquarters following the regime's rigged parliamentary elections, which at the time prompted Mubarak to say "let them have fun." See Esraa Abdel Fattah, "Loaded Victory: Egypt's Revolution and Where It Stands Post-30 June," in Meinrdus (ed.), *Liberalism in the Arab World*, p. 121.

[106] Ayman Nour, "Egypt's Choice is Clear: Democracy – or Chaos under Sisi," *Middle East Eye* (January 23, 2020), www.middleeasteye.net/opinion/repression-corruption-and-poverty-egypt-has-recipe-new-uprising)

once and for all[107], has not been a success. On September 20 and 21, 2019, thousands took to the streets to protest against al-Sisi across Egyptian cities, confirming that their fight for rights is not over. The protests followed an online video published by actor and contractor Mohammad Ali claiming that Sisi is engaged in flagrant corruption. "The Arab Spring is not over," says one activist. "It might not be making the news in any of the countries that could help us and others in the region achieve our dream of dignity and freedom, but activists and dissidents are still here, writing, listening, raising awareness, and protesting."[108] Surveys show activists are right to be hopeful. The Advocacy and Communications Director for Human Rights Watch's Middle East and North Africa office and one of the best investigative journalists in the region, Ahmed Benchemsi, reports, "… if we set aside media institutions and music celebrities, seven out of the 10 most followed Twitter accounts in Egypt are those of liberal commentators such as satirists Bassem Youssef and Belal Fadl or the secular politicians Mohamed ElBaradei, Hamdeen Sabahi, and Amr Hamzawy."[109]

And so the large crowds that gathered in Tahrir Square, the focal point of the 2011 uprising that toppled Mubarak, shouted again in 2019, "the people want to topple the regime" and "step down Sisi."[110] Of course this resulted in more crackdowns, as more than 4,000 individuals were arrested, including journalists, lawyers, and political leaders that had been in and out of prison before and throughout the Arab Spring, among them award-winning human rights lawyer Mahienour el-Massry, as well as prominent activists Esraa' Abdel-Fattah[111] and Alaa' Abdel Fattah.[112] But the goal remains, to move toward a liberal, peaceful, inclusive,

[107] For instance, Ayman Nour's Egyptian passport was not renewed, and he was accused of being a traitor and working against Egypt. See Mahmoud al-Shorbaji, "Hikim niha'i birafd tajdid jawaz safar ayman nour," *Masrawi* (June 6, 2020), www.masrawy .com/news/news_cases/details/2020/6/6/1803171)

[108] Author's conversation with Egyptian activist while visiting Dubai, May 2018.

[109] Ahmed Benchemsi, "Arab Liberalism Is Alive and Well, Thank You," *Free Arabs* (February 22, 2015), www.freearabs.com/index.php/ideas/102-stories/2166-jb-span-arab-liberalism-jb-span-is-alive-and-well

[110] Nadda Osman, "Egypt's Protests: Who Is Demonstrating and Who Is Being Arrested?" *Middle East Eye* (September 26, 2019), www.middleeasteye.net/news/ arrests-egyptian-anti-sisi-protesters-broken-down

[111] As mentioned earlier, Esraa Abdel Fattah was an active member of the Ghad Party and the Kefaya Movement, and was one of the initiators of the April 6 Movement. She also joined ElBaradei's National Association for Change in 2010, and co-founded the Egyptian Democratic Academy, which helped monitor the 2010 parliamentary elections.

[112] Osman, "Egypt's Protests"; "Egypt Detains Human Rights Lawyer Representing Anti-Sisi Protesters", *Middle East Eye* (September 22, 2019), www.middleeasteye.net/ news/egypt-detains-award-winning-human-rights-lawyer-representing-protesters

feminist, and humanist alternative that undermines the regime's narrative. Yet the regime is not going quietly, indeed, it added the BBC and Al Hurra TV channels to the list of 513 other websites already blocked in Egypt, and disrupted online messaging applications. Then there were the promises of political reform, including by the speaker of the parliament, who argued that repression is necessary to build a strong state and infrastructure.[113]

Still the opposition continues to push however. Thus in November 2019, member of the House of Representatives Ahmad Tantawi submitted a proposal for institutional reforms and to end Sisi's presidency in 2022 instead of 2024. On December 28, Muhammad Ali released the "Egyptian Consensus Document" with a list of main demands, which Ali claimed represented the consensus of a wide range of Egyptian opposition. The following day, the Egyptian National Action Group (ENAG), a group of Egyptians working to overthrow Egypt's military dictatorship, was launched with a consensus program to replace the Sisi regime. Ayman Nour has also helped create ENAG from exile.[114] The group reflects the liberal approach of inclusion and consensus creation. Nour announced that the group includes people from diverse political backgrounds including liberals, leftists, and Islamists who decided to "set [their] differences aside" in order to rid Egypt of its latest military dictatorship. The main values guiding ENAG are democracy, human dignity, justice, equality and freedom. Ayman explains that after more than six years of Sisi's vicious rule, the spirit that directed the Arab Spring has not faltered. It has only matured, and they are more determined than ever. In 2020, Nour addressed al-Sisi and his supporters:

You don't want to understand that there are no countries without disagreement in opinion and thought, and that disagreement is a healthy feature if it takes place within a democratic environment, and a binding social contract that does not eliminate any party and does not tie citizens' rights to the wishes of one leader ... I know that the problem of previous *mustabidin* (despots) and yourself is that you are arrogant and delude yourselves into thinking that you alone are patriotic while everyone else is a traitor, and that you are the reformers and the saviors, and that there are no reformists but you, and corruptors but those who

---

[113] Ezzeldine C. Fishere, "Egypt's Dictatorship Is Sitting on a Powder Keg," *Washington Post* (October 17, 2019), www.washingtonpost.com/opinions/2019/10/17/egypts-dictatorship-is-sitting-powder-keg/; MEE Staff, "Egypt's Parliament Speaker Favourably Compares Sisi to Hitler," *Middle East Eye* (October 2, 2019), www.middleeasteye.net/news/egypt-top-lawmaker-praises-hitler-parliament-speech

[114] "Egypt: Opponents of Sisi Launch Anti-Regime Group," *Middle East Monitor* (December 31, 2019), www.middleeastmonitor.com/20191231-egypt-opponents-of-sisi-launch-anti-regime-group/.

disagree with you … and the truth is that you are a disaster, and no good will come [to Egypt] unless you are gone …[115] [author's translation]

Like other liberal activists, Nour then asserted, "The Arab Spring is not over. What is less certain is how long it will take Western countries to realize how short-sighted they have been in failing the Egyptian people. The 'strongman policy' has only brought more instability and more support for extremists in the region. The costs may be much higher than the income from arms contracts. A genuine democratic transition will benefit everyone, especially compared with the chaos that will come if Sisi's rule continues."[116]

Other activists agree. Yehia Hamed writes, "I can clearly see something happening in our region. This wave of democratic unrest is not over and the counter-revolution allies have failed to convince Arabs everywhere that they can rule. The only means they use to silence anger are brutal ones. So far they have succeeded in keeping a lid on this kettle, but the time may soon come when they cannot – after the Covid epidemic dies down and the real impact of it on jobs and the economy makes itself felt."[117]

In this environment of political dictatorship, still-potent Islamism, poverty and widespread economic inequality, international betrayal of the liberal cause and a COVID-19 pandemic that has further empowered the despots, the future seems bleaker than ever. But it is within this bleakness that liberal activism is renewed and revitalized, and that lessons are learned for future opportunities. After all, liberalism seems almost an inevitable outcome of the autocratic setting, and thus ultimately inescapable.

Syria

According to an activist interviewed for this book, the Damascus Spring activists and intellectuals were not at all responsible for the protests that erupted across Syria in March 2011, rather, it is argued, those protests were the direct result of regime repression and a demonstration effect arising from the images of demonstrators rebelling in Tunisia, Egypt, Yemen, Libya, and Bahrain. The activist is not alone in his assertion. Multiple observers and analysts of Syrian politics agree that the

---

[115] Ayman Nour, "Al-Sisi ya'abbi-lnar wa nad'ual-'uqalaa bira fd siyasatihi," *Arabi21* (April 8, 2020), https://arabi21.com/story/1259526/أيمن-نور-السيسي-يلعب-بالنار-وندعو-العقلاء-لرفض-ممارساته

[116] Nour, "Egypt's Choice Is Clear."

[117] Hamed, "Joe Biden's Administration."

intellectuals and human rights advocates who have dedicated years and risked so much in their struggle to raise political awareness and provoke change in the country were not a meaningful force. And yet this narrative ignores the fact that leaders who were active during the Damascus Spring such as Michel Kilo, Riad Seif, Zaynab Lutafji, Suheir Atassi, and Razan Zaitouneh, were in the first demonstrations in 2011 and helped organize the first protests[118] as well as the first revolutionary committees (*tansiqiyat*). The demonstrators also demanded a number of rights that these intellectuals and advocates had nurtured for years: "the lifting of emergency laws, freedom, peace, democracy, dignity, and citizens' rights." Like in the Egyptian case, demonstrators focused on political liberalism rather than the need for economic egalitarianism and universal subsidies. They thus gave precedence to their political grievances, this despite the fact that the economic restructuring of the 2000s had been very hard on the poor and lower middle classes in both urban and rural settings, and had widened the gap between the rich and the poor while exponentially multiplying the wealth of a crony elite. Protestors expressed their adherence to "peaceful demonstrations" (*silmiyeh*), to freedom, to equality and justice, and to political inclusion. They chanted, "We are Syrians, we stand united," and their emphasis on unity and peace was a reminder to all that they stood together across socioeconomic cleavages against the repressive political order. When the regime started attacking the protestors, cities that included a majority of ethnic and religious minorities harbored mostly Sunni refugees, thus demonstrating "the protest movement's grassroots solidarity."[119]

The revolutionary spark that transformed the Syrian protests into a movement for complete political rupture started in the southern city of Dar'a, where 15 schoolboys had been arrested and tortured for anti-regime graffiti.[120] One hundred people were then killed as thousands

---

[118] Suheir Atassi, Razan Zaitouneh, and veteran activist Zaynab Lutafji were some of the first protestors in Damascus on February 22, 2011, protesting alongside about 150 others in support of the Libyan revolution. It was then that the slogan "traitor is he who kills his people" was shouted by Suheir Atassi. On her Facebook page she explains that it was Zainab Lutafji who whispered the slogan in her ear before everyone picked it up and started yelling it. Suheir Atassi was also one of the organizers of the protest at the Ministry of Interior in Damascus on March 16, 2011. Jonas Bergan Draege, "The Formation of Syrian Opposition Coalitions as Two-Level Games," *The Middle East Journal*, 70:2 (April 2016), p. 197.

[119] Joseph Daher, "Pluralism Lost in Syria's Uprising: How the Opposition Strayed from its Inclusive Roots," *The Century Foundation* (May 7, 2019), https://tcf.org/content/report/pluralism-lost-syrias-uprising/?agreed=1

[120] Radwan Ziadeh, "The Syrian Revolution: The Role of the 'Emerging Leaders'," in *Revolution and Political Transformation in the Middle East: Agents of Change* (Vol 1) (Washington DC: Middle East Institute, August 2011), p. 43.

took to the streets to protest the detention and torture of the boys. By the end of March, protests had spread to other cities, and by July 1st, more than 100,000 protestors gathered to openly question the legitimacy of the Syrian president Bashar al-Asad.[121] As demonstrations grew in size and multiplied, spreading across towns and the major cities including Aleppo, Hums, Hama and Damascus, so the actions of the military brigades grew and multiplied, with the aim of intimidating, detaining and killing the protestors. By May 2011, the Syrian military started besieging entire cities. And by September 2011, the country "had gone from hopeful popular demonstration to armed rebellion ...."[122] The UN estimates that in less than two years, more than 60,000 people were killed in Syria, most at the hands of the Syrian regime. The militarization of the revolt became almost a foregone conclusion as people felt the need to defend themselves against the regime's military and thugs (*shabiha*). By 2014, the UN announced that it could no longer keep track of the total number of deaths in Syria, an announcement that in effect allowed the Syrian regime and its patrons to do as they wished without outside scrutiny.

Activists Went to Work

In their attempts to rise to the magnitude of events and the possibility for change – change that had been thought to still be years away[123] – Syria's liberal opposition showed unity and reasserted their political positions against the regime by joining the protests. The first groups to materialize during the first year of the uprising were the Local Coordination Committees (LCC), the Syrian National Council (SNC), and The Free Syrian Army (FSA).[124]

---

[121] Mona Yacoubian, "Syria Timeline: Since the Uprising Against Assad," *United States Institute of Peace* (September 18, 2020), www.usip.org/syria-timeline-uprising-against-assad.

[122] El-Badawi, "Conflict and Reconciliation," p. 306.

[123] See the work of prominent activist Yassin al-Haj Saleh, *Al-thawra al-mustahila* (Beirut: al-mu'asasa al-'arabiya li al-dirasat wa al-nashr, 2017) in which he states that the "impossible revolution has taken place"!

[124] In addition to a left-leaning group, the National Coordination Council for Democratic Change (the NCC). The National Coordination Council for Democratic Change (NCC or NCB) was established soon after the LCC, in June 2011, with Hasan Abd al-Azim as its chairman. Although the NCC also imagined a liberal democratic Syria and worked to achieve that, the majority of those who signed the Damascus Declaration did not join it. Activists who had initially signed the NCC statement such as Michel Kilo then withdrew because its leaders were not able to unite a majority of the strands of the opposition and thus it remained more limited in its scope. Most of the 15 member parties in the NCC came from the leftist National Democratic Group, but the Bureau also included some Kurdish parties and independent intellectuals.

The LCC (*lijan al-tanseeq al-mahaliya* also known as *tansiqiyat*) were established in March 2011, as a loose umbrella network to coordinate on-the-ground activism. They included many of the Damascus Spring opposition leaders, as well as many youths, mostly university students who had witnessed and were actively part of and supported the Damascus Spring and its initiatives. The LCC eventually united under the presidency of their co-founder, lawyer, and human rights activist Razan Zaitouneh (more on Zaitouneh hereinafter).[125] Like their Egyptian counterparts, the LCC relied on social media, Skype rooms, and online communication and forums to consolidate their network, to coordinate protests, and to organize strikes and civil mutinies, to document war crimes and human rights abuses, and to keep the foreign media – banned from Syria at the start of the revolution – aware of events.[126] Activists were tech savvy and were able to breach the regime's media blackout and connect with the world's digital infrastructure. In so doing, they brought together a network of 70 groups responsible for managing the civil disobedience, for disseminating information, providing aid to those in need, as well as expanding and driving the movement all over Syria. They soon became the primary engine of the uprising and its mind and soul, playing a crucial role as it expanded into Damascus and its suburbs as well as into other cities such as Dar'a, Homs, Idlib, Baniyas, Hasakah, Qamishli, Hama, Raqqa and Suwaida, to name a few.

While these grassroots corps were not formally part of the political parties and groups of their predecessors, they were students and apprentices of the older generation of activists including young artists and actors, and they had formed groups and begun carrying out their activism around the need for liberal democratic change as early as 2009.[127] As stated above, they were especially active within schools and universities as well as in social and online forums, and asserted themselves as being the next generation of politically liberal activists in Syria. This generation also included Syrians in the diaspora (particularly in France, Britain, and Germany) who facilitated the activism as well as media outreach.

By 2012, there were around 400 coordinating committees doing work, this despite the regime's incredibly violent attempts to stop their efforts

---

[125] Fouad Gehad Marei, "Local Coordination Committees," in J. K. Zartman (ed.), *Conflict in the Modern Middle East: An Encyclopedia of Civil War, Revolutions, and Regime Change* (Santa Barbara, CA: ABC-CLIO, 2020), pp. 192–193.

[126] Zaina Erhaim, "How the Syrian Revolution Was Organized – And How it Unraveled," *Newlines Magazine* (March 16, 2021), https://newlinesmag.com/essays/how-the-syrian-revolution-was-organized-and-how-it-unraveled/

[127] Erhaim, "How the Syrian Revolution Was Organized."

and silence their leaders.[128] The committees were able to function partly by relying on their decentralized structure, and by focusing on neighborhoods, towns, and city suburbs – such as Dareya in Damascus – that they were familiar with and in which they had developed extensive and close knit networks of activists, journalists, and colleagues. These networks made it possible for them to escape the scrutiny and repression of a regime that had initially focused its efforts on controlling the cores of the major cities. Then each committee coordinated messages and tactics with other committees nationwide.

The LCC were able to gain the trust of many within and outside Syria because of the legitimacy that they gained by standing at the frontlines of the confrontation between the pro-democracy movement and the regime. Indeed, their members were the first to be imprisoned and to be killed; young activists such as Yahya Shurbaji who was a pacifist, Jihad Jamal, a journalist, and Hasan Azhari, a 5th-year pharmacology student, all arrested in 2012 and subsequently tortured to death.[129]

Communication became the most important tool to foster unity under a regime that aimed to choke off any political communication between activists and the general public inside and outside Syria, and that manipulated facts to disseminate false information and create alternative narratives. The LCC leaders quickly understood the need to push back against the regime's narrative. The LCC's bi-monthly newspaper titled *Rising For Freedom* (*tli'na 'al huriyeh* in colloquial Arabic) became an essential tool to set stories straight, to defend the cause of freedom and democracy and to raise the activists' morale, to promote peaceful resistance, and to share the LCC's social and political vision for Syria.[130] Another important newspaper was *Enab Baladi*, published online and in print in Dareya. *Enab Baladi* chronicled the revolution and imagined and planned for an eventual democratic and emancipated society. As one observer writes, "Incredibly, even after the regime recaptured Daraya and expelled its remaining inhabitants to Idlib in 2016, *Enab Baladi* continued to be published online – not simply as an homage to the town's memory, but as a necessary investment in the ongoing struggle against the regime … [as] emancipation begins in the imagination of Syria's dreamers and dissenters …."[131] Both *Rising for Freedom* and *Enab Baladi* continue to publish (on and off) alongside dozens of other blogs,

---

[128] Daher, "Pluralism Lost in Syria's Uprising."
[129] Erhaim, "How the Syrian Revolution Was Organized."
[130] For more on the magazine, see freedomraise.net
[131] Riad Alarian, "Imagining a Free Syria," *UNA-UK Magazine* (March 20, 2017), https://una.org.uk/imagining-free-syria

magazines, and newspapers that deal with the regime's misinformation, the displacement, the grief, and the loss, but also the hope and the work for human and citizens' rights and freedoms, and for discussing how the principles of constitutionalism and liberal democracy could (ultimately) be applied in the Syrian case.[132]

The LCC also organized social campaigns that helped in their efforts to build social capital and connect with and help the public, including those who had experienced torture and who were terrified of the regime's *shabiha* (thugs). Some of these campaigns include "Syria is Colorful," and "the Revolutionary Flag Represents Me," both initiatives launched to fight Islamist radicalization and the divisive narrative being propagated by the regime as well as the Islamists. Other initiatives are "Tomorrow Will be Better," which aims to help children and adults deal with the war and imagine a peaceful and bright future.[133] The committees focused on empowering women, providing food supplies, and on providing education and psychological support to children who were witnessing the instability and the violence first hand.

Initially, the LCC was against the militarization of the revolution, but by early 2012 it began to support it as they realized the extent to which the regime was willing to use violence against the civilian population and the peaceful protestors. They also began calling on the international community to actively take a stand against the oppressors within the region.

The LCC also assumed the responsibilities normally undertaken by government when services stopped in regime-controlled areas. So for example they acted as centers of civic authority, providing medical and legal services and administering humanitarian relief including distributing food supplies. They also helped form Local Administrative Councils in liberated territories, which relied on volunteers and which were self-governing, as well as delivering municipal services such as garbage collection and medical services. Further, they coordinated with the rest of the democratic movement as well as held democratic elections when they could.[134]

By August 2011, the increasing involvement of the Syrian Army in violently quelling the protests meant that some of the liberal dissenters were forced out of Syria in an attempt to avoid imprisonment, and thus

---

[132] Another prominent liberal Syrian newspaper that has provided Syrians with an online platform to discuss political issues since 2012 is aljumhuriya.net, which launched its English platform in 2016.

[133] "Local Coordination Committees of Syria" *Syria Untold* (June 24, 2014), https://syriauntold.com/2013/06/24/local-coordination-committees-of-syria/

[134] For more on Syria's Local Councils, see the National Coalition of Syrian Revolution and Opposition Forces website, at https://en.etilaf.org/

organized opposition meetings outside the country and with the help of Syrian expatriates. Thus the SNC was formed in Istanbul, Turkey on August 23, 2011. The SNC allowed the liberal opposition inside the country to re-unite with the exiled opposition, which was considered an integral part of the liberal opposition (see Chapter 3). This was not a new approach for the opposition – indeed, activist Ammar Abdulhamid and others often argued that the Syrian diaspora is an essential part of the Syrian opposition and that building a successful reform program relied on coordination between the inside and outside forces.[135] This approach is related to the autocratic reality within Syria, which had forced most political activists to leave their country even though they often wished to stay. Other activists were able to go in and out of Syria depending on the political environment at the time.

The SNC represented itself as the temporary leaders of the Syrian resistance and the coordinators of the transitional process toward a free and democratic Syria. Consisting of activists that had fought the regime for years, mostly the signatories of the Damascus Declaration such as Riad Seif, Suheir al-Atassi, and Michel Kilo, but also a number of Kurdish leaders who opposed the regime, representatives from the LCC, the Syrian Muslim Brothers, and independent and exiled liberals such as Bassma Kodmani, the SNC was considered a legitimate representative of the hopes and dreams of Syrians, and it enjoyed ample international support, at least at first. The SNC elected its first Chairman, Burhan Ghalioun, a prominent liberal activist and academic who lived and worked in France. In April 2012, more than 100 countries came together informally as the "Friends of Syria," and gave their recognition to and signaled their support for the SNC. It seemed as if Syrians finally had a strong, united actor that was going to work to create the liberal democratic home they had been dreaming and working for. The SNC goal was complete rupture with the autocratic order and its symbols. As they put it: to embody the aspirations of the Syrian Revolution, "to build a modern democratic, pluralistic, and civil state" by toppling the existing regime including all its operatives and symbols, supporting the peaceful revolution, representing all opposition forces and recognizing the diversity of the Syrian people.[136]

---

[135] Ammar Abdulhamid, "Syria: Mobilizing the Opposition," in Jeffrey Azarva, Danielle Pletka and Michael Rubin (eds.), *Dissent and Reform in the Arab World: Empowering Democrats* (American Enterprise Institute, 2008), p. 86, www.jstor.com/stable/resrep03025.14

[136] "Syrian National Council Mission and Program," www.syriancouncil.org/en/mission-statement.html

But morale started deteriorating quickly. While most of the members of the different groups agreed on upholding the principles of liberal democracy, they disagreed on how to achieve this goal within the volatile environment of the Syrian revolution. Some disagreed on the question of foreign intervention and on militarization of the revolution, others on whether they should engage in any dialogue with the Syrian regime and the Islamists. For instance, Syria's front-liners distrusted Western powers and the Gulf States and although they supported the use of arms "in cases of self defense and as a protection of peaceful protesters," they were not in favor of the overall militarization of the conflict. By contrast, the SNC leadership was more willing to work with the outside powers, was more connected with the Syrian expat communities, enjoyed cordial relations with Western and Gulf governments, saw the possibility for creating mutually serving agreements, and worked to attract international support to help topple the regime by force if necessary.[137]

The rise of the FSA, an affiliate of the SNC and composed of defecting soldiers who refused to fire on the peaceful protestors as well as civilians who took up arms to defend themselves, complicated and intensified the existing divisions, this despite the fact that most agreed that the FSA was needed to confront the violence that the regime was using against civilians. Like the LCC, the FSA too was composed of local, small units and lacked an actual central command, so much so that it could not agree nor effectively communicate a military strategy. At the same time, they were an organic extension of the revolution having emerged naturally to defend the civilian population, and represented the democratic aspirations of the protestors. Indeed, ideologically, unlike the radical Islamist militias that would soon emerge, most of the rebel fighters agreed to uphold the liberal principles of their civilian counterparts. They favored a secular and democratic system and process.[138] As for the more pious among them, they felt the need to reassert their commitment to a secular democratic movement, declaring that religion is for God and the homeland for all.[139]

The FSA would lose ground almost immediately following its creation. This is because Syria began witnessing the rise of more radical militias and less liberal activists, mostly radical Islamists, the majority of whom were released from Syrian prisons in 2011 by a regime looking

---

[137] Draege, "The Formation of Syrian Opposition," pp. 198–199.
[138] This was based on a survey conducted by the International Republican Institute (IRI) and Pechter Polls of Princeton in June 2012. See Daher, "Pluralism Lost in Syria's Uprising."
[139] Daher, "Pluralism Lost in Syria's Uprising."

to overwhelm the liberal opposition. Indeed, the secular and liberal factions of the FSA were no longer only fighting the regime, but the radical Islamists as well.[140] This unexpected turn of events in favor of an illiberal and rather violent group, which was aided by the Syrian authorities to put a halt to the liberal movement and their hopes-for transition, confused and further divided Syria's liberals.[141]

Like in Egypt, the liberals disagreed on the role and place of the Islamists (whether liberal or illiberal) within the opposition as well as within a future democratic Syria. The issue was increasing in importance as the SNC grew to include a large Islamist component, notably the Muslim Brothers but also a group of powerful businessmen who were affiliated with the Muslim Brotherhood and that had ties to international and regional actors.[142] This latter group kept a low profile and occupied one-quarter of the 310 seats in the council. And so while some liberals felt that the inclusion of the Islamists reflected the overall liberal principles of the Syrian opposition and its commitment to a secular and pluralistic political framework – a framework that the Syrian Muslim Brothers had themselves vouched for in March 2012 in a new "pledge and charter"[143] – and moreover argued that it was important that the SNC represent all currents within Syria, many were growing wary of the Islamists' influence within the liberal movement and argued that they were becoming too powerful for the SNC to remain a liberal democratic group.[144] To complicate the situation, the leaders' positions were also changing as time went on.

Indeed, time was not on the side of the liberals. The increased involvement of outside powers and the militarization of the revolution exacerbated their divisions and disenchantment. The disagreement over how to respond to foreign interference and the inclusion of the Islamists did not affect the liberals' consensus over the other guiding principles, though it did hinder their overall unity and ability to align around a consistent and well-defined program and roadmap, and thus to convince those

---

[140] Line Khatib, "The Pre-2011 Roots of Syria's Islamist Militants," *The Middle East Journal* 72:2 (Spring 2018), pp. 209–228; Line Khatib, "Syria, Saudi Arabia, the UAE and Qatar: The 'Sectarianization' of the Syrian Conflict and Undermining of Democratization in the Region," *British Journal of Middle Eastern Studies*, 46:3 (2019), pp. 385–403.

[141] Khatib, "The Pre-2011 Roots of Syria's Islamist Militants," pp. 209–211.

[142] Ammar Diub, "George Sabra ... Khitab Did al-Tarikh," *alaraby aljadid* (July 28, 2017), www.alaraby.co.uk; "The Syrian National Council," *Carnegie Middle East Center* (September 25, 2013), http://carnegie-mec.org/publications/?fa=48334

[143] "The Syrian National Council," *Carnegie Middle East Center* (25 September 2013), http://carnegie-mec.org/publications/?fa=48334

[144] Diub, "George Sabra ... Khitab Did al-Tarikh."

members of the opposition who were on the frontlines in Syria to fully rally behind them.[145]

Despite this however, the opposition inside Syria would eventually support the Free Syrian Army, and the pro-democracy movement would go on to issue in July 2012 two documents, a National Pact and a Joint Political Plan for the Transitional Phase. Yet the different groups were not able to come together as a unified body.[146] The SNC was also unable over the next few months to increase the representation of the front-liners and the growing civilian structures within Syria.[147] The result was that some of the LCC decided to leave the SNC until it reformed its organizational structure.

Meanwhile, those who were still inside Syria felt the need to continue their activism by becoming more direct and more defiant. Critics like cartoonist Ali Ferzat (see Chapter 3) depicted President Asad as a broken dictator, sitting on a broken armchair over a broken country.[148] Ferzat was part of the Damascus Spring, using his art to ridicule despotism and to advance principles of humanism, equality, and fairness. He was also emboldened by the democratic movement finally coming out into the open in all its might, and thus published a cartoon showing President Bashar al-Asad hitching a ride out of town with Colonel Muammar el-Qaddafi of Libya, who had just been toppled from power. The regime's response was rapid and brutal: masked gunmen pulled Ferzat out of his car and shattered his hands and fingers, thereby sending a clear message that his life was at risk if he continued to draw such cartoons. Like so many others, Ferzat had to leave Syria and continue his activism from abroad.[149]

Other artists, such as director Hatem 'Ali (considered the Godfather of Syrian drama), his wife Dala' Rahbi, who is a feminist writer and human rights activist, and well-known actors such as Fadwa Suleiman, Abdelhakeem Kutifan, Fares Helou, Jamal Suleiman, and May Skaf, all known critics of despotism and proponents of the liberal movement and the Damascus Spring, became victims of forced displacement when they sided with the protestors and supported their pleas for rupture with

---

[145] "The Syrian National Council," *Carnegie Middle East Center.*
[146] Ibid.
[147] Ibid.
[148] Jamie Merrill, "Syrian Cartoonist Ali Ferzat Turns Spotlight on UK's Failure to Take in More Refugees," *The Independent* (January 27, 2015), www.independent.co.uk/news/world/middle-east/syrian-cartoonist-ali-ferzat-turns-spotlight-uk-s-failure-take-more-refugees-10006638.html
[149] Ferzat was awarded the Sakharov Prize for Peace in 2012 and named as one of the 100 most influential people in the world by *Time* magazine.

the existing political order.[150] Fadwa Suleiman led the protests in 2011 and 2012, thus risking her life to voice her dissent and to counter the regime's claims that the protests are radical and sectarian[151], and to promote peaceful resistance to despotism: "Freedom has its price and we all have to chip in," she said.[152] May Skaf also took part in many of the protests and was arrested in August 2011 and subjected to torture. She was one of the first artists to challenge the government crackdown on the protestors, and went on to continue her political advocacy in Europe on behalf of the Syrian people.[153]

'Ali, Rahbi, Skaf, Helou, Kutifan, Fadwa Suleiman, and Jamal Suleiman, among others, were soon blacklisted and dismissed from the Syrian Artists Association. The regime was unable to tolerate their damaging insubordination and their intellectual and artistic resistance; yet it could not hide their work and their refusal after 2011 to be atomized and subsumed into the autocratic order. Nonetheless, they had to flee Syria. And so 'Ali left for Canada and continued to direct and produce critical works until his death in 2020, while May Skaf and Fadwa Suleiman fled to France where they continued their activism and became powerful and inspiring symbols of the revolution abroad until their death. Jamal Suleiman meanwhile escaped to Egypt, where he also continued his political resistance.[154] Helou and Kutifan fled to Europe. All of them used and continue to use their art and their fame to expose the impact of despotism and to help change the political culture in Syria and the region, but also to reveal the crisis of liberalism at the international level. May Skaf died in 2018 of a heart attack following news that two other dissidents

---

[150] Many other directors, actors, and artists can be mentioned here such as Muhammad Malas, Yara Sabri, and Khalid Taja.

[151] Fadwa Suleiman is of Alawi origins, a minority sect within Syria and Bashar al-Asad's own sect. Thus her background as a prominent Alawite made her message more impactful and dangerous to a regime that claims that the protests and the opposition in general advanced sectarian messages. A large number of protestors, activists, and intellectuals are of minority origins, such as Michel Kilo and May Skaf (Christian), Muhammad al-Maghout (Ismaili), and Hassan Abbas (Alawi) to name a few we have discussed in this book, but this is outside the scope of this study.

[152] Emily Langer, "Fadwa Suleiman, Syrian Actress Who Led Resistance to Assad Regime, Dies," *The Washington Post* (August 19, 2017),

[153] Sam Roberts, "Mai Skaf, Syrian Actress Who Defied Assad Regime, Dies at 49," *New York Times* (July 27, 2018), www.nytimes.com/2018/07/27/obituaries/mai-skaf-syrian-actress-who-defied-assad-regime-dies-at-49.html

[154] Suleiman's Syria Tomorrow Movement, a liberal party that was founded in 2016 in Egypt. Suleiman had planned on challenging the presidency of Bashar al-Asad in the 2021 elections if the Constitution was changed and the regime allowed competition, but the regime disallowed it by adding a requirement that the presidential candidate should have lived in Syria for 10 consecutive years prior to the elections, a requirement that most liberals cannot meet.

had died under torture in Damascus prisons. One blogger wrote, "Mai Skaf and the two prisoners all died together ... maybe because they all refused to live this ugly moment of Syrian history."[155]

As for Syria's other political activists and leaders, most were in self-imposed exile by 2012; yet they organized meetings in September and October 2012 in Doha, Qatar, during which Western governments urged Riad Seif – who was perceived as one of the most legitimate and credible figure of the Syrian liberal movement (see Chapter 3) – to create a new opposition council. On November 11, 2012, the National Coalition for Syrian Revolutionary and Opposition Forces (henceforth the National Coalition) was launched.

The National Coalition had a similar membership body to that of the SNC, which merged with it and was awarded 22 of the 63 seats in the Coalition's governing political council; other members of the SNC were given seats as independent national figures.[156] The National Coalition included the Free Syrian Army within its Military Council, but it was different from the SNC in that it gave more room to grassroots activists that had emerged on the ground. Mu'adh al-Khatib, a Damascene Sunni cleric, was elected president of the National Coalition, and Riad Seif and Suheir Atassi were elected vice presidents. The National Coalition was well received among the Friends of Syria countries: Turkey and France immediately recognized the coalition as "the legitimate leader of the Syrian people", while the United Kingdom and the United States followed suit soon afterwards.[157]

In an attempt to integrate everyone within the coalition, Islamists were also allowed to join – for example, Mohammad Alloush, who created the amy of Islam with his brother, Zahran Alloush.[158] Others participated in some meetings. The leaders of the SNC such as George Sabra (member of the liberal People's Democratic Party, the former communist party led by Riad Turk) and other activists such as Michel Kilo would at first justify the National Coalition's support of Islamist groups such as the Nusra Front by arguing that unlike the radical Islamists, these groups believed in compromise, democracy, and national consensus. In reality however, the issue of the influence of the Islamists and religion was not solved within the National Coalition, and would continue to divide the opposition.

---

[155] Phil Davidson, "Mai Skaf: Syrian Actor and Democracy Activist Exiled by the Asad Regime," *Independent* (July 30, 2018), www.independent.co.uk/news/obituaries/mai-skaf-may-skaf-syria-actor-assad-activist-exile-syrian-refugee-a8469876.html

[156] "The Syrian National Council," *Carnegie Middle East Center* (September 25, 2013), https://carnegie-mec.org/diwan/48334?lang=eng

[157] Draege, "The Formation of Syrian Opposition," p. 200.

[158] Zahran Alloush was arrested in 2009 and then released in 2011 from the Sednaya prison, a few months following the start of the revolution in Syria.

Inside Syria, the most active and recognized liberals continued to vanish at the hands of the security apparatus. Like in Egypt, the individual activists who had joined initiatives demanding democratic change would suffer enormously after 2013. One of those killed was a prominent activist, journalist, and civil society leader Raed Fares. Fares used satirical and witty banners to increase the world's understanding of the Syrian revolution, and his banners represented the thoughts and dreams of many of the Syrian protestors. For instance, one of the banners said, "It is not against a system of governance only, our revolution is against the infiltration of minds and against intellectual tyranny in all its forms" (April 12, 2013, author's translation).[159] The banners also denounced and poked fun at the absurdity of the regime's tactics in fighting the people: "Black Friday Special Offer: Whoever, Wherever You are, Bring your Enemy and Come To Fight in Syria For Free (Free Land and Free Sky), Limited Time Offer."[160]

Fares believed in the power of ideas to challenge injustice: "The revolution is an idea, and ideas cannot be killed with weapons," Fares asserted. In 2012, he started an organization called the Union of Revolutionary Bureaus in Idlib. The union supported local media projects and a free press, ran a radio station and a media center, ran a relief center and provided health and education services for women and young people. Fares believed in peaceful struggle against both dictatorship and the religious radicals, and held that the revolution in Syria was worth it despite its casualties, which he was very familiar with, because, he argued, it was the only way for Syrians to stop being treated like animals in Asad's farm.[161] He believed that the Asad regime terrorized Syrians twice, directly and then indirectly through the radicalism that succeeded the regime's terror on civilians. And yet Fares was hopeful and spread optimism around him, arguing that Syrians' peaceful ideas and quest for liberty and fairness would change the Arabs from the inside, by shattering monolithic discourses and monist systems: "that's why our revolution will change the Middle East," he asserted.[162]

[159] See "As'ilat al-thawra al-Suriya al-Mulihha fi Zikraha al-'Ashira … ru'iya siasiya wa shahadat haiyya," Markaz Harmoon lil-dirasat al-mu'asira (Harmoon Center for Contemporary Studies, March 16, 2021), www.harmoon.org/reports

[160] Photo of banner available in Marta Vidal, "Fighting for democracy and a free Syria," *Qantara.de* (November 22, 2019), https://en.qantara.de/node/38119

[161] Al-Manbar al-Suri with Musa al-Amr, "Interview with Raed Fares," *AL-Ghad al-Arabi* (March 24, 2014), www.youtube.com/watch?v=l9fqH5Km-ys

[162] Speech by Raed Fares, "Building a Free Syria one town at a time," *Oslo Freedom Forum* (May 23, 2017), https://oslofreedomforum.com/talks/building-a-free-syria-one-town-at-a-time-1).

Fares launched Radio Fresh in 2013. The Radio station was meant to warn residents about incoming bombs in order to minimize the casualties. But it turned out to be a station about everyday life in Idlib, about hope for a better future, and about building a free Syria one step and one city at a time.[163] Despite this positivity, he was too charismatic and popular to be left standing. Thus Fares and his cameraman and fellow activist, Hammoud Jneid, were shot dead in Kafranbel in Idlib in November 2018. "The smell of 50 years of oppression and pain is marked in my memory," he had said before the fatal incident.[164] When he died, a banner in English read, "'the assassination was the result of the world's indifference.' Another banner in Arabic read, 'They didn't kill you, you are still among us as a beacon of freedom.'"[165]

Another activist who dedicated her life to the quest for democracy and freedom in Syria was Razan Zaitouneh, a prominent human rights activist and lawyer who was awarded the Sakharov Prize for Freedom of Thought and the Anna Politkovskaya Award for defending human rights in 2011. Zaitouneh and other activists were forced into hiding at the start of the uprising because of their pro-democracy work as well as their reporting for the foreign media, which transgressed the regime's ban.[166] Zaitouneh was one of the main leaders of the liberal movement that remained inside Syria despite the deadly risk. She was a theorist as well as a committed practitioner, heading protests and co-founding along with her colleagues such as Mazen Darwish[167] the first LCC, as well as presiding over the entire network. She also created the Violations Documentation Center (VOC) in April 2011 in Damascus, and contributed to the founding of many other NGOs and citizens' initiatives, with a focus on empowering women and children. She published many articles and reports about issues of human rights, defended prisoners' rights and lobbied for civil liberties, and did not shy away from confrontation with the Syrian regime. Her popularity, charisma, sincerity, strength, and determination made her an especially powerful opponent of the regime, and in hindsight, the leader that many Syrians were looking for to unite them and guide them in their transition toward democracy.

[163] Raed Fares, "Building a Free Syria One Town at a Time," *Oslo Freedom Forum* (July 7, 2017), www.youtube.com/watch?v=OlWt-kI7_LQ

[164] Fares, "Building a Free Syria One Town at a Time."

[165] Vidal, "Fighting for Democracy and a Free Syria."

[166] Razan Zaitouneh, a human rights lawyer, spoke to Al-Jazeera English about the death toll caused by the regime in the city of Tall Kalakh and its growing pro-democracy movement (May 6, 2011).

[167] Syrian lawyer and activist and head of the Syrian Center for Media and Freedom of Expression. His wife Yara Bader is also an activist. Both spent time in jail in 2012, and felt compelled to leave Syria thereafter.

At the very start of the revolution, Zaitouneh said in a video: "we are confronting with peaceful protests, and freedom songs, and chants for a new Syria, one of the most brutal regimes of the region and the world. I am proud to be Syrian and to be part of these historical days, and of the greatness of my people."[168] [author's translation] She and her colleagues refused to leave the country despite knowing the risks of staying, dismissing the pleas of many colleagues asking them to flee to safeguard their lives.[169] Her husband, Wael Hamada, had been in prison for three months when Zaitouneh was forced into hiding underground for two years.[170] She finally moved to the Damascene suburb of Douma in 2013, which had fallen under the control of the rebels and the Army of Islam of Zahran Alloush.

That August, the VOC reported on the regime's use of chemical weapons against civilians in the Eastern Ghouta region, killing more than 1000 Syrians including 400 children. Razan wrote then, "I witnessed the massacre, I saw the bodies of men and women and children on the streets, I heard the screams of mothers when they found the bodies of their children" [author's translation]. In Douma, Zaitouneh also witnessed and fought against the rise of militant groups such as the Army of Islam and the Islamic State (IS or Daesh), who had begun fighting with each other to gain control over the territory and everybody within it, including reporting on their crimes. She also challenged their attempts to rule, refused to compromise with them, dissected their narratives, and revealed their abuses of power and their tyrannical ways: "We did not start a revolution and lose thousands of souls so that these monsters repeat the same history of injustice…they have to be held accountable just like the regime"[171] [author's translation], she explained.

Zaitouneh was kidnapped along with the activists Samira Khalil, Nazim Hamadi and her husband Wael Hamada, nicknamed the Douma Four, in December 2013 by men presumed to be from the Army of Islam.[172] Right before her kidnapping, Zaitounah was very active, talking to prisoners, and documenting the regime's torture especially within the military intelligence branches.[173] Her last tweet to the world was on December 1, 2013.

---

168 Quote from Lewis Sanders, Brigitta Schülke, Waffa Albadry and Julia Bayer, "Razan Zaitouneh … wajh al-thawra al-suriya al-mughayab," *Deutsche Welle* (March 15, 2021), https://bit.ly/3CGBjm8

169 Brigitta Schülke, Lewis Sanders and Waffa Albadry, "Video: The Missing Face of the Syrian Revolution," *DW news* (March 2021), https://fb.watch/4gzChmQG6Y/

170 Salma el-Hosseiny, "Syria: Reveal the Whereabouts of Razan, Samira, Nazem and Wa'el," *ISHR* (December 12, 2018), www.ishr.ch/news/syria-reveal-whereabouts-razan-samira-nazem-and-wael

171 Quote from "Razan Zaitouneh … wajh al-thawra al-suriya al-mughayab."

172 Zahran Alloush never admitted to the kidnapping.

173 https://twitter.com/razanz

Less than two years later, in October 2015, one of Syria's best-known cartoonists, Akram Raslan, was confirmed to have been killed by Syrian police. A fellow prisoner said that Raslan died in a prison hospital, possibly after torture. It had been three years since he was first taken into custody and four since the Syrian civil war began. Raslan's "colorful, almost optimistic scenes mocking corruption and senselessness set his work apart from his colleagues."[174] He was an inspiration to many Syrians. And more recently, the year 2020 saw three other prominent activists die: Hassan Abbas, the father of citizenship awareness in Syria, Michel Kilo, who had fought against tyranny under Asad the father and the son, and veteran lawyer-activist Habib Issa. The fate of these activists, including of the revolution's symbols Razan Zaitouneh, Raed Fares, Fadwa Suleiman and May Skaf, would come to be perceived as representing the fate of the peaceful and liberal revolution and its moral and intellectual prospects.

Loss of Control

With the loss of so many liberal leaders from both inside and outside Syria and the concomitant rise of the radicals, Syrian liberals would soon completely lose control of the revolution, and in the process of their own ability to shape the fate of Syria.[175] International actors, fighting for influence and control of Syrian territory that was now nearly entirely open to outside powers such as Russia, Iran, and Turkey would organize a series of "peace talks" in an attempt to control the situation on the ground and agree on zones of influence. Such attempts would include peace talks involving the UN and other international powers in Geneva, Vienna, and Riyadh, and mostly Russia, Turkey, and Iran in Moscow and Astana. While Geneva and Vienna had the goal of facilitating and creating the modalities of transition toward a democratic political regime, relying on UN Security Council resolutions 2118 and 2254[176], the Moscow and Astana meetings were focused on writing a new constitution by an appointed body, on negotiating and compromising with the regime and on accepting that it would be part of Syria's next phase. Further, the talks in Astana saw armed Islamist groups given more importance than the

---

[174] Asher Kohn, "The Syrian Cartoonists Who Live and Die by Their Pen," *Roads and Kingdoms* (November 20, 2015), https://roadsandkingdoms.com/2015/drawn-in-blood/

[175] See Documentary "Ahat al-Huriya," *Al-Jazeera* (March 12, 2014), https://youtu.be/yroOTxnkZJl

[176] Both resolutions call for a Syrian-led transition in addition to the creation of a new constitutional and legal order that would be subject to the approval of Syrians.

Syrian liberal opposition.[177] To many activists, the Moscow and Astana talks offered the Bashar regime the time and opportunity to stay on in power as they emphasized continuity and stability instead of rupture and liberal democratic change.[178] Nonetheless, the liberals' attempts to unite and come up with a tangible plan out of the crisis continued. The Syrian National Coalition and the inside leftist opposition, namely the NCC, reached a political agreement on July 23, 2015. But their efforts to unite and to reach a deal with the Syrian regime ultimately failed.

In 2015, Russian airstrikes sealed the fate of liberalism and the liberal movement in Syria, at least for the next few years. These airstrikes, launched against Western backed rebels and civilians on September 30, 2015, effectively turned the war in favor of the regime of Bashar al-Asad. It was in light of this that on October 20, Asad flew to Moscow to thank Russia for its involvement and military and advisory support. Then on November 14, 2015, the International Syria Support Group, which was composed of 17 countries and international bodies including the UN, the EU and the Arab League and also including Iran (a patron of the Syrian regime), met in Vienna to hammer out an agreement between the Syrian opposition and the regime. On December 18, 2015, the UN Security Council adopted Resolution 2254, which called for a transition to "credible, inclusive, and non-sectarian governance" within six months. It also scheduled the drafting of a new constitution and elections for a new government within 18 months.

February and April 2016 saw the UN host a third and fourth round of negotiations in Geneva between the regime and a new Syrian body called the High Negotiations Committee (HNC), which was a new broad umbrella body representing the opposition. But these talks broke down. A fifth round of indirect peace talks took place in Geneva in 2017, with participants including the regime, the HNC, the National Coalition, as well as two minor groups that are considered to be closer to the regime than to the liberal opposition, the Moscow and Cairo platforms. A sixth round took place in May 2017, and then a seventh and an eighth round in July and November 2017, with the ongoing stalemate underlining that Asad was unwilling to discuss a political transition, as was made clear in the observation that "nothing substantial will come out of the talks."[179]

---

[177] See "bayan hawla a'mal al-lajna al-dasturiya al-suriya", http://chng.it/8xBrT7Gv; "bayan hawla al-intikhabat al-suriya" (November 2020), www.ipetitions.com/petition/TheSyrianelections

[178] Ghassan Nasser, "Hiwar Ma'a Hussein Hamada: al'I'tilaf yu 'ani hashasha fi buni-yatihi al-tanzimiya wa huwa mabni min kital wa ahzab wahmiya," Harmoon Center (April 1, 2021), www.harmoon.org/dialogues

[179] "Syria War: Peace Talks Restart in Geneva," BBC news (May 16, 2017), www.bbc.com/news/amp/world-middle-east-39934868

The regime refused to discuss constitutional reforms and presidential elections, while the liberals within the different bodies refused to consider allowing Asad a future role in Syria.[180] In October 2019, the Syrian Constitutional Committee was created in Geneva, drawing together 50 people from the Syrian regime, the opposition and civil society groups to draft a new Constitution for Syria. This underlines then that the Syrian regime has become part of the transition whether the revolutionaries like it or not. The latest round of talks (at the time of writing) in Geneva to draft a new Constitution ended without progress in January 2021.[181] For Syrian liberals, there has been a need to look inside themselves, to try to come to terms with the loss, the betrayal, and the sadness, and to understand how they can learn from the failures and possibly even still safeguard their revolution. Understandably, some are more optimistic than others.

Why the Defeat?

In the Syrian case, as in the Egyptian case, a number of variables combined to facilitate the victory of the autocratic forces.

Firstly, the Syrian regime adopted a strategy of divide and rule, focusing on mobilizing its popular base through sectarian, tribal, regional, and clientelistic connections, releasing from prison radical Islamists who had been captured by the Syrian authorities while crossing the border from Iraq (and thus providing an opportunity for Islamists to join the movement for change, although with an entirely different agenda than the liberal movement). The regime's aim was to scare the public masses that change would mean fewer liberties, not more, and in so doing to ensure its ultimate goal of regime survival.

Secondly, the regime also soon realized that its usual tactics of cooptation, of harassing and detaining activists, banning communication, and blocking internet access, were not halting the movement. As a result, they opted to use incredible violence to repress the peaceful resistance, killing thousands of civilians, and imprisoning and killing the most well known of the activists and leaders who inspired and guided the peaceful protestors. Targeting the liberal and pro-democracy activists was meant to deny the protests their inclusive, humanitarian, feminist, democratic

---

[180] Abdallah al-Ghudwy, "George Sabra li-Zaman al-Wasl: Sira'at Muqbila fi al-Mu'arada," *Zaman Al-Wsl* (August 8, 2017), www.zamanalwsl.net/news/article/80760

[181] "UN Envoy on Stalled Syria Talks in Geneva: 'We Can't Continue Like This,'" *SWI* (January 30, 2021), www.swissinfo.ch/eng/unenvoy-on-stalled-syria-talks-in-geneva---we-can-t-continue-like-this-/46331318

and peaceful dimensions, dimensions that undermined the regime's pro-paganda that radicals were behind the protests.

Thirdly and more importantly, as in Egypt, the liberals' approaches to ensure their survival and encourage change within a repressive envi-ronment in fact decreased their chances of success in the short term. More specifically, their nonhierarchical and often noiseless approach, coupled with their reliance on self-sufficient, independent small groups, had allowed the liberals to maintain their presence, propagate their message, and effect change within the repressive environment of dictatorship from the 1970s onwards; but it became a hindrance to their ability to effectively present a leader and a united front post 2011. This is because the approach of working in atomized groups and circles as part of a horizontal rather than a vertical hierarchi-cal structure meant that decision-making was decentralized and that coordination/efforts to unite were slow and difficult. It became espe-cially difficult to agree on one set of leaders and one overall strategy, foundational texts, as well as inspiring speeches and messages. Thus the challenge became not how to agree on political principles, but on technicalities and on leadership, a problem that did not pose itself for example during 2000's Damascus Spring given that there was no need to present one leadership then. In fact if anything, multiplicity and diversity led to better outcomes. The issue of how to include the Islamists while curbing their illiberal trends only exacerbated the leadership problem.

Fourthly, in both Syria and Egypt, the intervention of foreign powers shifted the balance of power in favor of the despots. For instance, the for-eign military and advisory assistance and financial aid provided by Iran, the Hizbullah movement of Lebanon, and Russia (Russian troops were on the ground in Syria well before their official intervention in 2015) ultimately tipped the scale in favor of the despots. The Gulf countries, which had preferred to see the fall of the Syrian regime because of its pro-Iran predilections, still feared the rise of a democratic and liberal Syria and the propagation of liberal ideals within the region. They thus preferred to take a path that weakened the regime and its Iranian patron, while making sure the liberal democratic movement would not win the race.[182]

The interventions by illiberal powers with the aim of serving their geopolitical interests including undermining any liberal democratic movement success in the region was expected and debated within the liberal movement. The role of the established liberal democracies in

[182] Khatib, "Syria, Saudi Arabia, the UAE and Qatar," pp. 385–403.

undermining the movement was less expected by a majority, although it was consistent with historical patterns (see Chapter 1). Indeed, as with their Egyptian counterparts, established liberal democracies have been unwilling to give support to the Syrian protest movement and to its liberal intelligentsia, and have instead continued to prioritize the usual geopolitical considerations that see the survival of Asad as essential to maintain the current regional order, at the expense of ethical and moral priorities. They thus stood by as authoritarian regimes and their illiberal patrons violently suppressed the liberal movement and protests.[183] And in so doing, Western governments continued to perceive their interests in realist terms and to prioritize their own (short-term) stability while relying on the Gulf States, Iran, Turkey, and Russia to control the explosive situation, a strategy that ignored and undermined the Syrian people's pleas for democratic change, and minimized the incredibly severe humanitarian crisis within the country. In so doing, the Syrian crisis, more so than the Egyptian one, has exposed the hypocrisy at the heart of the international liberal order and regime.

Further, the established democracies' strategy has also ignored the actual implications of the Syrian crisis for the liberal democratic world. Only the establishment of the Islamic Caliphate in 2014 pushed the Obama administration to create a plan to defeat ISIS, and even then it was arguably largely motivated by the desire to stop the radical group from using terror tactics in the Western world. Yet at the same time, the American administration continued to deny the secular and pro-democracy Free Syrian Army battalions much-needed resources: the battalions were badly funded and not provided with the military assistance they needed, not even defensive assistance such as anti-aircraft missiles, even as the world witnessed the radical militarized factions emerging and taking over within Syria.[184] This can at least partly be attributed to the inability of the Syrian liberals to form the necessary coalitions at the domestic level to push for democratic change.

Thus domestic and regional conditions have certainly complicated decisions and undermined the liberal project, in particular the illiberalism of the Arab neighborhood. And yet the involvement of foreign powers in addition to domestic, regional, and international developments that put the focus elsewhere, in turn gave time for authoritarian rulers to adjust and increase their repressive methods against their people in order

---

[183] T. A. Börzel, "The Noble West and the Dirty Rest?" p. 526.
[184] Yezid Sayigh, "A Melancholy Perspective on Syria," Carnegie Middle East (April 8, 2014), https://carnegie-mec.org/2014/04/08/melancholy-perspective-on-syria-pub-55256

to ensure regime survival.[185] More importantly for this work, it exacerbated the sense of failure and guilt within the opposition, including a tendency to place blame on themselves and even for some to doubt the liberal project in its entirety, thus further weakening an already divided, frustrated, disillusioned, and demoralized opposition.

Hope Is Not Dead

The initial hope of the Arab Spring soon dissolved into renewed authoritarianism, with war being waged against civilians and widespread suffering across the country. Illiberal forces mobilized quickly and with all their might in the entire region: Russian bombs and Iranian and Syrian air strikes were dropped on the protestors in Syria; Saudi and Emirati air strikes against civilians took place in Yemen; Tribal warfare broke out in Libya; and, Islamist militancy whether by Shi'a or Sunni militias was coupled with the use of violence and repression, and triumphed over reason, freedom, rights, and communication. The region witnessed the demolition of entire cities, with refugees fleeing for often hard-to-reach unaffected zones. The world saw the images of defenseless people marching through the rubble of what were their homes, and heard about casualty figures not witnessed since World War II. Even in a city like Dubai that was seemingly unaffected by war, people feared the proximity to the inferno next door. Meanwhile in Egypt, the Gulf-sponsored military regime under Abd al-Fattah al-Sisi worked swiftly to consolidate its rule and to render political contestation impossible at the institutional level as it stripped parliament of any meaningful power and reverted to arbitrary detentions, harassment, and torture to silence pro-democracy activists at a scale that had scarcely been seen before.[186] The question thus arises: Is Arab liberalism defeated? Have autocrats successfully killed the liberal narrative and activism once and for all?

---

[185] For more on the autocrats' increased use of repression, see Maria Josua and Mirjam Edel, "The Arab Uprisings and the Return of Repression," *Mediterranean Politics* (February 18, 2021), https://doi.org/10.1080/13629395.2021.1889298. Also Aras and Oztig argue that rather than encouraging democratic change, the Arab Spring has "stimulated the learning process of authoritarian rulers" in other areas such as the Caucasus and Central Asia. Autocrats have thus increased the levels of repression targeting not only the protestors but the entire structure that has allowed the resistance movement to coordinate their efforts and to communicate. See Bulent Aras and Lacin Idil Oztig, "Has the Arab Spring Spread to the Caucasus and Central Asia? Explaining Regional Diffusion and Authoritarian Resistance," *Journal of Balkan an Near Eastern Studies* (February 16, 2021), https://doi.org/10.1080/19448 953.2021.1888249

[186] Beesan Kassab, "Why Is Sisi Afraid of the Constitution and Parliament," *Mada Masr* (September 15, 2015), www.madamasr.com/sections/politics/why-sisi-afraid-constitution-and-parliament.

History tells us that some actions can have paradoxical or hard-to-predict outcomes. The incredible levels of regime repression, aided by authoritarian powers such as Iran and Russia, could in the long run enhance the position of the liberals. After all, liberalism has emerged in the region, as was shown in the previous chapters, as a result of the experience of oppression and thrived despite the repression visited against it. In the words of Advocacy and Communications Director for Human Rights Watch's Middle East and North Africa office and investigative journalist Ahmed Benchemsi, "there are no indications that the liberals' power to inspire the Arab people has receded since 2011. In fact, it may have increased."[187] Benchemsi adds,

Even in Saudi Arabia, where the alliance between the ruling family and the Wahhabi establishment is more solid than ever, six out of the 10 most watched YouTube channels (telecom and gaming companies aside) are satirical shows produced by rebellious youth groups. By November 2014, the total views for the videos uploaded by these channels were no less than 915 million—with Saudi Arabia having only 30 million inhabitants. For those who care to look closer, many other surprising trends are taking over the Arab Internet, such as a surge in atheism via dedicated Facebook pages with tens of thousands of followers—unthinkable just five years ago—and gay rights groups popping up in every online corner. And each year, we hear of more attempts to move these groups from the virtual to the real world by staging gay pride parades in Arab cities.[188]

New generations of Arab liberals are rising and fighting assert others. "Many of those still fighting for the cause are building new businesses, publications, charities, startups and manifestos that they still believe can yield change – if not a revolution, for now."[189] Indeed, new movements and protests for democracy keep rising in the region, including in Egypt, Iraq, Lebanon, Syria, Tehran, and Istanbul. What this indicates then is that the Arab Spring is not over yet, it is simply regrouping, readjusting, and will continue to do so according to activists. Protestors see through the attempts by their governments to blame their miserable situations on the Imperialist West. In Syria, like in Egypt, activists on the ground have dealt with the immediate impact of the crisis, and many of those who are left, including those who have seen family members disappear or killed, have pledged to continue to struggle for liberal democracy, and to learn from their mistakes. In fact, as one observer puts it,

---

[187] Benchemsi, "Arab Liberalism Is Alive and Well, Thank You."

[188] Ibid.

[189] Elizabeth Dickinson, "What Happened to Arab Liberalism? Four Years after the Arab Spring, Activists Are Trying to Revive an Enfeebled Movement," *Politico Magazine* (December 17, 2014), www.politico.com/magazine/story/2014/12/arab-spring-anniversary-113637

The lesson has been learned: social pressure can indeed bring a bad ruler down, but ultimately democratic activism, as sincere as it may be, is not what it takes to prevail in a competition for power. Rather, the ultimate winners are those who have guns and deep pockets and, perhaps more importantly, can rely on solid, organized, and long-lasting networks—including at the grassroots level—to channel change in the direction they want. Unlike the young liberals, the Arab military and royal establishments have been amassing power and capital for decades. Such resources came in handy when these actors followed up on 2011's uprisings.[190]

Activists agree, they should have been better prepared, more organized, and better aware of the geopolitical reality around them. And yet, many believe that their struggle is not over yet. In 2015, the godfather of Syria's citizenship movement, Hassan Abbas wrote, "Call it whatever you want, criticize it as you wish, betray it, deceive it, divert it, dig the ground under its feet, color it, curse it, do whatever you want ... because as Galileo Galilei told his detractors, it still revolts despite everything, and it goes on, for it had started only to go on until it achieves that which the people want: a dignified life without injustice and without obscurantism."[191] Another prominent activist, Fayez Sara, wrote in 2020 on his Facebook account: "It wasn't just daring to dream, but seeking that which the Syrians will eventually reach, freedom, justice and equality despite everything"[192] [author's translation]

Yassin al-Haj Saleh, the husband of activist Samira Khalil, himself a social liberal activist, a writer, and a former political prisoner wrote,

Adequate punishment for crimes committed in Syria may never happen, yet we must not give up on justice.... As the decade comes to a close, I am faced with the dark truth that we live in a world far worse than we did 10 years ago – worse even than we dare admit to ourselves ... what are we to do now that those with the most power in the world [world powers] are devoid of the most instinctive of characteristics, compassion? ....I am Samira in her absence ... We have been crushed, true – but we create meaning from suffering. We struggle to the end, hope needs us as much as we need it. Our powerful enemies do not feel safe and secure unless we surrender ourselves to despair.[193]

[190] Benchemsi, "Arab Liberalism Is Alive and Well, Thank You."
[191] "Rahil Hassan Abbas ... al-thaqafa al-suriya takhsar safiraha," *Al-Mudun* (March 7, 2021), www.almodon.com/print/510245b1db1-8cac-447a-899e-ea8b01db740c/fd37c6b8-1eed-4e90-8ec0-1ee20eff76ab
[192] *"Ma kanat al-jur'a ila al-hilm faqat. Bal kanat sa'iyan ilayh wa sayasel al-suriyun ila al-huriya wa al-'adala wa al-musawat raghma kul al-dhuruf."*
[193] Yassin al-Haj Saleh, "Syria War: The Love of My Life Disappeared Six Years Ago, but Still I Cling to Hope", *Middle East Eye* (December 26, 2019), https://www.middleeasteye.net/opinion/syria-war-love-my-life-disappeared-six-years-ago-still-i-cling-hope.

When asked if she regretted the revolution, Syrian writer Suzanne Khawatimi said,

If the revolution hadn't happened, we would still be applauding the hero of fake victories, and be forced out to support rallies, and would watch the members of the National Assembly cheer the rise to power of Hafez al-Asad's grandson, and be silent about the arrests. Our youth would disappear without us being able to mention their names or ask about them, and we'd be insulted and silenced, and tremble when one of the security branches is mentioned. It is not a happy picture no matter what![194] [author's translation]

In line with this, right before his death in April 2020, veteran activist Michel Kilo wrote a letter to remind Syrians to unite in their struggle against tyranny and to focus on the demand for individual freedoms and citizens' rights.[195] What this underlines is that for many liberals, hope continues, as does the struggle.

Conclusion

Arab liberals were an essential and vital part of the Arab Spring having played a key role in shaping the narrative and the demands of the uprisings over a period of years. But their loosely organized horizontal and leaderless structures that were meant to shun elitist politics and to draw them closer to the public masses in order to better reflect wider needs and aspirations did not facilitate their position as the ultimate leaders of change, even if these characteristics had proven essential to their survival during previous decades of authoritarianism in the region. Further, the Egyptian and Syrian regimes' widespread use of imprisonment, forced exile, violence and killing of some of their most promising and trusted leaders left a big gap in the movements in each of the two countries – indeed, the people who were looking for assertive and clear leaders to follow and trust were in many ways left on their own. The result was that protestors and activists who risked their lives and at times those of their family members to protest authoritarianism and to achieve civil freedoms and rights were violently silenced. Further, the Islamization of the revolution and the intervention of foreign powers on the side of the despots

---

[194] "Al-thawra al-suriya fi zikraha al-'ashira: al-masira wa al-ma'alat," *Tli'na 'al Huriya* (March 16, 2021), https://bit.ly/3wFhIPH

[195] Kilo was buried in France. His headstone reads: "Michel Kilo 1940–2021: Writer, thinker, and Syrian politician who dedicated his life to defending his people and the values of freedom, of citizenship, of justice and of democracy" (author's translation from Arabic and French).

left the liberals divided, while the inability/unwillingness of the established democracies to take a stand against the terror and horror these regimes hurled at their people left many liberals in the two countries bitter, isolated and as a result often fatally compromised. Thus the Arab Spring, which brought out into the open the liberal element within Arab society and the possibility of change, also brought disarray as the existing regimes' resilience turned out to be stronger than anticipated by most.

And yet many Syrian and Egyptian activists agree that hope is not dead. New ways of organizing and of mobilizing will emerge, and a new generation will do a better job at putting an end to despotism and humiliation, with liberalism becoming the inevitable outcome of repressive and exploitative contexts. For now, the liberal movement will continue to struggle, but is highly unlikely to simply disappear. In the words of one activist, "they will wake up and see that we are all interconnected and allow us to achieve our dignity."

Conclusion

This book has aimed to refute the assumption and claims by many that Arabic-speaking liberals and Arab democratic liberalism have been an unimportant sociopolitical force, either nonexistent for long stretches of the period from the mid-1850s to around 2019 or at best inconsistently active and engaged. To do so, it has looked at the underground and often-overlooked actors and activities of liberal activism and counter-culture in addition to its more visible moments of activism and thought, and tried to present and assess its actual strength. More specifically, this book examined the efforts of key individual actors and groups, some of whom are assumed to be socialist, communist and even Islamist instead of liberal, tracing their sociopolitical activism, narratives, forms of reasoning, methods of outreach, following, and goals. It has particularly considered Syria and Egypt as focused case studies whose examination makes possible a deeper understanding of liberalism's trajectory in the two countries but also – given the countries' regional importance as well as the book's analysis of them within the larger regional context – gives some indication of trends within the Arab world. In so doing, it has sought to expand the understanding of liberalism in the region and more generally, as well as contribute to broadening conceptions of the region's sociopolitical landscape in the process.

The book has shown that Arab liberalism is different from Western liberalism even though it might have found inspiration in Western liberal intellectualism and politics. It is the direct outcome of Arab authoritarian contexts and repression, first the Ottoman and European, and then the "nationalist" authoritarian regimes of the 1950s and 1960s, both of which saw the rise of thousands of thinkers, intellectuals, activists, writers, teachers, doctors, lawyers, and artists aiming to push back the repressive state and demand rights. These individuals' ideas offered a transparent and hopeful environment with many significant sociopolitical transformations that demonstrated an Arab liberalism that is not simply imported but that developed over time and critically engaged with its context. These liberals were not, as claimed by some observers, disassociated from the region and aligned with the West. Indeed, they fought against the repression of the Western powers and imperialism, and advocated for homegrown solutions to local problems.

The era of the "nationalist" authoritarian regimes was/is so repressive that Arab liberalism had to reconsider and transform its previously elitist, paternalistic methods as well as its reliance on the institution of the State in order to achieve liberal democratic change. The rise of the authoritarian left was partly the result of modern realities that the region faced, including the inability of the liberals to secure a dignified independence from the colonial powers, but also population growth, a rising poverty gap, rural exodus, and a need to industrialize as quickly as possible, which meant that the most popular parties were no longer those advancing ideas of democracy, representative government, and civil liberties. Instead leftist ideas offering fast, seemingly effective, egalitarian, nationalistic, and totalizing solutions to the rising poor and middle class were gaining traction. But it is important to add here that authoritarian leftists were mostly able to gain power through adherence to the officer corps. Once in power, inspired by Soviet communism and European fascism, they focused on patriotism and unity, power and control of one's destiny as a nation through revolution, a strong political leadership, and societal change from above. And issues of fiscal health and social mobility took precedence over questions of liberty and citizens' rights. The result of these changes is that the ability to speak freely contracted quickly in Syria and Egypt, and throughout the region. By the 1960s, the ideas of the so-called enlightened thinkers of the region were effectively ignored, silenced, removed from schoolbooks, and eclipsed by both self-proclaimed republics and the region's conservative monarchies.

The era of classical liberalism would end sometime then. New voices of liberal intellectuals and activists would emerge with the realization that the liberal democrats not only failed to achieve change through the institution of the State but also lost their own privileged position in the process. These new voices began to focus on creating a vibrant civil society that would act as a buffer between the citizen and the State. The liberals' focus was thus slowly shifting away from enacting change from above – which had become impossible anyway – to creating a civil society that would enhance the power of the citizen and curb the powers of the State. In this new approach and logic, the State would still be expected to create an environment that would allow for such a civil society to emerge, but without the elitist paternalism of the earlier generation.

What this shows then is that a new generation of liberals was slowly recalibrating their methods in an attempt to continue their work. They turned toward social activism, toward nongovernmental institutions, which they founded, to issues of human and women's rights and to cinema, art and literature driven by a belief that a bottom-up approach is not just the only possible way but a necessary long-term strategy for awakening a free and democratic order. In so doing, the liberals were able to exist and to continue to work in the midst of some of the harshest autocratic settings, hidden in plain sight, while also helping to foster an environment in which liberalism could continue to exist, to speak, and to be nurtured despite its forced entanglement and painful confrontation within authoritarianism. The point was to provide for alternative spaces, to connect with others, even if in smaller groups, and to somehow reach the public so that it could help itself in line with political liberal ideals. Critique turned inward and engaged with the self instead of looking for outside reasons for failure. In so doing, Arab liberals advocated for the same values as most liberals outside the Arabic-speaking region: constitutionalism and representative parliaments, rotation of power, political and social pluralism, social justice and civil liberties, individual freedoms and human rights, and many other rights that are rooted in a liberal conceptualizations of power. But their thought and activism were also reflections of their contexts and subcultures. The outcome was and is an original liberalism that is focused on the specific issues that face the Arabic-speaking citizens, and that is inspired by the traditions, convictions, ethics, and overall culture of the region.

The 2000s witnessed the vigorous resurfacing of liberal notions and of liberal organization and political activism. This liberalism is a continuation of earlier liberalisms in the sense that some of its activists refer to previous liberals and assert continuity, but it is also a renewed version in the sense that it has a new approach and a renewed vision of how change should be achieved. Liberal political leaders integrated the intellectuals' calls to move beyond doctrinaire views in an attempt to acknowledge everyone and effectively include political opponents within conceptualizations of the nation. Thus by the 2000s, liberals and other pro-democracy groups shed their "dogmatic thinking" and asserted the need to coordinate with others in order to achieve a liberal democratic environment, which most activists were by this time calling for. Now they were rallying for rupture with the extant political order. The methodological and ideological fluidity that characterized this period was driven by an essentially liberal rationale. And while some of these ideas were already being asserted in the 1980s and 1990s, they increasingly lost their subtle or restrained nature and were in full flower during the 2000s. In this environment, political activists became united and led by their anti-totalitarian struggle, waiting for the spark of change.

That spark came in 2011. Arab liberals were an essential and vital part of the Arab Spring having played a key role in shaping the narrative and the demands of the uprisings over many years, as the book shows, and they were at the frontlines of the revolution. The first few months showed their vitality and their determined presence. But their loosely organized horizontal and independent structures, which were meant to shun elitist politics and to draw them closer to the public masses in order to better reflect wider needs and aspirations as well to ensure their survival during previous decades of authoritarianism in the region, did not facilitate their position as the ultimate leaders of change. Further, the Egyptian and Syrian regimes' widespread use of imprisonment, forced exile, violence and killing of some of the most promising and trusted liberal leaders left a big gap in the movements in each of the two countries. The liberals presented a threat that these regimes could not ignore, unlike their Islamist counterparts, who were perceived as possible allies or at least as useful foils by both the Syrian and Egyptian regimes. The result was that liberal activists were effectively silenced.

Further, the interventions of foreign powers on the side of the despots while the established democracies refused to take a clear stand against the terror and horror these regimes hurled at their own people left many liberals in the two countries bitter, isolated and as a result often fatally compromised. Thus the Arab Spring, which brought out into the open the liberal element within Arab society and the possibility of democratic change, also showed the existing regimes' and their patrons' (such as Russia and Iran) ability to terrorize, eliminate, and kill opponents. The Arab Spring also revealed the crisis of the democratic liberal order worldwide and showed that illiberal interventionism is not the only reason for the continued opression within these countries.

And yet many Syrian and Egyptian activists and youths agree that the quest for a liberal democratic order is not dead. New ways of organizing and of mobilizing will emerge, and a new generation will do a better job at putting an end to despotism and humiliation, with liberals hoping that liberalism turns out to be the inevitable outcome of repressive and exploitative contexts. For now, the liberal movement will continue to struggle, but is highly unlikely to simply disappear. Thus the story of liberalism in the region continues, with new ideas and new transformations still to develop and new chapters still to write.

Bibliography

Abdalla, Ahmed. *The Student Movement and National Politics in Egypt 1923–1973* (Cairo and New York: The American University of Cairo Press, 2008).

Abdalla, Nadine. "Youth Movements in the Egyptian Transformation: Strategies and Repertoires of Political Participation," *Mediterranean Politics*, 21, no. 1 (2016): 44–63, https://doi.org/10.1080/13629395.2015.1081445

Abdel Fattah, Esraa. "Loaded Victory: Egypt's Revolution and Where It Stands Post-30 June," in Ronald Meinardus (ed.), *Liberalism in the Arab World – Just a Good Idea?* (Cairo: Al-Mahrosa for Publishing, 2014): 115–128.

Abdel Kouddous, Sharif. "A Lifetime of Resistance in Syria," *The Nation* (September 1, 2011), www.thenation.com/article/archive/lifetime-resistance-syria/

Abdel Meguid, Ahmed, and Daanisch Faruqi. "The Truncated Debate: Egyptian Liberals, Islamists, and Ideological Statism," in Dalia F. Fahmy and Daanish Faruqi (eds.), *Egypt and the Contradictions of Liberalism: Illiberal Intelligentsia and the Future of Egyptian Democracy* (London: Oneworld Publications, 2017): 253–290.

Abdelrahman, Maha. *Civil Society Exposed: The Politics of NGOs in Egypt* (Cairo: American University of Cairo Press, 2004).

Abdulhamid, Ammar. "Syria: Mobilizing the Opposition," in Jeffrey Azarva, Danielle Pletka and Michael Rubin (eds.), *Dissent and Reform in the Arab World: Empowering Democrats* (American Enterprise Institute, 2008): 83–92, www.jstor.com/stable/resrep03025.14

Abou El Fadl, Khaled. "Egypt's Secularized Intelligentsia and the Guardians of Truth," in Dalia F. Fahmy and Daanish Faruqi (eds.), *Egypt and the Contradictions of Liberalism: Illiberal Intelligentsia and the Future of Egyptian Democracy* (London: Oneworld Publications, 2017): 235–252.

Abou El Fadl, Khaled. "The Ugly Modern and the Modern Ugly: Reclaiming the Beautiful in Islam," in Omid Safi (ed.), *Progressive Muslims: On Justice, Gender and Pluralism* (Oxford: Oneworld, 2003): 33–77.

Aboulenein, Ahmed. "Morsy Assumes Power: Sacks Tantawi and Anan, Reverses Constitutional Decree and Reshuffles SCAF," *Daily News Egypt* (August 12, 2012), https://dailynewsegypt.com/2012/08/12/morsy-assumes-power-sacks-tantawi-and-anan-reverses-constitutional-decree-and-reshufles-scaf/

Abu Rabi', Ibrahim. *Contemporary Arab Thought: Studies in Post 1967 Arab Intellectual History* (London: Pluto Press, 2003).

Abu Samra, Muhammad. "Liberal Critics, 'Ulama' and the Debate on Islam in the Contemporary Arab World," in Meir Hatina (ed.), *Guardians of Faith in Modern Times: 'Ulama' in the Middle East* (Leiden and Boston: Brill, 2009): 265–289.

Abu-'Uksa, Wael. *Freedom in the Arab World: Concepts and Ideologies in Arabic Thought in the Nineteenth Century* (Cambridge, UK: Cambridge University Press, 2016).

Abu Zayd, Nasr. *Critique of Religious Discourse*, 3rd ed. (Casablanca: Arab Cultural Center, 2007).

Abu Zayd, Nasr. *Mafhum al-Nas: Dirasa fi 'ulum al-Quran [The Concept of the Text: A Study of the Quranic Sciences]* (Cairo: al-Hay'a al-Misriyya al-'Amma li-l-Kitab, 1990).

Adam, Luay. *Watan fi Watan: Muhammad al-Maghut* [A Nation within a Nation: Muhammad al-Maghut] (Damascus: Dar al-Mada, 2001).

Adwan, Mamdouh. "Mamdouh Adwan athna' *mu'tamar itihad al-kutab al-'arab* 1979." *YouTube,* uploaded by SyrianGirl47 (July 1, 2011), www.youtube .com/watch?v=Zb1dbHuSgv8

Agencies in Damascus. "Haitham Maleh Jailed for Three Years by Syrian Court," *The Guardian* (July 4, 2010).

Ahmari, Sohrab. "The Failure of Arab Liberals," *Commentary Magazine* (May 1, 2012), www.commentarymagazine.com/articles/the-failure-of-arab-liberals/

Ahmed, Leila. *Women and Gender in Islam* (New Haven: Yale University Press, 1992).

Ajami, Fouad. *The Arab Predicament: Arab Political Thought and Practice since 1967* (Cambridge, UK: Cambridge University Press, 1981).

Ajami, Fouad. "The Arab Road," *Foreign Policy,* no. 47 (Summer 1982): 3–25.

Alaimo, Kara. "How the Facebook Arabic Page 'We Are All Khaled Said' Helped Promote the Egyptian Revolution," *Social Media + Society* (July–December 2015).

Alarian, Riad. "Imagining a Free Syria," *UNA-UK Magazine* (March 20, 2017), https://una.org.uk/imagining-free-syria

Al-Akhdar, Al-'Afif. *Al-Mithaq al-'Aqlani* (PUBLISHER, 2007), https://elaph .com/ElaphWeb/ElaphWriter/2007/11/281513.html

Al-Anani, Khalil. "Egypt's Democratization: Reality or Mirage?" *Open Democracy* (May 9, 2005), www.opendemocracy.net/en/article_2491jsp/

Al-Aqqad, 'Abbas Mahmud. *Al-Hukum al-Mutlaq fi al-Qarn al-'Ishreen [Absolutist Governance in the 20th Century]* (Cairo: 1929).

Al-Aqqad, 'Abbas Mahmud. *Hitler fi al-Mizan [Hitler in the Balance]* (Cairo, 1940).

Al-Ashmawi, Muhammad Said. *Usul al-shari'a*, 4th ed. (Cairo: Maktabat Madbuli al-Saghir, 1996).

Arabic News. "Al-Atasi Forum and the Culture of Fear," *Arabic News* (March 13, 2001), www.arabicnews.com/ansub/daily/day/010313/2001031316.html

Albrecht, Holger. *Raging Against the Machine: Political Opposition under Authoritarianism in Egypt* (Syracuse, NY: Syracuse University Press, 2013).

Al-Barnamij Al-Siyasi. National Democratic Gathering (December 20, 2001), mafhoum.com/press2/77taj.htm

Al-Ghudwy, Abdallah. "George Sabra 'li-Zaman al-Wasl': Sira'at Muqbila fi al-Mu'arada," *Zaman Al-Wsl* (August 8, 2017), www.zamanalwsl.net/news/article/80760

Al-Hafiz, Yasin. *Al-A'mal al-kamilah li-Yasin al-Ḥafiẓ* (al-Ṭab'ah 1. ed.). (Beirut: Markaz Dirasat al-Waḥda al-'Arabiya, 2005).

Al-Hafiz, Yasin. *Al-La 'aqlaniya fī al-siyasa: Naqd al-siyasat al-'Arabiyah fī al-marḥalah ma ba'da al-Naṣiriya* (al-Ṭab'ah 1. ed., Mufakkir al-'Arabi). (Beirut: Dar al-Ṭali'a lil-Ṭiba'ah wa-al-Nashr, 1975).

"Al-Haqiqa al-Gha'iba: al-kitab allazi qatala Faraj Fouda." *Kharej al-Nas.* Al-Jazeera TV (September 17, 2017).

Ali, Kecia. *Sexual Ethics and Islam: Feminist Reflections on the Quran, Hadith and Jurisprudence* (Chino Valley, AZ: Oneworld, 2006).

Ali, Souad. *A Religion, Not a State: Ali 'Abd al-Raziq's Islamic Justification of Political Secularism* (Utah: University of Utah Press, 2009).

Al-Kawakibi, 'Abd al-Rahman. *Ṭaba'i' al-Istibdad wa-Masari' al-Isti'bad* [The Nature of Despotism], second edition with introduction by Muhammad Imarah (Cairo, Egypt: Dar al-Shorouk, 2009).

Al-Khayyir, Abd al-Aziz. "A Conversation with 'Abd al-'Aziz al-Khayyir." *YouTube,* uploaded by DayPressNews (July 20, 2013), www.youtube.com/watch?v=BIOe6nwupsQ

"Al-liberaliyun al-arab wa al-dimucratiya." *Fi al-'umq.* AlJazeera, (May 12, 2014), www.youtube.com/watch?v=U_K_w7meM9E

Al-Maghut, Muhammad. *Al-a'mal al-shi'riya* (Damascus: Dar al-Mada, 2006).

Al-Maghut, Muhammad. *Day'at Tishrin.* (Damascus, 1974).

Al-Maghut, Muhammad. *Kasak ya Watan.* (Damascus, 1978).

Al-Muwatana, Sada. "Sada al-muwatana: watha'iqi 'an al-munadel 'Abd al-'Aziz al-Khayyir." *YouTube,* uploaded by Sada Almuwatana Prog (November 2, 2012), www.youtube.com/watch?v=JDcHOeSPWSk

Al-Nabulsi, Shakir. *Man hum al-libiraliyun al-arab al-judud wa ma huwa khitabuhum* (2004).

Al-Qassemi, Sooud S. "Qatar's Brotherhood Ties Alienate Fellow Gulf States," *Al Monitor* (January 23, 2013), www.al-monitor.com/pulse/originals/2013/01/qatar-muslim-brotherhood.html#ixzz3a7KolL8a

Al-Raziq, Ali Abd. *Al-Islam was usul al-hukum: bahth fi al-khilafa wa al-hukuma fi al-Islam* [Islam and the Foundations of Governance: A Study of the Caliphate and Government in Islam], with commentary by Mamduh Haqi (Beirut, Lebanon: Dar Maktabat al-Hayat, 1925).

Al-Ruwaini, 'Abla. *Haka al-ta'er saadallah wanus* (Cairo: dar meret, 2005).

Al-Saleh, Asaad. "Approaching Sa'dallah Wannus's Drama: The Manifestos of a New Arab Theater," *Alif: Journal of Comparative Poetics,* no. 39 (Annual 2019): 190–205.

Al-Sawwah, Wael. "Hassan 'Abbas wa Rabi' Dimashq: al-quwwa al-na'ima," in Fayez Sara (ed.), *Hassan 'Abbas bi-'uyun mu'asira* (Partners: November 2020): 22–34.

Al-Shorbaji, Mahmoud. "Hikim niha'i bi-rafd tajdid jawaz safar Ayman Nour," *Masrawi* (June 6, 2020), www.masrawy.com/news/news_cases/details/2020/6/6/1803171

Al-Shubashi, Sharif (interview). "Al-hijab: hal al-mar'a 'ora kay nughatiha?" *fi falak al-mamnu'*. France 24 (November 25, 2016).

Al-Turk, Riad. "The Old Man of the Syrian Opposition," *Fanack.com* (October 23, 2018), https://fanack.com/syria/faces/riad-al-turk/?gclid=EAIaIQob ChMIvLT98-GX5wIVELbICh10TgIlEAAYASAAEgJ89_D_BwE

Al-Wardani, Mahmud. "Al-Islam wa usul al-hukum li al-shaykh Ali Abd al-Raziq: al-kitab allazi wallada alaf al-kutub," *Al-Khaleej newspaper* (UAE), File 32, No 7534 (January 4, 2000).

Amnesty International, *Smothering Freedom of Expression: The Detention of Peaceful Critics* (June 6, 2002), www.refworld.org/docid/3cff2aa74.html

Amnesty International, *Syrian Refugee Crisis by Cartoonist Ali Ferzat* (May 18, 2020), www.amnesty.org.uk/syrian-refugee-crisis-cartoonist-ali-ferzat

Anderson, Leslie. "The Authoritarian Executive? Horizontal and Vertical Accountability in Nicaragua," *Latin American Politics & Society*, 48, no. 3 (Summer 2006): 141–169.

"Anwar Sadat Issues 'Law of Shame,' Veto Gate (Egypt), 22 January 2014." Translated by Kevin Moore, *The Edinburgh Arabic Initiative* (February 9, 2014), edinburgharabicinitiative.wordpress.com/2014/02/09/anwar-sadat-issues-law-of-shame/

"April 6 Youth Movement," *Carnegie Endowment* (September 22, 2010), https://carnegieendowment.org/2010/09/22/april-6-youth-movement-pub-54918

Arab Center for Research and Policy Studies (ACRPS). *The Arab Opinion Index*, www.dohainstitute.org/en/ProgramsAndProjects/Pages/programDe-tailedpage.aspx?PageId=4

"Arab Reform Issues: Vision and Implementation." *The Alexandria Statement* (Bibliotheca Alexandrina: March 2004), https://al-bab.com/albab-orig/albab/arab/docs/reform/alex2004.htm

Aras, Bulent, and Lacin Idil Oztig. "Has the Arab Spring Spread to the Caucasus and Central Asia? Explaining Regional Diffusion and Authoritarian Resistance," *Journal of Balkan and Near Eastern Studies* 23, no. 3 (February 16, 2021): 516–532, https://doi.org/10.1080/19448953.2021.1888249

Arslanian, Ferdinand. "The Left in the Syrian Uprising," in Hinnebusch and Imady (eds.), *The Syrian Uprising: Domestic Origins and Early Trajectories* (London and New York: Routledge, 2018).

"As'ilat al-thawra al-Suriya al-mulihha fi zikraha al-'ashira...ru'iya siasiya wa shahadat haiyya," *Markaz Harmoon lil-dirasat al-mu'asira* (Harmoon Center for Contemporary Studies, March 16, 2021), www.harmoon.org/reports/ ذكرا-في-الملحة-السورية-الثورة-أسئلة

Atassi, Karim. *Syria, the Strength of an Idea: The Constitutional Architectures of Its Political regimes*, Translated from French by Christopher Sutcliffe, (Cambridge: Cambridge University Press, 2018).

Azimi, Negar. "Egypt's Youth Have had Enough," *OpenDemocracy.net* (August 31, 2005), www.opendemocracy.net/en/enough_2794jsp/

Bahgat Korany. "Restricted Democratization from Above: Egypt," in Bahgat Korany, Rex Brynen and Paul Noble (eds.), *Political Liberalization and Democratization in the Arab World: Comparative Perspectives* (vol. 2) (Boulder Colorado: Lynne Rienner, 1998): 39–69.

Bar'el, Zvi. "60,000 Political Prisoners and 1,250 Missing: Welcome to the New Egypt," *Haaretz* (September 11, 2016), www.haaretz.com/middle-east-news/.premium-60-000-political-prisoners-and-1-250-missing-welcome-to-the-new-egypt-1.5440308

Baron, Beth. *Egypt as a Woman: Nationalism, Gender, and Politics* (Berkley, CA: University of California Press, 2007).

Barr, Cameron W. "Syrians Test New Signs of Freedom," *The Christian Science Monitor* (February 13, 2001), www.csmonitor.com/2001/0213/p1s4.html

Barut, Jamal. *Ḥarakat al-tanwir al-'arabiyya fi al-qarn al-tasi' 'ashar: halaqat halab dirasa wa-mukhtarat [The Arab Enlightenment Movement in the Nineteenth Century: A Study and Extracts from the Aleppo Circle]* (Damascus, Syria: the Syrian Ministry of Culture Publications, 1994).

Batatu, Hanna. *Syria's Peasantry, the Descendants of its Lesser Rural Notables, and their Politics* (Princeton, NJ: Princeton University Press, 1999).

Batatu, Hanna. *The Old Social Classes and the Revolutionary Movements in Iraq* (Princeton: Princeton University Press, 1978).

Batatu, Hanna. "Some Observations on the Social Roots of Syria's Ruling Military Group and the Causes of its Dominance," *Middle East Journal* 35, no. 3 (1981): 331–344.

"Bayan hawla al-intikhabat al-suriya" (November 2020), www.ipetitions.com/petition/TheSyrianelections

Beinin, Joel and Zachary Lockman. *Workers on the Nile: Nationalism, Communism, Islam and the Egyptian Working Class* (Princeton, NJ: Princeton University Press, 1998).

Bellin, Eva. "Reconsidering the Robustness of Authoritarianism in the Middle East: Lessons from the Arab Spring," *Comparative Politics*, 44, no. 2 (January 2012): 127–149.

Bellin, Eva. "The Robustness of Authoritarianism in the Middle East: Exceptionalism in Comparative Perspective," *Comparative Politics*, 36, no. 2 (2004): 139–157.

Benchemsi, Ahmed. "Arab Liberalism Is Alive and Well, Thank You," *Free Arabs* (February 22, 2015), https://web.archive.org/web/20150812095527/www.freearabs.com/index.php/ideas/102-stories/2166-jb-span-arab-liberalism-jb-span-is-alive-and-well

Benchemsi, Ahmed. "Invisible Atheists: The Spread of Disbelief in the Arab World," *New Republic* (April 24, 2015), https://newrepublic.com/article/121559/rise-arab-atheists

Berman, Paul. *Terror and Liberalism* (New York: W. W. Norton, 2003).

Binder, Leonard. *Islamic liberalism: A critique of development ideologies.* (University of Chicago Press, 1988).

Bitar, Karim Emile. "Arab Liberals Must Realize that the Enemies of Their Enemies Aren't Necessarily Their Friends," *Your Middle East* (March 12, 2014), https://yourmiddleeast.com/2014/03/12/arab-liberals-must-realize-that-the-enemies-of-their-enemies-arenaet-necessarily-their-friends/

Britannica, The Editors of Encyclopaedia. "Isma'il Pasha." *Encyclopedia Britannica*, www.britannica.com/biography/Ismail-Pasha, Accessed June 8, 2021.

Browers, Michaelle. *Political Ideology in the Arab World: Accommodation and Transformation* (New York: Cambridge University Press, 2009).

Brown, Nathan, and Kristen Stilt. "A Haphazard Constitutional Compromise," *Carnegie Endowment for International Peace* (April 11, 2011), https://carnegieendowment.org/2011/04/11/haphazard-constitutional-compromise-pub-43533

Brown, Nathan. *The Rule of Law in the Arab World: Courts in Egypt and the Gulf* (Cambridge University Press, 1997).

Brownlee, Jason. "The Decline of Pluralism in Mubarak's Egypt," *Journal of Democracy*, 13, no. 4 (2012): 6–14.

Brözel, T. A. "The Noble West and the Dirty Rest? Western Democracy Promoters and Illiberal Regional Powers," *Democratization*, 22, no. 3 (2015): 519–535.

Brumberg, Daniel. "Islamists and the Politics of Consensus," *Journal of Democracy*, 13, no. 4 (2002): 109–115.

Brumberg, Daniel. "The Trap of Liberalized Autocracy," *Journal of Democracy*, 13, no. 4 (2002): 56–68.

Carothers, Thomas. "The End of the Transition Paradigm," *Journal of Democracy*, 13, no. 1 (2002): 5–21.

Caten, George. "Harakat Kifaya al-misriya tatajawaz al-ahzab al-aydiyologiya," *al-Hiwar al-Mutamaden*, No. 1238 (June 24, 2005).

Cavatorta, Francesco and Paul Aarts. *Civil Society in Syria and Iran: Activism in Authoritarian Contexts* (Boulder and London: Lynne Rienner Publishers, 2012).

Cavatorta, Francesco and Vincent Durac. *Civil Society and Democratization in the Arab World: The Dynamics of Activism* (New York: Routledge, 2011).

Cavatorta, Francesco. "The EU and the Arab world: Living up to the EU's normative expectations," *The Arab Spring of discontent: A collection from e-International relations* (2011): 14–17.

Center for Human Rights Legal Aid, *Freedom of Academic Research* (Cairo: September 1996), www.wluml.org/node/262

Centre Arabe de Recherches et d'Etudes Politiques de Paris (CAREP). www.carep-paris.org/

Chalcraft, John. *Popular Politics in the Making of the Modern Middle East* (New York: Cambridge University Press, 2016).

Cody, Edward. "Sadat Presses Bill to Punish Dissent," *The Washington Post* (February 21, 1980).

"Court to consider withdrawing Ayman Nour's Citizenship," *The Cairo Post* (January 23, 2014), https://archive.vn/20140131075204/http://thecairopost.com/news/78414/politics/court-to-consider-withdrawing-ayman-nours-citizenship#selection-465.7-469.203

Daher, Joseph. "Pluralism Lost in Syria's Uprising: How the Opposition Strayed from its Inclusive Roots," *The Century Foundation* (May 7, 2019), https://tcf.org/content/report/pluralism-lost-syrias-uprising/?agreed=1

Dannreuther, Roland. "Russia and the Arab Spring: Supporting the Counter-Revolution," *Journal of European Integration*, 37, no. 1 (2015): 77–94.

Davidson, Phil. "Mai Skaf: Syrian Actor and Democracy Activist Exiled by the Asad Regime," *Independent* (July 30, 2018), www.independent.co.uk/news/obituaries/mai-skaf-may-skaf-syria-actor-assad-activist-exile-syrian-refugee-a8469876.html

Dawn, C. Ernest. *From Ottomanism to Arabism: Essays on the Origins of Arab Nationalism* (Urbana: University of Illinois Press, 1973).

Debeuf, Koert. "From Arab Spring to Arab Revolution: Three Years of ALDE Representation in the Arab World," in Ronald Meinardus (ed.), *Liberalism in the Arab World – Just a good idea?* (Cairo: Al-Mahrosa for Publishing, 2014): 157–167.

Deeb, Marius. "Labour and Politics in Egypt, 1919–1939," *International Journal of Middle East Studies*, 10, no. 2 (May 1979): 187–203.

"Detainee Goes on Hunger Strike after Two Years' Imprisonment for Writing Unpublished Theological Research Paper." *Egyptian Initiative for Personal Rights* (July 4, 2005), https://eipr.org/en/press/2005/07/detainee-goes-hunger-strike-after-two-years%E2%80%99-imprisonment-writing-unpublished. Press Release.

Dickinson, Elizabeth. "What happened to Arab Liberalism? Four years after the Arab Spring, activists are trying to revive an enfeebled movement," *Politico Magazine* (December 17, 2014), www.politico.com/magazine/story/2014/12/arab-spring-anniversary-113637

Duib, 'Ammar. "George Sabra...Khitab Did al-Tarikh," *Alaraby Aljadid* (July 28, 2017), www.alaraby.co.uk/جورج-صبرا-خطاب-ضد-التاريخ

Draege, Jonas Bergan. "The Formation of Syrian Opposition Coalitions as Two-Level Games," *Middle East Journal*, 70, no. 2 (Spring 2016): 189–210.

Dunne, Michele, and Amr Hamzawi. "Egypt's Secular Political Parties: A Struggle For Identity And Independence," *Carnegie Endowment* (March 31, 2017), https://carnegieendowment.org/2017/03/31/egypt-s-secular-political-parties-struggle-for-identity-and-independence-pub-68482

Dunne, Michele. "Interview with Wael Nawara, Secretary General of the Ghad," *Carnegie Endowment* (November 3, 2010), http://carnegieendowment.org/sada/41861

Egyptian Initiative for Personal Rights. *Freedom of belief and the Arrests of Shi'a Muslims in Egypt* (August 2004), available on EIPR.org, https://eipr.org/en/publications/freedom-belief-and-arrests-shia-muslims-egypt

"Egypt Detains Human Rights Lawyer Representing anti-Sisi Protesters," *Middle East Eye* (September 22, 2019), www.middleeasteye.net/news/egypt-detains-award-winning-human-rights-lawyer-representing-protesters

"Egypt Elections: Democratic Front Party," *Carnegie Endowment* (September 20, 2011), http://egyptelections-carnegieendowment.org/2011/09/20/al-ghabha-al-dimuqrati-the-democratic-front-party

"Egypt's Morsi rescinds controversial decree," *AlJazeera* (December 9, 2012), www.aljazeera.com/news/2012/12/9/egypts-morsi-rescinds-controversial-decree

"Egypt's National Salvation Front," *BBC News* (December 10, 2012), www.bbc.com/news/world-middle-east-20667661

"Egypt: Opponents of Sisi Launch Anti-Regime Group," *Middle East Monitor* (December 31, 2019), www.middleeastmonitor.com/20191231-egypt-opponents-of-sisi-launch-anti-regime-group/

"Egypt's Parliament Speaker Favourably Compares Sisi to Hitler," *Middle East Eye* (October 2, 2019), www.middleeasteye.net/news/egypt-top-lawmaker-praises-hitler-parliament-speech

Eickelman, Dale F., and James Piscatori. *Muslim politics* (Princeton, NJ: Princeton University Press, 1996).

'Eid, 'Abd al-Razzak. "Al-nukhab al-suriya wa taraf al-ikhtiar bayn al-dimucratiya wa al-libraliya!" *Shafaf al-Sharq al-Awsat* (August 5, 2005), www.metransparent.com/old/texts/abdelrazak_eid/abdelrazak_eid_syrian_elite_democracy_and_liberalism.htm

'Eid, 'Abd al-Razzak and Muhammad 'Abd al-Jabbar. *Al-dimucratiya bayn al-'ilmaniya wa al-islam* (Damascus: Dar al Fikr, 1999).

El-Badawi, Emran. "Conflict and Reconciliation: 'Arab liberalism' in Syria and Egypt," in Dalia F. Fahmy and Daanish Faruqi (eds.), *Egypt and the Contradictions of Liberalism: Illiberal Intelligentsia and the Future of Egyptian Democracy* (London: Oneworld Publications, 2017).

El Deeb, Sarah. "A Sinister Night for 3 Women in Egypt Protest Wave," *Associated Press* (November 28, 2013), https://apnews.com/article/423356fa778644638db78ebad821b4f8

El-Ghobashy, Mona. "Egypt Looks Ahead to a Portentous Year," *Middle East Report* (February 2, 2005).

El Haddaji, Hicham. "The Congruent Critique of Despotism in 'Abd Al-Rahman Al-Kawakibi and Shaykh 'Ali Abdel-Raziq," *AlMuntaqa*, 1, no. 3 (2018): 92–103, https://doi.org/10.31430/almuntaqa.1.3.0092. Accessed August 5, 2020.

El-Hosseiny, Salma. "Syria: Reveal the Whereabouts of Razan, Samira, Nazem and Wa'el," *ISHR* (December 12, 2018), www.ishr.ch/news/syria-reveal-whereabouts-razan-samira-nazem-and-wael

El-Mahdi, Rabab. "Egypt: A Decade of Ruptures." In Lina Khatib and Ellen Lust (eds.), *Taking to the Streets: The Transformation of Arab Activism* (Washington: John Hopkins University Press, 2014).

El-Mahdi, Rabab. "Enough: Egypt's Quest for Democracy," *Comparative Political Studies*, 44, no. 5 (June 2009): 1011–1039.

Elmasry, Mohamad. "Egypt's protests: Sisi's Iron Fist is No longer Enough," *Middle East Eye* (September 30, 2019), www.middleeasteye.net/opinion/egypt-protests-sisi-iron-fist-is-no-longer-enough

El-Naggar, Mona. "Equal Rights Takes to the Barricades," *New York Times* (February 1, 2011), www.nytimes.com/2011/02/02/world/middleeast/02iht-letter02.html

El Saadawi, Nawal and Heba Raouf Ezzat. *Al-Mar'a wa al-Din wa al-Akhlaq* [*Women, Religion and Ethics*.] (Beirut: Dar al Fikr, 2000)

El Sheikh, Mayy. "A Voice of Dissent in Egypt is Muffled but not Silent," *The New York Times* (May 2, 2014), www.nytimes.com/2014/05/03/world/middleeast/an-egyptian-voice-of-dissent-is-muffled-but-not-silenced.html

Erhaim, Zaina. "How the Syrian Revolution was Organized—And How it Unraveled," *Newlines Magazine* (March 16, 2021), https://newlinesmag.com/essays/how-the-syrian-revolution-was-organized-and-how-it-unraveled/?f bclid=IwAR0gw1j8MtRDblGQu44Zk4gAUQ22dbxbFWoG34Wq1DoYmr 7mALN56oRHA

Fadel, Leila. "Examining the Years since Egypt's Arab Spring," *NPR Morning Edition* (February 11, 2015), www.npr.org/2015/02/11/385396424/examining-the-4-years-since-egypts-arab-spring

Fadl, 'Essam. "Asharq Al-Awsat talks to Egypt's April 6 Youth Movement founder Ahmed Maher," *Asharq al-Awsat* (February 10, 2011), https://eng-archive.aawsat.com/theaawsat/features/asharq-al-awsat-talks-egypts-april-6-youth-movement-founder-ahmed-maher

Fahmy, Khaled. *All the Pasha's Men: Mehmet Ali, His Army and the Making of Modern Egypt* (Cairo: American University in Cairo Press, 2002).

"Farag Fouda: Nakun aw la-Nakun." *Muni'a Min al-Tadawul, Al-Ghad TV* (July 29, 2019).

Fares, Ra'ed. "Building a Free Syria One Town at a Time," *Oslo Freedom Forum* (May 23, 2017), https://oslofreedomforum.com/talks/building-a-free-syria-one-town-at-a-time-/

Fares, Raed. "Building a free Syria One Town at a Time." *YouTube*, uploaded by Oslo Freedom Forum (July 7, 2017), www.youtube.com/watch?v=OlWt-kI7_LQ

Fares, Raed. "Liqa' sareeh ma'a Ibn Kafranbel, Ra'ed al-Fares, yuhawiruhu Mousa Al-Omar." *YouTube*, uploaded by Mousa Al-Omar (March 24, 2014), www.youtube.com/watch?v=l9fqH5Km-ys

Faruqi, Daanish, and Dalia F. Fahmy. "Egyptian liberals, from revolution to counterrevolution," in Fahmy and Faruqi (eds.), *Egypt and the Contradictions of Liberalism: Illiberal Intelligentsia and the Future of Egyptian Democracy* (London: Oneworld Publications, 2017): 1–27.

Fathallah, Najlaa. "Yusri Nasrallah: 'amr sakhif' tahwil al-fan li-khidmat al-siyasa," *Alrai Media* (October 7, 2007), www.alraimedia.com/article/419252

Fathi, Yasmine. "SCAF's Proposal for Constitution 'Abuses Will of the People,' Charge Critics," *Ahram Online* (November 3, 2011), https://english.ahram .org.eg/NewsContent/1/0/25802/Egypt/0/SCAFs-proposal-for-constitution-abuses-will-of-the.aspx

Fawcett, Edmund. *Liberalism: The Life of an Idea*, 2nd ed. (Princeton and Oxford: Princeton University Press, 2018).

Fawcett, Edmund. *Liberalism: The Life of an Idea* (Princeton, NJ: Princeton University Press, 2015).

Fishere, Ezzeldine C. "Egypt's dictatorship is sitting on a powder keg," *Washington Post* (October 17, 2019), www.washingtonpost.com/opinions/2019/10/17/egypts-dictatorship-is-sitting-powder-keg/

Franjiya, Samer. "Al-irth al-mudamer li niqad al-liberaliyin al-'arab'" [The destructive legacy of the critics of "Arab Liberals"], *Al-Hayat newspaper* (May 9, 2015).

Freeden, Micheal. *Ideologies and Political Theory: A Conceptual Approach* (Oxford and New York: Oxford University Press, 1996).

Freeden, Micheal. *Reassessing Political Ideologies: The Durability of Dissent* (London and New York: Routledge, 2001).

Fuda, Farag. *Al-Haqiqa al-gha'iba*, 3rd ed. (Cairo: Dar al-Fikr, 1988).

Fuda, Farag. *Al-Irhab* (Cairo: Dar Misr al-Jadida, 1988).

Fuda, Farag. *Al-Nadhir* (Cairo: Dar Misr al-Jadida lil-Nashr wal-tawzi, 1983).

Fuda, Farag. *Hiwar hawla al-'almana* (Cairo: Dar al-Nashr, 1986).

Fuda, Farag. *Nakun aw la nakun* [To be or not to be] (Cairo: Dar Misr al-Jadida, 1988).

Gengler, Justin, Mark Tessler, Darwish al-Emadi, and Abdoulaye Diop. "Civil Society and Democratization in the Arab Gulf," *Mideast Foreign Policy*, (July 25, 2011), https://foreignpolicy.com/2011/07/25/civil-society-and-democratization-in-the-arab-gulf/

George, Alan. *Syria: Neither Bread nor Freedom* (London: Zed Books, 2003).

Gershoni, Israel, and James Jankowski. *Egypt, Islam, and the Arabs: The Search for Egyptian Nationhood, 1900–1930* (London: Oxford University Press, 1986).

Gershoni, Israel, and James Jankowski. *Confronting Fascism in Egypt: Dictatorship versus Democracy in the 1930s* (Stanford, California: Stanford University Press, 2010).

Gershoni, Israel. "Egyptian Liberalism in an Age of 'Crisis of Orientation': al-Risala's Reaction to Fascism and Nazism, 1933–39," *International Journal of Middle East Studies*, 31, no. 4 (1999): 551–576.

Gershoni, Israel. "Liberal Democratic Legacies in Modern Egypt: The Role of the Intellectuals, 1900–1950," *IAS* (2012), www.ias.edu/ideas/2012/gershoni-democratic-legacies-egypt

"Ghad al-Thawra Party," *Al-Ahram Online* (December 3, 2011), http://english.ahram.org.eg/News/26694.aspx

Ghaliyoun, Burhan. "Rad 'ala al-liberaliyin al-'arab," *Voltairenet* (July 5, 2005), www.voltairenet.org/article90638.html

Ghonim, Wael. *Revolution 2.0: The power of the people is greater than the people in power. A memoir* (New York, NY: Houghton Mifflin Harcourt, 2012).

Gordon, Joel. "Egypt's new liberal crisis," in Dalia F. Fahmy and Daanish Faruqi (eds.), *Egypt and the Contradictions of Liberalism: Illiberal Intelligentsia and the Future of Egyptian Democracy* (London: Oneworld Publications, 2017): 317–335.

Gordon, Joel. *Nasser's Blessed Movement: Egypt's Free Officers and the July Revolution* (New York: Oxford University Press, 1992).

Greenfield, Danya, and R. Balfour, *Arab Awakening: Are the US and EU Missing the Challenge?* (Washington, DC: Atlantic Council, 2012).

Guazzone, Laura and Daniela Pioppo. *The Arab State and Neo-Liberal Globalization: The Restructuring of the State in the Middle East* (Reading, UK: Ithaca Press, 2009).

Guerin, Orla. "Revolution a Distant Memory as Egypt Escalates Repression," *BBC News* (December 9, 2014), www.bbc.com/news/world-30381292

"Haitham el-Maleh," *Carnegie Middle East Center* https://carnegie-mec.org/syriaincrisis/?fa=48368&lang=en

Hamed, Yehia. "Joe Biden's Administration Should Start Listening to all Egyptians," *Middle East Eye* (November 17, 2020), www.middleeasteye.net/opinion/joe-bidens-administration-should-start-listening-all-egyptians

Hanssen, Jens and Max Weiss (eds.) *Arabic Thought Beyond the Liberal Age: Towards an Intellectual History of the Nahda* (Cambridge University Press, 2016).

Hassan, Oz. "Undermining the Transatlantic Democracy Agenda? The Arab Spring and the Saudi Arabia's Counteracting Democracy Strategy," *Democratization*, 22, 3 (2015): 479–495.

Hatina, Meir and Christoph Schumann (eds.). *Arab Liberal Thought after 1967: Old Dilemmas, New Perceptions* (New York: Palgrave Macmillan, 2015).

Hatina, Meir. "Arab Liberal Discourse: Old Dilemmas, New Visions," *Middle East Critique*, 20, no. 1 (Spring 2011): 3–20.

Hatina, Meir. "Arab Liberal Thought in Historical Perspective," in Meir Hatina and Christoph Schumann (eds.), *Arab Liberal Thought After 1967: Old Dilemmas, New Perceptions* (New York: Palgrave Macmillan, 2015).

Haugbølle, Rikke Hostrup, and Francesco Cavatorta. "Will the Real Tunisian Opposition Please Stand Up? Opposition Coordination Failures under Authoritarian Constraints," *British Journal of Middle Eastern Studies*, 38, no. 3 (2011): 323–341.

Hearst, David, and Abdel-Rahman Hussein. "Egypt's Supreme Court Dissolves Parliament and Outrages Islamists," *The Guardian* (June 14, 2012), www.theguardian.com/world/2012/jun/14/egypt-parliament-dissolved-supreme-court

Hearst, David. "Interview with Egyptian Opposition Leader Ayman Nour," *Middle East Eye* (March 14, 2015), www.middleeasteye.net/news/exclusive-interview-egyptian-opposition-leader-ayman-nour

Heydemann, Steven. "Mass Politics and the Future of Authoritarian Governance in the Arab world," *The Arab Thermidor: The Resurgence of the Security State*, POMPES Studies (December 16, 2014), https://pomeps.org/mass-politics-and-the-future-of-authoritarian-governance-in-the-arab-world

Heydemann, Steven. *Upgrading authoritarianism in the Arab World* (Analysis Paper No. 13, Saban Center for Middle East Policy at the Brookings Institution, 2007).

Hinnebusch, Raymond A. "Calculated Decompression as a Substitute for Democratization: Syria," in B. Korany, R. Brynen and P. Noble (eds.), *Political Liberalization and Democratization in the Arab World, Vol. 2: Comparative Experiences* (Boulder, Colorado and London: Lynne Rienner, 1998): 223–240.

Hinnebusch, Raymond A. "Liberalization without Democratization in 'Post-Populist' Authoritarian States," in Nils August Butenschøn, Uri Davis and Manuel Sarkis Hassassian (eds.), *Citizenship and the State in the Middle East* (Syracuse: Syracuse University Press, 2000): 123–145.

Hinnebusch, Raymond A. "Syria: From 'Authoritarian Upgrading' to Revolution?" *International Affairs*, 88, no. 1 (2012): 95–113.

Hinnebusch, Raymond A. "The Reemergence of the Wafd Party: Glimpses of the Liberal Opposition in Egypt," *International Journal of Middle East Studies*, 16, no. 1 (1984): 99–123.

Hourani, Albert. *A History of the Arab Peoples* (Faber and Faber, 1991).

Hourani, Albert. *Arabic Thought in the Liberal Age, 1798–1939* (Cambridge: Cambridge University Press, 1983).

Hourani, Albert. *Arabic Thought in the Liberal Age, 1798–1939* (Oxford: Oxford University Press, 1962).

How to Start a Revolution. Directed by Ruaridh Arrow, performance by Ahmed Maher, Jamila Raqib, Ausama Monajed and Gene Sharp (TVF International, September 18, 2011), www.howtostartarevolution.org/

Huntington, Samuel. *The Clash of Civilizations and the Remaking of World Order* (New York: Simon and Schuster, 1996).

Hussein, Taha. *Fi al-shi'r al-jahili [On pre-Islamic poetry]* (Cairo: Dar al-kutub al-masriyyah 1926).

Hussein, Taha. *Mustaqbal al-thaqafa fi Misr [The Future of Culture in Egypt]* (Cairo: Matba 'at al-Ma'aref wa Maktabat Masr 1938).

"Interview with Bashar al-Asad," *Asharq al-Awsat* (February 8, 2001) https://al-bab.com/documents-section/interview-president-bashar-al-assad-0. Accessed June 29, 2021.

Jamal, Amaney. *Barriers to Democracy: The Other Side of Social Capital in Palestine and the Arab World* (Princeton, NJ: Princeton University Press, 2007).

Jamil, Abd al-Sami'. "Kuluhum Qatalu Farag Fouda hayan, kuluhum yakhshunahu al'an mayitan," *Daqaeq* (May 14, 2020).

Jankowski, James. "The Egyptian Blue Shirts and the Egyptian Wafd, 1935–1938," *Middle Eastern Studies*, 6, no. 1 (January 1970): 77–95.

Josua, Maria, and Mirjam Edel. "The Arab Uprisings and the Return of Repression," *Mediterranean Politics* (February 18, 2021), https://doi.org/10.1080/13629395.2021.1889298

Kamrava, Mehran (ed.). *Innovation in Islam: Traditions and Contributions* (Los Angeles: University of California Press, 2011).

Kassab, Beesan. "Why is Sisi afraid of the constitution and parliament," *Mada Masr* (September 15, 2015), www.madamasr.com/en/2015/09/15/feature/politics/why-is-sisi-afraid-of-the-constitution-and-parliament/

Kassab, Elizabeth Suzanne. "The Arab Quest for Freedom and Dignity: Have Arab Thinkers Been Part of It?" *Middle East Topics and Arguments*, Vol. 1 (May 1, 2013), https://meta-journal.net/article/download/1038/988/

Kassab, Elizabeth Suzanne. *Contemporary Arab Thought: Cultural Critique in comparative Perspective* (New York: Columbia University Press, 2010).

Kassem, Maye. *Egyptian Politics: The Dynamics of Authoritarian Rule* (Boulder, CO: Lynne Rienner, 2004).

Kawakibi, Salam. Personal Interview. By Line Khatib (2019 and 2021).

Kawakibi, Salam. *Syrie: malgré la débâcle militaire, la renaissance de la société civile* (Carep Paris, October 2020), www.carep-paris.org/wp-content/uploads/2020/10/Syrie_malgre_la_debacle_militaire_la-renaissance_de_la_societe-civile_Salam_Kawakibi.pdf

Kedourie, Elie. *Democracy and the Arab Political Culture* (London: Frank Cass, 1994).

Kermani, Navid. "From Revelation to Interpretation: Nasr Hamid Abu Zayd and the Literary Study of the Quran," in Suha Taji-Farouki (ed.), *Modern Muslim Intellectuals and the Quran* (Oxford University Press, 2004): 169–192.

Khatib, Line. "Challenges of Representation and Inclusion: A Case Study of Islamic Groups in Transitional Justice," in K. J. Fisher and R. Stewart (eds.),

Transitional Justice and the Arab Spring (London and New York: Routledge, 2014): 131–145.

Khatib, Line. "The Pre-2011 Roots of Syria's Islamist Militants," *The Middle East Journal* 72, 2 (Spring 2018): 209–228.

Khatib, Line. "Syria, Saudi Arabia, the UAE and Qatar: The 'Sectarianization' of the Syrian Conflict and Undermining of Democratization in the Region," *British Journal of Middle Eastern Studies* 46, no. 3 (2019): 385–403.

Khoury, Philip S. "Syrian Political Culture: A Historical Perspective," in Richard T. Antoun and Donald Quataert (eds.), *Syria: Society, Culture, and Polity* (New York: State University of New York Press, 1991): 13–27.

Khoury, Philip S. *Syria and the French Mandate: The Politics of Arab Nationalism, 1920–1945* (Princeton University Press, 1987).

Khoury, Philip S. *Urban Notables and Arab Nationalism: The Politics of Damascus, 1860–1920* (Cambridge University Press, 1983).

Kienle, Eberhard. *The Grand Delusion: Democracy and Economic Reform in Egypt* (London: I. B. Tauris, 2001).

"'Kifaya' in Egypt," *The Washington Post* (March 15, 2005) p. A22, www.washingtonpost.com/wp-dyn/articles/A35379-2005Mar14.html

Kilo, Michel. "Michel Kilo Yatakalam athna' mu'tamar itihad al-kutab al-'Arab 'am 1979." *YouTube,* uploaded by SyrianGirl47 (July 1, 2011), www.youtube.com/watch?v=Hx9rxdNPqwE

Kilo, Michel. "Shahadat: Mishel Kilo," *al-Nahj* 40 (1995).

Kilo, Michel. "Syria.. the road to where?" *Contemporary Arab Affairs*, 4, no. 4, (2011): 431–444.

Kirkpatrick, David D. "Army Ousts Egypt's President; Morsi Is Taken into Military Custody," *The New York Times* (July 3, 2013), www.nytimes.com/2013/07/04/world/middleeast/egypt.html

Kodmani, Hala. *Abd al-Rahman al-Kawakibi, Du despotism et autres textes.* (Arles: Actes Sud, 2016).

Kohn, Asher. "The Syrian Cartoonists who live and die by their pen," *Roads and Kingdoms* (November 20, 2015), https://roadsandkingdoms.com/2015/drawn-in-blood/

Korany, Bahgat. "Restricted Democratization from Above: Egypt," in Bahgat Korany, Rex Brynen and Paul Noble (eds.), *Political Liberalization and Democratization in the Arab World: Comparative perspectives* (vol. 2) (Boulder Colorado: Lynne Rienner, 1998): 39–69.

Krämer, Gudrun. "Islam and Pluralism," in Rex Brynen, Bahgat Korany and Paul Noble (eds.), *Political Liberalization and Democratization in the Arab World: Theoretical Perspectives* (vol. 1) (Boulder, Colorado: Lynne Rienner, 1996): 113–128.

Kubba, Laith. "Arabs and Democracy: The Awakening of Civil Society," *Journal of Democracy*, 11, no. 3 (2000): 84–90.

Kurzman, Charles (ed.). *Liberal Islam: A Sourcebook* (New York: Oxford University Press, 1998).

Langer, Emily. "Fadwa Suleiman, Syrian actress who led resistance to Assad regime, dies," *The Washington Post* (August 19, 2017), www.washingtonpost.com/local/obituaries/fadwa-suleiman-syrian-actress-who-led-resistance-

to-assad-regime-dies/2017/08/18/78f12b44-841d-11e7-b359-15a3617c
767b_story.html

Laroui, Abdallah. *The Crisis of the Arab Intellectual: Traditionalism or Historicism?* (Berkeley and Los Angeles: University of California Press, 1976).

Lee, Robert, Lihi Ben Shitrit. "Religion, Society, and Politics in the Middle East," in Ellen Lust (ed.), *The Middle East*, 13th ed. (Los Angeles, London, Singapore, Washington DC: Sage, 2014).

Lesch, Ann M. "The Authoritarian State's Power over Civil Society," in Fahmy and Faruqi (eds.), *Egypt and the Contradictions of Liberalism: Illiberal Intelligentsia and the Future of Egyptian Democracy* (London: Oneworld Publications, 2017): 121–174.

Lesch, David W. *The New Lion of Damascus: Bashar al-Asad and Modern Syria* (New Haven and London: Yale University Press, 2005).

Leverett, Flynt. *Inheriting Syria: Bashar's Trial by Fire* (Washington, DC: Brookings Institution Press, 2005).

Lewis, Bernard. *What Went Wrong: Western Impact and Middle Eastern Response* (Oxford and New York: Oxford University Press, 2002).

"Local Coordination Committees of Syria" *Syria Untold* (June 24, 2014), https://syriauntold.com/2013/06/24/local-coordination-committees-of-syria/

Loza, Pierre Roshdy. *The Case of Abu Zayd and the Reactions it Prompted from Egyptian Society* (Georgetown University: Masters' Thesis, 2013).

Lust-Okar, Ellen. *Structuring Conflict in the Arab World: Incumbents, Opponents, and Institutions* (Cambridge: Cambridge University Press, 2005).

Lynch, Marc. *Voices of the New Arab Public* (New York: Columbia University Press, 2006).

MacFarquhar, Neil. "Mubarak Pushes Egypt to Allow Freer Elections," *The New York Times* (Febuary 27, 2005), www.nytimes.com/2005/02/27/world/middleeast/mubarak-pushes-egypt-to-allow-freer-elections.html

"Macron gave Sisi France's highest award on Paris visit: official," *France 24* (December 10, 2020), www.france24.com/en/live-news/20201210-macron-gave-sisi-france-s-highest-award-on-paris-visit-official

Mardam Bey, Salma. *La Syrie et la France: bilan d'une équivoque (1939–1945)* (Paris: l'Harmattan, 1994).

Mardam Bey, Salma. *Syria's Quest for Independence 1939–1945* (Reading, UK: Ithaca Press, 1994).

Mady, Abdel-Fattah. "Student Political Activism in Democratizing Egypt," in Dalia F. Fahmy and Daanish Faruqi (eds), *Egypt and the Contradictions of Liberalism: Illiberal Intelligentsia and the Future of Egyptian Democracy* (London: Oneworld Publications, 2017): 199–232.

Maghraoui, Abdelslam M. *Liberalism without democracy: nationhood and citizenship in Egypt, 1922–1936* (Durham and London: Duke University Press, 2006).

"Main Case of the Month: Aref Dalila," *English Pen*, https://pen.org/advocacy-case/aref-dalila/

Majed, Ziad. "A dialogue with Zakaria Tamer" (translated by Syrian Translators group), *Ziad Majed's Blog* (June 5, 2021), https://freesyriantranslators.net/2012/07/22/a-dialogue-with-zakaria-tamer-2/

Makdisi, Ussama. *The Culture of Sectarianism: Community, History, and Violence in Nineteenth Century Ottoman Lebanon* (Berkeley, CA: University of California Press, 2000).

Marei, Fouad Gehad. "Local Coordination Committees," in J. K. Zartman (ed.), *Conflict in the Modern Middle East: An Encyclopedia of Civil War, Revolutions, and Regime Change* (Santa Barbara, CA: ABC-CLIO, 2020).

Marsot, Afaf Lutfi al-Sayyid. *Egypt's Liberal Experiment: 1922–1936* (Berkeley: University of California Press, 1977).

Marrash, Francis. *Ghabat al-Haqq* [The Forest of Justice] (c. 1865).

Massad, Joseph. "Al-irth al-mudamer li al-liberaliyeen al-'arab," *Al-Akhbar newspaper* (April 7, 2015).

Massad, Joseph. "The destructive legacy of Arab Liberals," *The Electronic Intifada* (March 30, 2015), https://electronicintifada.net/content/destructive-legacy-arab-liberals/14385

McDonald, Andrew. "Ali 'Abd al-Raziq: A profile," *Jadaliyya* (September 4, 2018), www.jadaliyya.com/Details/37930

Meijer, Roel. "Liberalism in the Middle East and the Issue of Citizenship Rights," in Meir Hatina and Christoph Schumann (eds.), *Arab Liberal Thought After 1967: Old Dilemmas, New Perceptions* (New York: Palgrave Macmillan, 2015): 63–81.

Meijer, Roel. *The Quest for Modernity: Secular Liberal and Left Wing Political Thought in Egypt, 1945–1958* (New York and London: Routledge, 2002).

Meital, Yoram. "The Struggle Over Political Order in Egypt: The 2005 Elections," *The Middle East Journal*, 60, no. 2 (April 2006): 257–279.

Merrill, Jamie. "Syrian Cartoonist Ali Ferzat Turns Spotlight on UK's Failure to Take in More Refugees," *The Independent* (January 27, 2015), www.independent.co.uk/news/world/middle-east/syrian-cartoonist-ali-ferzat-turns-spotlight-uk-s-failure-take-more-refugees-10006638.html

Michel Kilo's Commandments to the Syrian People, *Zaman al-Wasl* (19 April 2021) https://en.zamanalwsl.net/news/article/62110/

Middle East Intelligence Bulletin, *Statement by 99 Syrian Intellectuals*, 2, no. 9 (October 5, 2000), www.meforum.org/meib/articles/0010_sdoc0927.htm

Middle East Watch, *Syria Human rights Workers on Trial*, 4, no. 5 (March 1992).

Middle East Watch, *Syria Unmasked: The Suppression of Human Rights by the Asad Regime* (New Haven: Yale University Press, 1991).

Morayef, Heba. "Reexamining Human Rights Change in Egypt," *Middle East Report* 274 (Spring 2015).

Moubayed, Sami. "Farewell Mohammad al-Maghut," *Mideast views* (April 3, 2006), https://web.archive.org/web/20110714091009/www.mideastviews.com/articleview.php?art=104

"Muhammad al-Maghut." *Adab al-Sujun*, AlJazeera (April 10, 2006).

Mukheylef, Ahmad Ali. "Dawr harakat Kifaya fi 'amaliyat al-taghyir al-siyasi fi Misr 'am 2011," *Majalat Buhuth al-Sharq al-Awsat*, N. 45 (March 2020).

Murphy, Caryle. *Passion for Islam: Shaping the Modern Middle East the Egyptian Experience* (New York, London: Scribner, 2002).

Nagler, Michael. "Lamp in the Storm," *Yes magazine* (July 30, 2012), https://web.archive.org/web/20190829144859/www.yesmagazine.org/peace-justice/syria-lamp-in-the-storm

"Najlaa Fathi tarfud taqdim dawr walidat khalid said: Azhab ila midan al-tahrir mutakhafiya" *Elfann* (March 13, 2012), www.elfann.com/news/show/1010465

Nasser, Ghassan. "Al-thawra al-suriya fi zikraha al-'ashira: al-masira wa al-ma'alat," *Tli'na 'al Huriya* (March 16, 2021), https://freedomraise.net/المس-العاشرة-ذكراها-في-السورية-الثورة/.

Nasser, Ghassan. "Hiwar Ma'a Hussein Hamada: al-I'tilaf yu 'ani hashasha fi buniyatihi al-tanzimiya wa huwa mabni min kital wa ahzab wahmiya," *Harmoon Center for Contemporary Studies* (April 1, 2021), www.harmoon.org/dialogues/بني-في-هشاشة-يعاني-الائتلاف-حمادة-حسين/.

Nasser, Ghassan. "Khairi al-Zahabi: al-dimucratiya wa al-muwatana huma al-bawaba al-wahida li-khalas suriya," *Harmoon Center for Contemporary Studies* (January 28, 2021), www.harmoon.org/dialogues/هم-والمواطنة-الديمقراطية-الذهبي-خيري/.

National Coalition of Syrian Revolution and Opposition Forces. https://en.etilaf.org/

Nawara, Wael. "Why General Sisi Should Not Run for President of Egypt," *Al-Monitor* (September 20, 2013), www.al-monitor.com/originals/2013/09/generalsisipresidentelection.html?amp

"No Room to Breathe: State Repression of Human Rights Activism in Syria." *Human Rights Watch*, 19, no. 6(E) (October 2007), www.hrw.org/reports/2007/syria1007/syria1007webwcover.pdf

Noueihed, Lin, and Alex Warren. *The Battle for the Arab Spring: Revolution, Counter-revolution and the Making of a New Era* (New Haven and London: Yale University Press, 2012).

Nour, Ayman. "Al-Sisi yal'ab bi-l nar wa nad'u al-'uqalaa bi rafd siyasatihi," *Arabi 21* (April 8, 2020), https://arabi21.com/story/1259526/ممارساته-لرفض-العقلاء-وندعو-بالنار-يلعب-السيسي-نور-أيمن

Nour, Ayman. "Egypt's Choice is Clear: Democracy – or Chaos under Sisi," *Middle East Eye* (January 23, 2020), www.middleeasteye.net/opinion/repression-corruption-and-poverty-egypt-has-recipe-new-uprising

"Nour Vows to Lead Egypt Opposition," *AlJazeera* (September 20, 2005), www.aljazeera.com/amp/news/2005/9/20/nour-vows-to-lead-egypt-opposition

Osman, Nadda. "Egypt's Protests: Who is Demonstrating and Who is Being Arrested?" *Middle East Eye* (September 26, 2019), www.middleeasteye.net/news/arrests-egyptian-anti-sisi-protesters-broken-down

Parties and Movements, "Democratic Alliance for Egypt," *Jadaliyya* (November 18, 2011). www.jadaliyya.com/Details/24648

Patterson, Molly, and Kristen Renwick Monroe. "Narrative in Political Science." *Annual Review of Political Science* 1, no. 1 (1998): 315–331.

Peel, Michael, Camilla Hall, and Heba Saleh. "Saudi Arabia and UAE prop up Egypt regime with offer of $8bn," *Financial Times* (July 10, 2013), www.ft.com/content/7e066bdc-e8a2-11e2-8e9e-00144feabdc0

Perthes, Volker. *Syria under Bashar al-Asad: Modernization and the Limits of Change* (London and New York: Routledge).

"President Bush Visits Prague, Czech Republic, Discusses Freedom," Office of the Press Secretary, *White House Archives* (June 5, 2007), speech available at, https://georgewbush-whitehouse.archives.gov/news/releases/2007/06/20070605-8.html

Qadaya wa shahadat, No.1 (Spring 1990).

"Rahil Hassan Abbas... al-thaqafa al-suriya takhsar safiriha," *Al-Mudun* (March 7, 2021), www.almodon.com/culture/2021/3/7/سفيرها-تخسر-الثقافة-عباس-حسان-رحيل

Ramadan, Oula and Yassin Swehat. *Muqarabat 'an al-mujtama' al-madani al-Suri* [Approaches to Syrian civil society] Al-Jumhuriya.net (October 15, 2020), www.aljumhuriya.net/en/content/approaches-syrian-civil-society

Reid, Donald. "The National Bar Association and Egyptian Politics, 1912–1954," *The International Journal of African Historical Studies,* 7, no. 4 (1974): 608–646.

Roberts, Sam. "Mai Skaf, Syrian Actress Who Defied Assad Regime, Dies at 49," *New York Times* (July 27, 2018), www.nytimes.com/2018/07/27/obituaries/mai-skaf-syrian-actress-who-defied-assad-regime-dies-at-49.html

Roumani, Rhonada. "Syria Launches Crackdown on Dissent," *The Christian Science Monitor* (May 25, 2006), www.csmonitor.com/2006/0525/p06s01-wome.html

Rutherford, Bruce K. *Egypt After Mubarak: Liberalism, Islam and Democracy in the Arab World* (Princeton, NJ: Princeton University Press, 2008).

Sachedina, Abdulaziz. *The Islamic Roots of Democratic Pluralism* (New York: Oxford University Press, 2001).

Sadiki, Larbi. "Popular Uprisings and Arab Democratization," *International Journal of Middle East Studies* 32, no. 1 (2000): 71–95.

Sadiki, Larbi. *The Search for Arab Democracy: Discourses and Counter-Discourses* (New York: Columbia University Press, 2004).

Safi, Omid (ed.). *Progressive Muslims: On Justice, Gender and Pluralism* (Oxford: Oneworld, 2003).

Safi, Omid. "Progressive Islam," in Coeli Fitzpatrick and Adam Hani Walker (eds.), *Muhammad in History, Thought, and Culture: An Encyclopedia of the Prophet of God* (Santa Barbara: ABC-CLIO, 2014).

Said, Edward. *Orientalism* (New York: Vintage Books, 1978).

Said, Jawdat. *Al-din wa al-qanun: ru'ya qur'aniya* (1998).

Said, Jawdat. Interviewed by Abdul-Jabbar al-Rifa'ee. *Current Islamic Issues* (April 1998), www.jawdatsaid.net/en/index.php?title=Current_Islamic_Issues

Said, Jawdat. *Iqra' wa rabika al-akram,* Abhath fi sunan taghyir al-nafs wa al-mujtama' (Damascus, 1988).

Said, Jawdat. "Jawdat Said." *YouTube,* uploaded by Golan Films (Bir Ajam, May 30, 2011), www.youtube.com/watch?v=9VUN6Cj2B5o

Said, Jawdat. *Kun ka-ibn adam* (Damascus, 1996).

Said, Jawdat. "Law kan al-din bi al-'aql," *Al-Majala* (n.d.), www.jawdatsaid.net/index.php?title=بالعقل_الدين_لوكان.

Said, Jawdat. *Lima haza al-ru' b kuluh mina al-islam wa keyfa bada'a al-khawf?* [Why is Such Dread from Islam? (publisher's proposed translation)] (2006).

Said, Jawdat. *Mazhab ibn Adam al-awal* [The doctrine of the first (or better) son of Adam] (1966).

Said, Jawdat. *Mazhab ibn Adam al-awal: mushkilat al-'unf fi al-'amal al-siyasi,* 5th ed. (Beirut: Dar al-Fikr, 1993). Available at www.jawdatsaid.net/index.php?title=الخامسة_الطبعة_آدم_ابن_مذهب_مقدمة.

Said, Jawdat. *Mushkilat al-'unf fi al-'amal al-siyasi; Iqra' wa rabika al-akram* (1988).

Said, Jawdat. "The role of religious actors in peace-building," *Islam, Christianity and Europe* (2009–2010), www.jawdatsaid.net/en/index.php/The_role_of_religious_actors_in_peace-building. Seminar

Said, Jawdat. "Personal Interview." By Line Khatib (2017)

Saleh, Yassin al-Haj. "Syria War: The Love of My Life Disappeared Six Years Ago, but Still I Cling to Hope," *Middle East Eye* (December 26, 2019), www.middleeasteye.net/opinion/syria-war-love-my-life-disappeared-six-years-ago-still-i-cling-hope?

Saleh, Yassin al-Haj. *Al-thawra al-mustahila* (Beirut: al-mu'asasa al-'arabiya li al-dirasat wa al-nashr, 2017).

Sanders, Lewis, and Brigitta Schülke, Waffa Albadry and Julia Bayer. "Razan Zaitouneh...wajh al-thawra al-suriya al-mughayab," *Deutsche Welle* (March 15, 2021), www.dw.com/ar/المُغيَب-السورية-الثورة-وجه-زيتونة-رزان/a-56854643

Sayigh, Yezid. "A Melancholy Perspective on Syria," *Carnegie Middle East* (April 8, 2014), https://carnegie-mec.org/2014/04/08/melancholy-perspective-on-syria-pub-55256

Schölch, Alexander. *Egypt for the Egyptians! The Socio-Political Crisis in Egypt 1878–1882* (London: Ithaca Press, 1981).

Schülke, Brigitta, Lewis Sanders and Waffa Albadry. "Video: The missing face of the Syrian revolution," *DW news* (March 15, 2021), https://fb.watch/4gzChmQG6Y/

Schumann, Christoph (ed.). *Nationalism and Liberal Thought in the Arab East: Ideology and Practice* (London: Routledge, 2010).

Schumann, Christoph. "The 'failure' of radical nationalism and the 'silence' of liberal thought in the Arab World," in Schumann (ed.), *Nationalism and Liberal Thought in the Arab East: Ideology and Practice* (New York and London: Routledge, 2010).

Schumann, Christoph. *Liberal Thought in the Eastern Mediterranean: Late 19th Century Until the 1960s* (Leiden, The Netherlands: Brill, 2008).

Scott, James C. *Domination and the Arts of Resistance: Hidden Transcripts* (New Haven and London: Yale University Press, 1990).

Selim, Gamal M. "Egypt under SCAF and the Muslim Brotherhood: The Triangle of Counter-Revolution," *Arab Studies Quarterly*, 37, no. 2 (Spring 2015): 177–199.

Seurat, Michel. *Syrie, l'Etat de barbarie* (Paris: Presses Universitaires de France, Kindle Edition, 2015).

Sfeir, George. "Basic Freedoms in a Fractured Legal Culture: Egypt and the Case of Nasr Hamid Abu Zayd," *Middle East Journal*, 53, no. 2 (1998): 402–414.

Shaaban, Ahmad B. *Raffat al-farasha, Kifaya: al-Mady wa al-Mustaqbal* (Cairo: Kefaya Publications, 2006).

Shahin, Emad El-Din. "Sentenced to Death in Egypt: How I Became Defendant 33—yet another casualty of the return to military rule," *The Atlantic* (May 19, 2015), www.theatlantic.com/international/archive/2015/05/death-sentence-egypt-emad-shahin/393590/

Shapiro, Samantha M. "Revolution Facebook-Style," *The New York Times Magazine* (January 22, 2009), www.nytimes.com/2009/01/25/magazine/25bloggers-t.html

Sharabi, Hisham. *Arab Intellectuals and the West: The Formative Years 1875–1914* (Baltimore, MD: John Hopkins University Press, 1970).

Sharp, Gene. *From Dictatorship to Democracy: A conceptual framework for liberation.* 1st English language edition. (Bangkok, Thailand: Committee for the Restoration of Democracy in Burma, 1994).

Shehata, Dina. "Youth Activism in Egypt," *Arab Reform Initiative* (October 23, 2008).

Shehata, Dina. *Islamists and Secularists in Egypt: Opposition, Conflict and Cooperation* (London and New York: Routledge, 2009).

Sherry, Virginia. "Syria: The Price of Dissent." *Human Rights Watch*, vol. 7, no. 4, (July 1995), www.hrw.org/reports/1995/Syria.htm

Shorbagy, Manar. "Understanding Kefaya: The New Politics in Egypt," *Arab Studies Quarterly*, 29, no. 1 (Winter 2007): 39–60.

Sika, Nadine. "Youth Political Engagement in Egypt: From Abstention to Uprising," *British Journal of Middle Eastern Studies*, 39, no. 2 (2012): 181–199.

Sing, Manfred. "Arab Post-Marxists after Disillusionment: Between Liberal Newspeak and Revolution Reloaded," in Meir Hatina and Christoph Schumann (eds.), *Arab Liberal Thought After 1967: Old Dilemmas, New Perceptions* (New York: Palgrave Macmillan, 2015): 155–157.

Sivan, Emmanuel. "Arab Nationalism in the Age of Islamic Resurgence," in Israel Gershoni and James Jankowski (eds.), *Rethinking Nationalism in the Middle East* (Columbia University Press, 1997).

Sivan, Emmanuel. "The Clash within Islam," *Survival: Global Politics and Strategy*, 45, no. 1 (2003): 25–44.

"Statement of the 1000." *Committees for the Revival of Civil Society in Syria* (Syria, 2001). Web Archive. Retrieved from the Library of Congress, https://webarchive.loc.gov/all/20060517183030/www.mowaten.org/politics/politics-home.htm

Stork, Joe. "Egypt's Political Prisoners," *Open Democracy* (March 6, 2015), www.hrw.org/news/2015/03/06/egypts-political-prisoners

Stork, Joe. "Three Decades of Human Rights Activism in the Middle East and North Africa: An Ambiguous Balance of Sheet," in Joel Beinin and Frederic Vairel (eds.), *Social Movements, Mobilization, and Contestation in the Middle East and North Africa*, 2nd ed. (Stanford, California: Stanford University Press, 2013): 83–106.

"Syrian National Council Mission and Program," *Syrian National Council*, www.syriancouncil.org/en/mission-statement.html

Syrian National Policy Group. Petition "Bayan hawla a'mal al-lajna al-dasturiya al-Suriya [To have a meaningful implementation of the Security Council Resolutions in Syria]," (October 2020), http://chng.it/8xBrT7Gv

"Syrian Opposition Figure Asma al-Faisal Dies in Canada," *Enab Baladi* (January 8, 2018), https://english.enabbaladi.net/archives/2018/01/syrian-opposition-figure-asma-al-faisal-dies-canada/

"Syria War: Peace Talks Restart in Geneva," *BBC news* (May 16, 2017), www.bbc.com/news/amp/world-middle-east-39934868

"Tahta al-mijhar—Ahat al-Huriya." *YouTube*, uploaded by AlJazeera Channel (March 12, 2014), www.youtube.com/watch?v=yroOTxnkZJI

Tamer, Georges. "Nasr Hamid Abu Zayd," *International Journal of Middle East Studies*, 43, no. 1 (2011): 95–193.

Tamir, Zakariya. *Tigers on the Tenth Day and Other Stories* [translator: Denys Johnson-Davies] (London: Quartet Books, 1985).

"Tashwish al-Mu'arada," Ayman Nour's Facebook page, https://fb.watch/6qOR_iVZQq/

Tessler, Mark, and Amaney Jamal. "Citizen Attitudes in Selected Arab Countries About Whether Democracy is the Best Form of Government," *Arab Barometer Project* (2010), www.arabbarometer.org

"The Beirut-Damascus Declaration," *Free Syria* (July 12, 2006). Web Archive, https://web.archive.org/web/20080207083503/www.free-syria.com/en/load-article.php?articleid=6924

"The situation in the Middle East," Resolution 1680, United Nations Security Council (May 17, 2006) UN doc 06-35177, http://unscr.com/en/resolutions/doc/1680

"The Syrian National Council," *Carnegie Middle East Center* (September 25, 2013), http://carnegie-mec.org/publications/?fa=48334

Thomassen, Bjørn. "Notes Towards an Anthropology of Political Revolutions," *Comparative Studies in Society and History* 54, no. 3 (2012): 679–706.

Thompson, Elizabeth. *How the West Stole Democracy from the Arabs: The Syrian Arab Congress of 1920 and the Destruction of Its Historic Liberal-Islamic Alliance* (New York: Atlantic Monthly Press, 2020).

Tibi, Bassam. *Arab Nationalism: Between Islam and the Nation State* (New York: Palgrave Macmillan, 1997).

Tli'na 'al Huriya [FreedomRaise], https://freedomraise.net/

"UN envoy on stalled Syria talks in Geneva: 'we can't continue like this,'" *SWI swissinfo.ch* (January 30, 2021), www.swissinfo.ch/eng/unenvoy-on-stalled-syria-talks-in-geneva---we-can-t-continue-like-this-/46331318

Vidal, Marta. "Fighting for democracy and a free Syria," *Qantara.de* (November 22, 2019), https://en.qantara.de/node/38119

Wa hunak ashia' kathira kan yumken an yatahadath 'anha al-mar' [There are many things one can talk about.]. Directed by Omar Amiralay. ARTE (1997).

Wall, Melissa and Sahar el-Zaher. "'I'll Be Waiting for You Guys': A YouTube Call to Action in the Egyptian Revolution," *International Journal of Communication* 5 (2011), www.researchgate.net/publication/298060207_I%27ll_Be_Waiting_for_You_Guys_A_YouTube_Call_to_Action_in_the_Egyptian_Revolution

Wannous, Sa'dallah. "Ana al-Janaza wa al-mushayi'un ma'an" [*I am the funeral and the bereaved*]. *al-A'mal al-kamila* (Damascus: Al Ahali, 1996).

Wannous, Sa'dallah. *Bayanat li-masrah 'arabi jadid* (Beirut: dar al-fikr al-jadid, 1988).

Wannous, Sa'dallah. *Haflat Samar min ajl Khamsa Huzeiran* (1968) [A Soirée for the 5th of June] translated by Roger Allen. The Mercurian 5.2 (Fall 2014), https://the-mercurian.com/2016/06/17/soiree-for-the-fifth-of-june/

Wedeen, Lisa. *Ambiguities of Domination: Politics, Rhetoric, and Symbols in Contemporary Syria* (Chicago and London: University of Chicago Press, 1999).

Weismann, Itzchak. *Abd al-Rahman al-Kawakibi: Islamic Reform and Arab Nationalism* (London: OneWorld, 2015).

"We will not be silenced: April 6, after court order banning group," *Ahram Online* (April 28, 2014), https://english.ahram.org.eg/News/100015.aspx

"Who's who: Michel Kilo," *The Syrian Observer* (September 27, 2013), https:// syrianobserver.com/EN/who/34536/whos_who_michel_kilo.html

Wiktorowicz, Quintan. "The Salafi Movement in Jordan," *International Journal of Middle East Studies*, 32, no. 2 (2000): 219–240.

Wilson, John F. "Modernity and Religion: A Problem of Perspective," in William Nicholls (ed.), *Modernity and Religion* (Waterloo, Ontario: Wilfrid Laurier University Press, 1987): 9–18.

Wittes, Tamara Cofman. "The 2005 Egyptian Elections: How Free? How Important?" *Brookings* (August 24, 2005), www.brookings.edu/research/ the-2005-egyptian-elections-how-free-how-important/?amp

Yacoubian, Mona. "Syria Timeline: Since the Uprising Against Assad," *United States Institute of Peace* (January 1, 2021), www.usip.org/ syria-timeline-uprising-against-assad

Yazbeck, Dalia Ghanem, and Vasily Kuznetsov. "The 'Comrades' in North-Africa," in Nicu Popescu and Stanislav Secrieru (eds.), *Russia's Return to the Middle East: Building Sandcastles?* (Luxembourg: EU Institute for Security Studies, 2018): 73–82.

Youssef, Bassem. "Egypt's secularists repeating Islamists' mistakes," *CNN online* (July 20, 2013), www.cnn.com/2013/07/19/opinion/youssef-egypt-political-upheaval/

Youssef, Bassem. "Scaling Free Speech: The Reputation and Replication of AlBernamag." *YouTube*, uploaded by Concordia (Programming Partner: The Tahrir Institute for Middle East Policy) (October 14, 2015), www .youtube.com/watch?v=H0RK-yhZsZQ

Zachs, Fruma. *The Making of a Syrian Identity: Intellectuals and Merchants in Nineteenth Century Beirut* (Leiden and Boston: Brill, 2005).

Zaitouneh, Razan [@razanz], http://mme.cm/WWTT00 عر @NOW_ar." *Twitter* (December 1, 2013), https://twitter.com/razanz/status/407151933191761921

Ziadeh, Farhat J. *Lawyers, the Rule of Law, and Liberalism in Modern Egypt* (Stanford: Hoover Institution, 1968).

Ziadeh, Radwan. "Power and Policy in Syria: Intelligence Services," *Foreign Relations and Democracy in the Middle East* (London: I. B. Tauris, 2012).

Ziadeh, Radwan. "The Syrian Revolution: The Role of the 'Emerging Leaders'," in *Revolution and Political Transformation in the Middle East: Agents of Change* (Vol 1) (Washington DC: Middle East Institute, August 2011).

Zisser, Eyal. "A False Spring in Damascus," *Orient*, 44, no. 1 (2003): 39–62.

Zisser, Eyal. *Commanding Syria: Bashar al-Asad and the first years in power* (London and New York: I. B.Tauris, 2007).

Zubaida, Sami. "Civil Society, Community, and Democracy in the East," in Sudipta Kaviraj and Sunil Khilnani (eds.), *History and Possibilities* (Cambridge: Cambridge University Press, 2001): 232–249.

Index

Printed by Printforce, United Kingdom